THE IMAGINATIVE ARGUMENT

The Imaginative Argument

A PRACTICAL MANIFESTO FOR WRITERS

Frank L. Cioffi

PRINCETON UNIVERSITY PRESS

Princeton and Oxford

LIBRARY OF CONGRESS CATALOGING-IN-PUBLICATION DATA

Cioffi, Frank L., 1951–
The imaginative argument : a practical manifesto for writers / Frank L. Cioffi.
p. cm.
Includes bibliographical references and index.
ISBN 0-691-12289-X (acid-free paper) — ISBN 0-691-12290-3 (pbk.)
1. Persuasion (Rhetoric)—Problems, exercises, etc. 2. English
language—Rhetoric—Problems, exercises, etc. 3. Report writing—Problems,
exercises, etc. I. Title.
PE1433.C56 2005
808′.042—dc22 2004057500

British Library Cataloging-in-Publication Data is available

This book has been composed in Adobe Garamond, Bluejack, and Raphael

Printed on acid-free paper. ∞

pup.princeton. edu

Printed in the United States of America

3 5 7 9 10 8 6 4 2

ISBN-13: 978-0-691-12289-2 (cloth)

ISBN-10: 0-691-12289-X (cloth)

ISBN-13: 978-0-691-12290-8 (pbk.)

ISBN-10: 0-691-12290-3 (pbk.)

FOR KATHLEEN CIOFFI

whose love exceeds imagination, and whose courage
and insight brook no argument

Writing isn't about talent. It's about devotion,
it's about practice.

—Naomi Shihab Nye

Not he is great who can alter matter, but he
who can alter my state of mind.

—Ralph Waldo Emerson,
"The American Scholar"

By imagination the architect sees the unity of a building
not yet begun, and the inventor sees the unity and
varied interactions of a machine never yet constructed, even a
unity that no human eye can ever see, since when the
machine is in actual motion, one part may hide the
connecting parts, and yet all keep the unity of the
inventor's thought. By imagination a Newton sweeps
sun, planets, and stars into unity with the earth and the
apple that is drawn irresistibly to its surface, and
sees them all within the circle of one grand law.
Science, philosophy, and mechanical invention have little
use for fancy, but the creative, penetrative power of
imagination is to them the breath of life, and the
condition of all advance and success.

—*Funk and Wagnalls New Standard Dictionary*
of the English Language

CONTENTS

PREFACE

Written argument, which logically explains and defends a controversial idea, seems to be disappearing as a form of discourse. Here I offer a manifesto for the protection, for the nurturance, of this endangered species. Why? Because argument deserves to survive and flourish. It should be taught more rigorously in schools, in colleges and universities. It should enter the public conversation, informing and being informed by ordinary human feelings and actions. An essential part of a complex web of culture, argument shares an environment with analysis, evaluation, understanding, knowledge. Yet it's too often shackled and bound by the immuring vocabulary of Greek words, life-sentenced to the dustiness of classrooms, relegated to the aerie-like confines of the Ivory Tower or cinderblock facsimiles thereof: the mad-discipline in the attic—or on the very edge of campus, anyway!

This manifesto calls not so much for revolution, as for evolution, or at least reform: a reenvisioning of what writers and scholars, producers of ideas and creators of new knowledge, ought to be doing and ought to be teaching others. It also calls for you, the writer, to do something perhaps a little different from what you've previously been taught.

"Argument" and "imagination" are not typically (or at least not traditionally) conjoined, but doing so infuses written argument with value. You need not only to imagine an audience but to imagine what kinds of questions that audience might raise. You also need to imagine what does not at present exist: a response that truly emerges from within yourself, and that would therefore be different from anything else yet written or thought, as different as each individual is from every other. And further, if such a process takes place, you will acknowledge and take into account the viewpoints of others. This process, I'm arguing here, will advance knowledge as it promotes your own understanding; in addition, it's a process that values and validates the individual as he or she emerges within a context of a larger, projected audience—the group to which that individual speaks, and whose influence constrains, limits, and at the same time engenders the very creativity of the solitary mind.

The organizing idea behind this volume is not just the argument but the "imaginative argument." Look up "imaginative argument" in a search engine—all of the hits use the term as if it were an absolute, a summum bonum. And yet how rarely is imagination taught in conjunction with argument! I want to stress that writers always have choices about how to say things, about what to say, about when to say what. Unlike social situations, which call for very quick thinking and occasional blurting out of the wrong thing or suppression of the right response—you know, until twenty minutes later, when it's too late—writing is something that you can think about, revise, recast, or expeditiously handle with the "delete" key. I am trying to suggest in the following pages that you as a writer should attempt to form not just an argument about an issue, a text, a situation, but an *imaginative* argument—one that (perhaps) has not been offered many times before, one that (perhaps) involves a new use of language or ideas, one that (perhaps) employs a novel range or mix of source materials. Or something else—really, who knows what?—it's imaginative, unforeseeable. And you are not doing this just to be weird and ornery; rather, you are trying to see the issue in a new way—a way that will be interesting, partly because it's unexpected, but at the same time graspable and credible because it is offered in a formal, serious, logically structured manner.

Here's how I would characterize the status quo: you, the proverbial student in the chair, do not want to write argument. You do not want to risk statements that could be attacked, refuted, made mockery of—or even assertions that you hold so strongly they provide a point of vulnerability. And your timidity is not a surface timidity: it goes as deeply into your mind as it does into your educational past. You've been schooled to tread the paper path of least resistance; to repeat ideas that you've been indoctrinated with; to parrot even the language of authorities you supposedly value; to rarely attack a problem from a fresh, vital vantage point, or even look at it through a personal, quirky, inventively eccentric optic.

But I want you to do more than just sit there. A lot more. One of your most important intellectual endeavors should be figuring out what you genuinely feel and think about something. Don't just try to anticipate what others might want you to think—or even what people you respect and admire might themselves think or want you to think. Determine your own angle, your own true beliefs. This takes some ingenuity. It is not easy to say what you think or feel about complex issues. If it were, they wouldn't be complex issues. In a way, writing argument consists in looking at evidence that supports both what attracts you about something and what you might find confusing, repulsive, elusive; it consists in trying to figure out, as you sort through contradictory evidence, what it is that matters—not just to you, but to an audience as interested, as invested, as you are.

Against me stands a long and still flourishing tradition of repeating the already-established and oft-reiterated. Indeed, much of our educational system envisions the dispensing of such truth—"facts"—as its primary goal. Charles Dickens's famous pedagogue from *Hard Times*, Thomas Gradgrind, embodies this teaching philosophy:

> "Now what I want is, Facts. Teach these boys and girls nothing but Facts. Facts alone are wanted in life. Plant nothing else, and root out everything else." (1)

Surely Dickens exaggerates for humorous effect. But now 150 years later, many people still believe in a Gradgrindian educational philosophy. Recently, when I was team-teaching a course on political theory, I was asked to lecture about writing. I basically presented (in vastly compressed form) what follows in this volume you are now holding. I explained how it was necessary to have not just an argument but an imaginative argument; how my auditors needed to form their own ideas and make their own judgments; how they needed to see the texts as being ones that spoke to them as those texts spoke from a remote past; how each generation, indeed, each individual, must come to terms with those texts and must argue why those terms matter to an audience. The professor in charge of the course, who had been looking uncomfortable for the entire eight minutes I was speaking, stood up quickly at the bell. She said, "Yes, yes, that's all true. But we also want to make sure that in your papers it's clear that you GOT IT, that you've understood the texts." What she wanted was, in a word, belief—and catechistic proof thereof.

I know that many institutions within our culture strongly resist change, do not encourage Doubting Thomas figures, and demand, instead, just this kind of belief. Seventeenth-century Irish poet John Denham wrote a couplet characterizing this position—the exact opposite to my own—and in the mid–nineteenth century, the grammarian Goold Brown quotes Denham with approbation:

> Those who have dealt most in philological controversy have well illustrated the couplet of Denham:
>
> The Tree of Knowledge, blasted by disputes
> Produces sapless leaves in stead of fruits. (iii)

For Denham, as for Brown, the facts of knowledge are inviolate— only damaged by debate, undermined, rendered lifeless or sterile by "gainsayers." He suggests here (and elsewhere in the 1668 poem "The Progress of Learning" Brown quotes from) that controversy weakens any understanding of divine creation, fatally blights "The Tree of Knowledge." Disputatiousness "blasts" away its beauty and wonder. Instead of having something we can hold on to, eat from, benefit from, we have a ravaged tree, on its way toward death. In short, Denham and Brown make a plea for the value of knowledge unencumbered by debate and controversy.

This quasi-Gradgrindian conception of knowledge not only informs the philosophy of many teachers today (who want to make sure that you've "GOT IT") but generally appeals to authority figures because it allows them to claim an unimpeachable authority. I'd argue that when authority figures take this position, you probably have good reason to distrust them, whether they be teachers or writers, the media or the Supreme Court, your favorite Web site or the president. To squelch chat limits freedom of thought, limits freedom. Goold Brown evidently wanted just that kind of unimpeachable authority, writing for an audience that he felt needed to know the precepts—the "facts"—of English grammar, rather than all the anxiety-provoking controversies surrounding those precepts (probably my political theorist colleague felt the same about her role in our class).

By contrast, I expect a little more than "facts." The genre of argument demands more than just evidence that you as students "GOT IT"—as in *fact*, the facts themselves often need to be argued for, or are under some dispute, and the "it" (of "got it")—a notoriously slippery entity—eludes, gambols, dances away at the touch of an eyebeam or the utterance of a single remark. "It" must be captured, coaxed, looked at from many angles, and possibly unmasked. In short, I argue here that the truth consists not so much of an "it," or of "facts," as of propositions that need to be defended and proven to be—provisionally, within a certain sociohistorical context—true.

While this is not the place to enter the debate about the relative nature of truth, it seems to me profoundly essential to question and think about how truths are arrived at. Lewis Carroll contends, in a memorable exchange between Alice and Humpty Dumpty, that the powerful make the truth; they can make words mean whatever they want them to mean:

> "When *I* use a word," Humpty Dumpty said in a rather scornful tone, "it means just what I choose it to mean—neither more nor less."
>
> "The question is," said Alice, "whether you can make words mean so many different things."
>
> "The question is," said Humpty Dumpty, "which is to be master—that's all." (274)

I know this might at first appear sinister, but I see it in a positive way. The power that Humpty alludes to can reside within you as the writer: you are master. You can persuade others of your position, even though you do not have billions of dollars, or enormous influence in the media, or a job in the White House's West Wing. You can establish a truth via arguing for it.

Establishing a truth involves negotiating its terms; it involves other minds, other subjectivities. Is there a truth "out there" that you can "discover"? Maybe, maybe not. As Wallace Stevens writes, "Where was it one first heard of the truth? The the." But just because there might be no eternal truth—or if there is, it's ever-elusive—this doesn't mean we all live in solipsistic, subjective, closed-off universes, either, worlds where we just make up whatever we want. Indeed, while our subjectivities are rarely congruent, they surprisingly often overlap, intersect, or asymptotically approach each other. Your job as a writer is to push the borders of your own subjectivity in the direction of others, just as you simultaneously determine where others' subjective worlds touch, overlap, and impinge on your own. I can't promise you that the truth you discover will be apodictic or eternal, or even that all these subjectivities neatly interlock, but your argument, your work—if it's been done honestly and thoroughly— will have the capacity to make an impact and effect change, not only on others but also on you, on your world.

A very fundamental human act undergirds and empowers this activity of arguing for truth. It's one that you see in children all the time, one that might even be annoying: the relentless asking of questions of all kinds. Just as a child might ask again and again, "Why?" until the parent finally shushes him or her with a "Because that's the way it works," or "Just because. Now leave me alone!" so you as thinkers and writers should be asking question upon question. You should be terminally curious; your curiosity should follow you to your graves. (I'll let you imagine the kinds of epitaphs this might engender.) You should ask questions that will help you understand, assess, contextualize, make sense of a given situation, a given idea, text, or topic. And these questions should reach outward—"What do others say?"—at the same time that they should delve within: "How do I feel about this?" Questioning allows you to open yourself to possibilities—an action that characterizes genuinely creative thought.

"Opening yourself" means that you must scrutinize, if you can, all of your preconceptions, your closely held beliefs, even your notions of good and bad, of evil and saintly, of right and wrong. You shouldn't let these notions ossify into hardened cerebral monuments. You should be constantly interrogating them, problematizing them—at least in your writing, if not in your life. In the process of asking questions, provided that they really probe the issues, you suddenly recognize your personal stake in the topic. No longer is writing about x or y a dry, or for that matter wet, perspiration-inducing academic exercise, but rather a way of discovering and inventing your "take" about something—and then wanting to share that with others, wanting to transform their subjective worlds as you define and reshape your own.

In some sense, then, what follows here is a book not only about how to make arguments, how to structure them in formal writing, and how to use your language to make them vivid, memorable, striking, and forceful. It's not just meant to set out some rules that can be followed like formulas or flowcharts. It's also, I hope, a book that tries to inspire you to want to write argument *because argument matters*. It's a book about creativity, a book about how to identify and imagine a present and a future audience for one's ideas.

But will any of these ideas survive twenty, thirty, five hundred years? A colleague of mine, Teresa Vilardi, recently asked this very question of a group of forty or so writing teachers, and we were all much unsettled. Is a book about writing necessarily ephemeral, since it engages issues of pedagogy, which seem lodged in a bounded, narrow time stratum? How will these discussions of the Internet, of doing on-line research, of writing in university courses, of style and fallacies and figures of speech, play out when no books are published, when brick-and-mortar universities have ceased to exist, when ever-more-scarily interactive versions of the Internet become the major conduit of entertainment, information, and knowledge, and when education has taken on a form that we, primitive denizens of the double 0's of the twenty-first century, can now hardly imagine? I'm not sure. But I expect that many human qualities—in fact, most of what we are now—will perdure and last; and still in the future, as in the past, people will have varying degrees of creativity, independence of mind, confidence in themselves, originality.

So let me offer this manifesto-like assertion, which I'm hoping will be as applicable a hundred years hence as it was a hundred years ago, or as it is today: cherish your curiosity, your individual insight— even if it hurts. To adopt an argumentative way of thought is to be intellectually alive, constantly wondering, thinking; it's tantamount to existing in a realm of provisionality and uncertainty, to seething, almost to enduring a kind of disease. I know this is more than merely unsettling. And I hasten to add that it has become an essential part of our worldview. Playwright Tom Stoppard succinctly captures this idea in his play *Jumpers*: "Copernicus cracked our confidence and Einstein smashed it: for if one can no longer believe that a twelve-inch ruler is always a foot long, how can one be sure of relatively less certain propositions, such as that God made the Heaven and the Earth?" (74). When our own confidence is cracked, it augurs loss; it provokes instability, anxiety, even alarm. That's in part why you hate to make arguments. That's why many teachers adopt Gradgrind's philosophy and why so many of you remain rooted to your chairs, listening to the "facts."

But let's join Stoppard and abandon "confidence." Instead, look toward anxiety as a tool for thought. Anxiety—about the way things work, about the way things seem to be, about how to explain a book, a person, or a universe—forms the basis for writing argument, for creating new knowledge. I wanted to write that all the important new knowledge—the new discoveries, breakthroughs, and inventions—are still to come, are yet to emerge in a distant if hazy future. I'm just not sure that's true. It might be. But think about the future, for it is your writing that will help create it, and before you can create it, you must challenge not only the present but your own capacity to supersede it.

*   *   *

The chapters that follow—on audience, invention, the thesis, the writing process, research, style—all strive to persuade you that having an argument is necessary, but not quite sufficient; good, but not quite good enough. You have to have an imaginative argument. Chapter 1 defines the genre and differentiates it from other nonfiction writing. Chapter 2, on audience, suggests that as you envision your audience, you simultaneously create it by offering readers not what they expect but what they really want: new knowledge. Chapter 3, on the writing process, strives to show how one must actively work toward creation of an essay of the kind being suggested: it's not something that emerges, Athena-like, whole from one's brain; it must be thought about, imagined, tested out, revised. Chapters 4 and 5, which cover the idea of thesis, lay out conventional thesis strategies and show how these often function as only "pseudo-theses"—and as such are deficient. By contrast, the truly argumentative thesis is more potentiality than actuality—and serves to open up new areas of questioning. Chapter 6 examines the paragraph—a paper in miniature. Expanding on the paper in miniature, chapters 7 and 8 discuss structure and development of the entire essay, claiming that the key to creating strong, argumentative papers is, first, to pose the most interesting kinds of questions—and then to attempt answering the most provocative, most unanswerable question of them all: what I term the "macro-question." Chapter 9 examines a special version of the argument, the research paper, showing how the best research makes you, the writer/researcher, change your mind and arrive at new insights in the process.

Chapters 10 and 11 stress the need to say things in an imaginative and forceful way. Chapter 10, for example, covers some figures of speech and demonstrates how to use various rhetorical patterns in order to give your language greater impact. It also lays out logical fallacies, ways of "cheating at argument" that I suggest you learn to recognize in others and avoid in your own work—they should not be used by responsible writers. Their use in fact represents, at best, intellectual complaisance; at worst, a demented version of imagination. Chapter 11, on style, offers ways to craft a distinctive, interesting style, including both prohibitions and suggestions. I provide eleven brief snippets of essays by renowned stylists and show what makes them worthy of inclusion here—indeed, worthy of awe. In a concluding chapter to this "practical manifesto," I urge you to embrace a version of fuzzy logic that I call "fuzzy subjectivity"—a new way of thinking and imagining that has the capacity to effect change.

ACKNOWLEDGMENTS

Writing a book of this kind recalls and revivifies many people from my past to whom I owe a debt of gratitude. My late parents, Nan and Lou Cioffi, met in a creative writing class at New York University and aspired to be great writers. They inculcated in me and my twin brother, Grant—to whom I also owe incalculable thanks—an abiding respect for the written word and love for the literary, the artistic, and the beautiful. My uncle, also named Frank Cioffi, who assumed the role of my intellectual father when my own father died in 1968, has had an influence on me and my thinking that is too enormous to estimate. I often quote him in the following pages, and his spirit hovers in some sense above this all. I hope he forgives me errors in my own logic, my limited scope, my too-oft-infelicitous phrasing. On him, hence on me, the influence of his wife, my Aunt Nalini, has also been profound: to her I extend thanks beyond measure.

Many people influenced me in college. Professor Lawrence Evans of Northwestern University first alerted me to the importance of style and organization in writing, and took a great interest in helping me with the development of my own prose. Peter Michelson and the late Stephen Spender, both professors of creative writing at Northwestern, encouraged my work and provided a format for the analysis of others' work, a format that I still use today in my classes. To Robert E. Gross, of Indiana University, I owe gratitude for writing instruction, as I do to Scott Russell Sanders, whose commentary on my work forms a model of superb professorial judgment. Professor Georges Edelen of Indiana University inculcated in me the importance of an "argumentative edge" in writing. I also owe gratitude to the late Professor Timothy J. Wiles, whose ideas and insights occur and reoccur to me so often that they form part of my permanent mental landscape. Professors Donald J. Gray, Murray Sperber, S. C. Fredericks, Ihab Hassan, H. James Jensen, and David Bleich were enormously influential and at the same time amazingly patient with me, as I tried to formulate my ideas and invent myself as a writer and member of the teaching profession in the late 1970s and early 1980s. Their lucid and extraordinary writing and teaching still provide me with models toward which I aspire.

My colleagues at the Princeton University Writing Program, especially David Thurn, Kerry Walk, Ann Jurecic, Victor Ripp, Ahmet Bayazitoglu, Amanda Irwin-Wilkins, Anne Caswell-Klein, Kimberly Bohman, and David Cutts not only helped me formulate my ideas but provided a forum and an audience for those ideas as I refined them over the course of my four years' teaching in the Ivy League. At Bard College, Rob Whittemore, Joan Retallack, and Teresa Vilardi helped provide me with insights into a way of teaching writing that engages both sides of the brain and that engages students as well.

My one colleague at both Princeton and Bard, Sandra R. Friedman, I want to single out for especial thanks, as she not only listened to me read aloud long portions of this book but also carefully read and commented on its entirety.

To Kathryn Watterson and Alfred E. Guy, Jr., I also want to extend especial thanks, as they offered detailed and apposite commentary on the entire manuscript and gave me the kind of constructive criticism that genuinely reshaped this book and my thinking.

I thank my students at Princeton University, who have used as a textbook several different versions of *The Imaginative Argument* and who provided countless suggestions and comments, many of which I found useful to incorporate into these pages. Especial thanks to Ryan Marrinan and Lisa Korn, who allowed me to use their excellent papers in my appendix.

Thanks also to Jerzy Limon, Andrzej Ceynowa, David Malcolm, and Beata Williamson, colleagues at the University of Gdańsk who helped me in countless ways both here and in Poland, and who supported my academic endeavors; to Patrice Caldwell of Eastern New Mexico University, who generously helped me clarify many of my ideas about writing and teaching, to Jeff Ginsberg, who assisted in the editing of an early version of the book; to Carole Breheny, of Madison High School, who had the kindness to call this text a "survival manual" and used an early version of it in the English department that she chairs; to Carol Cook, for her genuine insights into teaching and writing; to Mike Tweedle and Christine Poon, who patiently listened to and helped me refine my lucubrations about writing, and who always challenged me vocabulistically; to John Sand, Joe Powell, Anne Buckley, Anthony DeCurtis, Bruce Fredrickson, Liahna Armstrong, Donald W. Cummings, and Philip Garrison, who stood by me in difficult times and always engaged and encouraged my ideas; and to Jessica Kennedy Delahoy, Peter Gruen, and Valerie Meluskey, teachers all and colleagues who were brought together in a profoundly wonderful and I expect long-lasting way. Thank you, too, to Caroline and Helmut Weymar, whose unfailing generosity and kindness helped me through ill-health—indeed, I composed much of this book while working under their roof.

And an enormous debt of gratitude and thanks to Princeton University Press's Lauren Lepow, who was both my copyeditor and my production editor. Her attention to detail, expression, logic, and ideas was superb—indeed, humbling. And great thanks and goodwill to Peter J. Dougherty, whose faith in this project and belief in me have been unshakable and long-lasting. I feel rewarded that he's not only my editor but now a friend.

*　　　*　　　*

I would like to thank the following authors and publishers for permission to use quotations from their works:

Erving Goffman, *Stigma: Notes on the Management of Spoiled Identity.* Copyright © 1963 by Prentice-Hall, Inc.; copyright renewed © 1991 by Simon & Schuster, Inc. Reprinted with the permission of Simon & Schuster Adult Publishing Group.

Bela Hap, "Structuralist Meta-Analysis," translated by Gyula Kodolányi, in *Essaying Essays: Alternative Forms of Exposition*, edited by Richard Kostelanetz (New York: Out of London Press, 1975). Used by permission of Gyula Kodolányi.

Charles Frazier, introduction to *The Book of Job*, King James Version (New York: Grove, 1999). Used by permission of Grove/Atlantic.

David Foster Wallace, "Consider the Lobster," *Gourmet*, August 2004. Used by permission of David Foster Wallace.

THE IMAGINATIVE ARGUMENT

1

An Introduction to the Writing of Essays

So much writing surrounds us that the textual environment has emerged as a complex and supremely detailed subuniverse. We as readers inhabit it as we take it in. All over the place—on billboards, bottle caps, cereal boxes, the Internet; in magazines, newspapers, books—the written word proliferates. Yet the writing of short essays, "themes," or "term papers" seems to be an activity confined to students. Poor, beleaguered students. Louis Menand, an essayist and literary historian, claims that term-paper composition is "one of those skills in life that people are obliged to master in order to be excused from ever practicing them again" (92). One naturally wonders what other skills Menand has in mind, but his point stands. Outside the college classroom, there is little direct use for writing of the kind done therein. The short, exploratory, focused, argumentative essay has only one secure home: academia.

But that's OK. I argue that the academic argument, the subject of this text, forms the central and most important kind of nonfiction writing that you should master, even if you don't get a chance to use it after graduating from college. It's important not only because it draws on elements of all the other forms of nonfiction writing and hence will allow you to move to any of those forms relatively easily. It also replicates the method by which ideas are created. It teaches you to think.

That's my belief, anyway. Mastering the type of writing I outline here will help not just students who want to become professional writers or professors but also those of you who work in any position that requires honest, sustained appraisal or scrutiny of issues, ideas, people, texts, or situations. It's a kind of writing that replicates the kind of thought needed to uncover, as much as possible, The Truth. Such essays look not only for *confirmatory* evidence (that is, evidence to support a given position) but for *disconfirmatory* evidence as well, and they end up using both kinds of evidence to develop their ideas. They aim not merely to persuade but to give as fair and honest and complete an analysis as possible. For it is only such a fair and honest analysis, only such a careful appraisal of alternative and competing positions, only such a scrupulous but dispassionate scrutiny, that will serve the highest goal: the advancement of knowledge.

While this kind of essay attempts to advance human knowledge, writing it will also help you increase and clarify your own thoughts and insights, even about things that you thought you were already quite sure of. Sometimes, for example, you will have feelings and insights about an issue or a book or a film, but won't exactly know what they are—what they stem from, on what assumptions they might be based, or how they might connect with those of others. But writing the argumentative essay requires both that you articulate thoughts about an issue or text, and that you organize your inchoate feelings and insights into a form accessible to others and yourself. Moreover, writing this kind of essay allows you to understand argumentation, a form of discourse that will be useful in any situation that requires analysis.

But let's first take a look at more immediately recognizable and familiar kinds of writing. It seems to me that there are at least three discrete and historically established types of nonfiction writing, all of which differ from the kind of essay I describe here. The first might be called "essay as literature." Some universities offer a "creative nonfiction" course, in which you write personal essays or opinion pieces— these might resemble essays from magazines such as *Harper's* or the *Atlantic*, or from journals such as the *American Scholar*, *Creative Nonfiction*, or *Raritan*. This literary genre of nonfiction, sometimes called "belles lettres," forms part of our Literary Tradition. It might include the works of Montaigne, Samuel Johnson, Addison and Steele, Margaret Fuller, Thomas Carlyle, Ralph Waldo Emerson, Matthew Arnold, Annie Dillard, and many others. The essay as work of art—the essay as creative work—memoirs, autobiographies, and other kinds of "creative nonfiction" might fall under this rubric. Courses examining (and requiring) such writing are often offered by English departments or in creative writing programs.

Other university courses are widely available (often called "Technical Writing") on the second major type of nonfiction writing, namely, "informative writing," a type of writing used in industry. Such writing intends primarily to convey information, not necessarily in a literary or artful manner, and often of relatively trivial or quotidian varieties—instruction manuals for our gadgets and appliances, software documentation so that we know how to use computer programs, statutes, warning labels, that sort of thing. Such writing also includes some reportage—journalism. It is also the language of much business writing, such as memos, reports, announcements. Hence writing courses are often taught in schools of journalism or in business departments.

And finally, the third main category of nonfiction has as its primary goal persuasion: this writing attempts to make you do something, take a particular position, vote for a candidate or issue, buy a particular car or drug or deodorant. Such writing appears in political speeches, legal cases, and advertising: it will use any tactic imaginable—whether logic, or blatant appeals to guilt or emotion, or even threats of various kinds—to persuade its audience. Writing of this kind often forms the subject for courses in mass communication or media studies departments.

I hasten to add that these categories are by no means as clearly separated or nonoverlapping as I've made them out. Much informative writing seeks to persuade. Journalism can be "artful" and literary. Belletristic writing is often informative, as are some political speeches or even advertisements. But the general categories hold up, I think—even if we look at the kind of writing available on the Internet, which no doubt makes up a sizable moiety of what Americans read today.

Though all of these differ from each other, they do share some similarities as well. For example, writers in all these subgenres work with a certain audience—and its expectations—clearly in mind. They all rely on a series of conventions that writers must respect—what kind of format to use, what level of formality, what tone to adopt, what kinds of syntax, language, and vocabulary to employ. They all have a readily apparent organizational structure, which should be more or less clear from the outset.

Where does the "academic argument" fit in here? I would suggest that it hovers somewhere in the middle, drawing on common aspects of nonfiction writing—it is attentive to audience, conventions, tone, language, organization. But it also shares some specialized qualities with each of these three subgenres. The academic argument pays considerable attention to the way things are stated—it aims not necessarily to "be" art but to state its points in a creative manner, a manner that has the artist's or craftsperson's sensitivity to form, precision, image. It also must convey some information, some facts; it roots itself in the actual. Finally, the academic argument aims to persuade, but not to persuade at any cost—it strives to convince through the use of logical argumentation, giving as fair, honest, and complete an analysis as possible.

In fact, the essays that I require in classes must do more than just impress, convey information, or persuade. They try to uncover the truth of a situation and try to convince—in an artful way—a specific audience of this truth. Not surprisingly the staple of "scholarship," this kind of writing resembles what professors—in many various disciplines—must themselves do.

What is their writing like? While an academic argument does express its author's opinion, this opinion is more than "just an opinion," a knee-jerk response, or an unexplored prejudice. Rather, academic argument offers a point of view buttressed by evidence. It provides an educated, considered, and reasoned opinion—an opinion not just offered or asserted but argued for.

Professors argue their point of view, seeking to persuade, but they additionally examine other scholars' works and situate their writing within what might be called the "dialectical discourse"—in opposition to some works and in partial agreement with others. They convey information, drawing on considerable secondary resource material. Such writing tends to be "formal," and it almost always appeals primarily to specialized audiences, such as those for *New Literary History* (literary theorists), *Paeduma* (scholars studying medieval works), *Urology* (medical doctors who specialize in urology), or *Behavioural and Brain Sciences* (psychologists, philosophers, neurologists).

These "presumptive audiences" consist of other specialists in the field, and scholars can take for granted that those audiences will all be dwelling within what Carl Becker calls the same "climate of opinion": their frames of reference will be similar, and they will share at least some notion of the value and scope of the subject matter. They will be interested in the argument.

The argument essay contains five key components:

1. It contains a formal statement of an argumentative position (a **thesis**), something that answers a vitally important **question** in an unexpected, insightful way.
2. It develops and draws **support** for its position from external sources ("facts," "evidence," "warrants," "examples") of various kinds.
3. Its **organization** or **structure**, internally consistent and intuitive, logically and progressively shows—without using fallacious argument—both the content and complexity of its main idea and how that main idea can be supported.
4. It seeks out, examines, and answers reasonable ideas that oppose it, that would attempt to refute its thesis, or subpoints, i.e., "**con arguments**" or counterarguments.
5. Its **conclusion** amplifies and enhances the thesis—is an idea that can be proposed now that the paper has explained and explored the thesis. The conclusion shows a change in the thesis—a "$\triangle T$" (see chapter 5).

Throughout, I want to stress that the very writing of the essay itself—the process of writing—has just as much value as the finished product. And while that finished product may well form the basis for a published article or essay, the thought, the writing, the doing, the slaving-away-at-the-keyboard effort that the finished essay required emerges as the more valuable result. Ultimately, too, you need to realize that this effort of writing a paper is even more rewarding and meaningful than the grade or than what the professor has to say about the finished product. In a variation on the old saw "The spoils is the game, not the victory," I want to offer "Writing finds its rewards in the I'm-writing, not the I've-written." Now getting you to believe this—that will be the difficult part.

THE ARGUMENT ESSAY DEFINED

In a way it is unfortunate that we need to use the term "argument" to describe a kind of writing, for "argument" most typically means a heated dispute, an altercation, a verbal fight. Actual fights may indeed follow the verbal fight of an "argument" too—an argument is a serious, emotional, and confrontational experience. It's worse than a spat, more angry than a discussion, more heated than a mere debate.

But forget all that. None, or little, of it really applies here. Instead, here (and in other textbooks about argumentation), "argument" refers to a kind of discourse, an organized verbal attempt to persuade an audience through the use of logic and reason. Obviously there are other ways to persuade people—ranging from torture and coercion, on one hand, to cajolery, satire, burlesque, or advertisement, on the other. But logical argument—if you will permit a value judgment—is the most civilized, the most high-minded mode. It's the mode suggested here, anyway, and logical argument has its own system of rules and prohibitions, its own structure, and its own ontology, much of which I will attempt to delineate in the following pages.

Written argument may take many forms. For example, a description might strive to show a new way of looking at something, such as a poem, a system of government, or a tax loophole; a classification would place something in a large, organizational matrix or system; an evaluation makes a judgment about something based on comparison of that thing with a stipulated ideal type; a proposal might suggest a future course of action or a present problem that needs to be addressed; a comparison-contrast might compare two different things, issues, ideas, or texts in an effort to illuminate something about one or both of them; a cause-effect paper might show how a situation or state of affairs could lead to or cause another; a definition might argue for a new way of characterizing something. In his *Rhetoric* Aristotle gives twenty-eight valid "topics" for argument, but these can for the most part be distilled into the seven modes I have suggested above.

These modes—description, classification, evaluation, proposal, comparison-contrast, cause-effect, and definition—give you the structure or subgenre of your whole paper, but they don't tell you in any detail what you actually have to do. Basically, working within these modes, your paper needs to *explain something*. Usually a paper will attempt to explain something relatively difficult—something in need of explanation—but sometimes the simplest things only *seem* simple. On closer inspection, they reveal themselves as not quite so simple and hence really do need to be explained.

Let me be more specific and offer some strategies that you might use when you attempt to explain. While these strategies are not mutually exclusive—indeed, many overlap—I nonetheless offer them as examples of what an argumentative paper can usefully do by way of explaining. Your paper can do one or more of the following:

1. *Interpret.* An interpreter usually renders one language into another, and in some sense that is what an interpretation paper does as well. It argues meaning or elucidation of something difficult and perhaps obscure. It translates one version of English into a more accessible version. You might focus on some aspect of language, in such an analysis, or you might look at what various "key words" mean. This involves more than merely defining them—indeed, you might conceive of what special meanings the words have in the context of the work. For example, when the philosopher John Rawls writes about "the veil of ignorance," you need to know what kinds of things he has in mind with respect to creating a fair system of organizing a society. You also need to know dictionary definitions of words. On one exam I took, I was given a poem, "The Chambered Nautilus," and asked to explicate it. My task was made far easier by the fact that I for some reason knew the nautilus to be a type of seashell. Make sure that you look at all aspects of a work, including the title! For example, the short poem "Little children you all may go / But the one you are hiding will fly" makes some sense on its own, but its title, "Song of Primitive Man Chipping Out an Arrowhead," gives it a different meaning altogether. When Marshall McLuhan chose his famous book title, *The Medium Is the Massage*, what did he mean?

2. *Uncover assumptions.* Often there are assumptions that need to be unpacked or unmasked. Whether an essay examines a speech, a paleontological theory, a novel, or a yacht, there are underlying assumptions and elements inherent in the makeup of each of these genres (speech,

theory, novel, yacht), as well individual variations from novel to novel, or yacht to yacht, for example. This kind of paper would argue not just that certain underlying assumptions exist, but that they function in some interesting, elaborate, or perhaps sinister way. Sometimes an author's words themselves embody preexisting theoretical commitments. In fact, even the author might not know these implicit assumptions or they are so deeply rooted in the psyche that all of us might be unaware of them. But looking for these is often a useful, even sobering task.

3. *Reveal significant patterns.*   A paper might argue both for the existence of patterns of some kind (giving examples to support its assertions) and for the idea that such patterns are meaningful, important ones. These patterns can be linguistic (repetition of certain words, sentence structures, or images), thematic, generic, or even stylistic. You might, for instance, discover some pattern that could explain how a building works—say, the use of curves or of the number six in the Chrysler Building. Or you could find something interesting about word-pattern in a novel. For example, Martin Amis, while reading *Crash* by J. G. Ballard, notes that the author uses certain keywords many times: "perverse" sixteen times, "geometry" twenty-one times, "stylized" twenty-six times. These curious repetitions seem to suggest something about the author's sensibility, as does the fact that, for example, in Ben Franklin's autobiography, the word "ingenious," or some variation thereof, appears more than thirty times.

But pattern finding need not be limited to word counting. Georg Simmel points out that in Shakespeare's plays the minor characters tend to be killed by outside forces, while the major characters seem to die as a result of internal problems. An interesting pattern—what does it mean? You might ask yourself, too, whether there is a pattern evident in the way that the author handles certain kinds of characters or situations. Is there a pattern of action that seems to predominate with reference to the way a plot unfolds? Does it remind you of other patterns of action? Sometimes such a paper can compare the patterns of the subject with overarching pattern-generating schemes, such as those provided by history, sociology, psychoanalysis, feminism, myth.

4. *Reveal pattern breaks.* This kind of paper would have to incorporate elements of (3) above, but it takes the revelation of patterns a step further, showing how the apparent patterns are not always followed and are either purposely or inadvertently violated. It might then speculate why the patterns break down.

5. *Recontextualize.* Such a paper shows how, when looked at in another context—one provided by current events, other works, a new idea or explanatory scheme—a work, idea, or artifact takes on a wholly new meaning. Simply, it views the work—poem, story, whatever—as part of a larger structure. For example, all movies, novels, poems, plays, or books about terrorism must be seen in a new light since the events of September 11, 2001. On a less political note, you might look at a painting or sculpture, for example, in light of its initial reception, or in light of what was going on in the artist's life (or the life of his/her social class, or the life of the artist's nation) at the time it appeared.

6. *Generalize.* Such a paper argues that the system, text, artifact, or thing under scrutiny represents a larger, more expansive universal. For example, the new security measures at airports represent how we as citizens have lost the War on Terror. The proliferation of prescription drug commercials on television suggests a larger reliance on drug use as a way of life. Fiction can be generalized this way too: a story might be about a woman, but this story could perhaps be explained as being about the plight of every woman—or every person. A story about looking for a parking space might be seen as being about something as general as the nature of quests. A story about a boy's disappointment with his visit to a mall Santa Claus might be seen as a story about growing up and coming to terms with the alloyed quality of anticipated pleasure. Another way to think about this would be to see certain elements of a piece of writing

or a situation as being metaphorical, as representing something else. (The extreme version of such a tactic is the allegorization of experience that many cultures adopt. And allegory is "one story that is really another, very different story," to use Henry James's definition. Almost all of *Aesop's Fables* are allegories, for example.)

7. *Argue for effect.*   This paper might argue for how something has an impact on a reader, viewer, participant. It tries to show how the elements of whatever is under analysis have a direct (or not-so-direct) connection to the way people respond to that subject.

8. *Extrapolate.*   A paper might take the argument of an essay or the general "message" of a work and show its silliness, ridiculousness, or nonsensicality by extending it to its logical next or last step. Your paper would demonstrate and explain the work's weakness, shallowness, or incoherence. (Usually people employ this strategy, "reductio ad absurdum," to attack other arguments or philosophical propositions.)

Overall, you need to remember, though, that whatever strategy you employ—and some things seem to be more amenable to certain strategies than others—your paper needs to argue for something not obvious, not taken for granted, not superficial, not readily conceded. You want to reveal something that you have in some genuine sense *discovered*. Your paper will prove why what you have discovered has resonance and importance. At the same time you don't want to "explain away" the text or subject matter: your essay will not replace or supplant what it is that you are writing about. Remember that if you feel that you've explained everything, then probably something is wrong with the angle you have taken. As the critic and writer Murray Sperber often warns, avoid creating a critical machine that grinds to hamburger everything in its path!

Keep in Mind That . . .

Your own writing is not intended to be a reiteration of the class's or the instructor's ideas. Rather, the papers being written here should be an elaboration, an extension, and an expression of your own ideas. Your own voice—your own insights—should predominate. It is, however, necessary to understand and build on the ideas of the texts, class, and instructor; to ignore these or to present them as your own (or as silly and jejune) would be a mistake. But overall, most instructors appreciate creativity and originality of insight rather than mere recasting or parroting of previously expressed ideas. External sources, too, should not usurp or displace your own voice in the course of an essay; rather, they should be used to bolster, to contextualize, to delineate, and to sharpen your own position. This of course may vary from class to class—probably some classes do require both acceptance and reiteration of the ideas of the instructor and texts: they want you to demonstrate that you "got it," to quote my erstwhile colleague. Yet finally it's up to you to figure out to what extent you are expected to be entirely original and to what extent you just need to demonstrate that you have understood and can reproduce the various concepts (reading materials, ideas from lectures) in a class.

2

Audience, or For Whom Are You Writing?

An audience—a group of people sitting in the room while we talk—usually listens somewhat, usually gives some indication of their response to what we say. They can applaud or laugh, hiss or whistle, chew gum, throw spitballs, have their own little side conversations, or read a newspaper. In one class I taught, a woman who was eating a jawbreaker fell asleep, and the huge piece of candy popped out of her mouth and bounced onto the desk in front of her, waking her up. For the speaker, the feedback is often immediate.

With writing, though, the person or persons on the receiving end—also called the "audience"—tend not to give us immediate feedback. I am now alone in a room. A fan whirrs overhead, and cars motor by on the street below my open window. To whom might I actually be writing? Why, I'm writing to myself. But at the same time, I have to keep in mind others who might read the words that appear right now on my screen before me. Who are they? How will they respond? Will they understand what I'm saying? Find it interesting? Read to the next paragraph, even to the end of the book? Because I want them to do this, I need to respect and consider their needs and interests. I need, in short, to appeal to them. And before doing this, I have to figure out who they might be.

When most people sit down to write, all too rarely do they deeply, self-consciously consider the variety of audiences, the interests and proclivities of the people who read their writing, the things that the audience will respond to (and what they might incorrectly respond to), or what the audience genuinely wants from the writing. Such considerations might be thought to border on the trivial—to be almost too obvious to bother with. But I want to suggest that these considerations are of enormous importance, especially in the writing of arguments. You need to figure out what that audience is like before you can set about persuading them of anything. And your first consideration, I think, should be the kind of language you use—the way you put together words on the page, the way you sequence them and punctuate them and spell them; their rhythm; their sound.

LANGUAGE USE

When writing a personal letter or email, you probably keep the recipient in mind; if you're writing a more "professional" missive, report, or paper, you might think about omitting personal references, the personal pronoun, slang, abbreviations, or even contractions. But the kind of language you use, its "correctness," the level of vocabulary, the length and variety of your sentences—these should all be conscious choices. Your language does more than merely help to bolster the argument you're explicitly making—it makes an argument in and of itself. If it is concise, crisp, accurate, and well edited, it carries persuasive force independent of your argumentative strategy. If, by contrast, it contains many errors in usage and punctuation, uses short, all-too-similarly-structured sentences, employs slang, misspelled words, and other nonstandard forms, it tends to undermine your argument.

Indeed, you need to make this rhetorical decision about "correctness." You need to control that particular variable, because whether you make this decision consciously or not, *your audience will interpret it as a conscious choice!* Your audience will respond not just to your ideas but to the way you say them. A paper rife with small errors might suggest that the writer is careless, hurried, or perhaps even uneducated. And while merely correcting the spelling and usage of a weak, empty, or old-hat paper will not turn that particular sow's ear into a Prada bag, it will nonetheless provide your work with something like entry-level credibility for an audience. Writing "correct" prose—on the sentence level—may seem a minor issue, but it is important insofar as readers often judge a writer by the accuracy or slovenliness of his or her usage (sometimes erroneously called "grammar"), or by the precision with which the writer follows "The Rules of Usage."

Hence even if you have a very subtle and penetrating argument but use what might be perceived as inappropriate language in presenting it, your audience might automatically stopper its ears. Your language use might well suggest that you don't have anything important or intelligent to say; it might, in short, stigmatize you from the get-go. Let me translate this same idea into "inappropriate" (in this case, oral) language to demonstrate how it changes:

It's like when you write, you know, it's **not** like just the *stuff* you think of, y'know, like your *ideas*, like your *insights*, like y'know, all the *content* and all, but it's other things that, like, get heard too by y'r audience, y'know? It's like they see y'r writing as being, like, not just y'know, the *stuff*, dude, but like, it's like the *words*, too, are im*por*tant. Hey, you know, I can see, like—the im*por*tant things, of course, but like, you know there are people out there who they don't, like, really *get* it, y' know? It's like they don't *listen*, y' know, unless you speak, like, the same way they do, and you know, here at **college, it's like—dude—they don't.**

Paradoxically, The Rules of Usage don't exist per se. Usage, similar in many ways to other aspects of writing discussed here, varies quite widely, adjusts to differing situations, and even within a given context involves few black/white, wrong/right issues. Perhaps you have noticed that many published, even formal essays deviate from The Rules. Writers often creatively violate the norms of "correct" usage, or they press on the margins of correctness to make a certain point or to refine their own distinctiveness. Hence using their writing as a model might be problematic. Keep in mind, too, that most of the writing we encounter in our daily lives does not abide by strict principles of formal usage: advertising, journalism, street signs, operating instructions, Web sites, poetry, fiction, "creative nonfiction," and letters or emails all have their own grammar, syntax, and vocabulary ("btw," "lol," "fwiw"), their own range of the conventional and acceptable. Such writing might have considerable value, but we cannot look to it for reliable models of academic writing. Nor can we look to speech as a model for writing: things we say are typically more colloquial, more redundant, and more imprecise than things we write.

Some people have objected that I am too rigid with the level of correctness that I call for—that I should allow for an "imaginative" spelling or punctuation, one violating the so-to-speak norm. While I'm sure most people advancing this argument do so a bit disingenuously, I do want to say that, yes, you certainly can be imaginative in any way that you see fit. Many great writers distort language—I'm thinking of James Joyce, Gertrude Stein, William Faulkner—and recent writers, too, such as Russell Hoban (in his novel *Riddley Walker*), David Bunch (in *Moderan*), or David Foster Wallace (in *Infinite Jest*) use self-consciously deviant spellings, syntax, or punctuation. The American philosopher William James—himself a masterful writer—allegedly railed against people "who opposed spelling reform with purely conservative arguments" (2:19). He even championed, to an extent, English "spelt spontaneously." He writes Henry Holt in a letter of 1894,

> Dear Holt, —The Introduction to filosofy is what I ment—I dont no the other book.
> I will try Nordau's Entartung this summer—as a rule however it duzn't profit me to read Jeremiads against evil—the example of a little good has more effect.
> A propo of kitchen ranges, I wish you wood remoov your recommendation from that Boynton Furnace Company's affair. We have struggld with it for five years—lost 2 cooks in consequens—burnt countless tons of extra coal, never had anything decently baikt, and now, having got rid of it for 15 dollars, are having a happy kitchen for the 1st time in our experience—all through your unprinsipld recommendation! You ought to hear my wife sware when she hears your name!
> I will try about a translator for Nordau—though the only man I can think of needs munny more than fame, and cood n't do the job for pure love of the publisher or author, or on an unsertainty. (*Letters* 2:19)

James did not continue in this vein, I feel compelled to add. In fact, how long would you continue to read this book were its spelling similar to the above? Again, everything about your writing communicates something, regardless of what you intend it to communicate. And "spelling reforms" such as those in James's letter communicate—what?—a lack of gravitas? A lack of concern with getting points across? A lack of respect for the audience? The misspellings so call attention to themselves that they probably serve more to distract than to reform.

Of course most of you already speak and write fundamentally sound and correct English. For example, you don't use sentences such as

*A of ran terrific inherent about plunge his the creates to.

But English, like all languages, has its own sublanguages, dialects, and variations. "Good" English in one context is not appropriate in other contexts. In this book, I try to use fundamentally "formal," correct English—not always the kind of English you might speak (or even write), but the kind that you probably want to be able to master in your academic career. And I am acutely aware, too, that experts do not always agree about what makes for "correct" English. It might be said that "formal" English serves as a default language in situations where you don't really know what kind of language your audience would consider the most appropriate. Using this kind of English will not stigmatize you—or, for that matter, work to your advantage—in every situation, but it's still the safest, most neutral, for you to regularly employ.

LANGUAGE AS MARKER

Some students of language contend that language use carries class markers of very specific kinds. Such markers may or may not be important to you. For example, the sentence

*Me and him went out to the storage unit to get some props.

does not convey that the speaker has a formal education. Educated people might use such sentences, perhaps in order to belie their actual social status—or perhaps because they don't realize how much their language reveals about them. Similarly, a number of usages and pronunciations convey class distinction, according to some linguists:

*We ain't got no shortage of problems around here.

*Between you and I, it's a relief to have rain.

*He doesn't want to do that hisself.

All of these are easy to understand, but many linguists have highlighted such usages as being "non-upper-class" or the kinds of usages that only uneducated persons might employ. While I am not sure that class distinctions evidenced by language use are obvious to everyone, it does seem manifestly clear that people judge you by your language use. I leave it to your own judgment when to use one type of English rather than another. Of course, using "correct" language might itself be stigmatizing at times. If we lived in a classless society or one in which classism, prejudice against members of another (usually lower) class, did not exist, none of this would matter. But that day seems, sadly, far off.

And I don't want to be in the position of claiming that using "incorrect" English will exclude you from the successful stratum of society, or from positions of power or authority. (Consider the many "Bushisms" generated by President George W. Bush.) Western society is so complex and the kinds of success and power so multifarious that labeling one language, formal English, as the tongue of successful people would be imprudent—in fact, just plain wrong. However, I think university students need to know some of the aspects of formal, standard English (a prescriptive grammar) that they can regularly employ in the appropriate situations. It doesn't take that long to learn the fundamentals of usage, what to do, what to avoid.

Some students have contended that I'm teaching them not just English but how to be English teachers. I concede the point. It is likely that most of you will teach language to others—whether to fellow workers, your children, or students in a classroom here or in another country. So yes, I am trying in some ways to prepare you to teach English. I'm hoping this skill will prove valuable. Maybe the best thing that will come of your study, though, will be a greater awareness of the language you use and the impact it makes.

IMAGINING THE AUDIENCE

Now that I have you productively self-conscious (or maybe just worried) about how you use language, you have to start thinking about what you want to say and whom you are addressing. You must spend some time imagining your audience, determining as much as possible its values and preferences. You want to find out what that audience is like, what it expects from your writing, how homogeneous or specialized it is, and what formal and linguistic parameters you must respect. Some students feel that such audience-determination suggests dishonesty, as if they were being asked to give the audience only what it wants to hear. But that is not the case. With a hostile audience, for example, you need to present your argument in a much different way from what you'd use were you facing an indifferent, neutral, or friendly audience. But in no case am I recommending that you be dishonest. I'm not suggesting that you abandon your position or ideas in order to pander to what the audience wants. Rather, I want you to assess your audience so that you might more effectively shape and organize your argument.

At the same time, though, that you imagine the audience, you need to imagine (or reimagine) yourself. What image of yourself do you want to convey? Well, who are you? Here and at many other points in the writing process you will need to confront this question, indeed do something by way of self-assessment or self-analysis. You won't, for example, need or want to project the entirety of your personality or experience in your writing. I don't want to convey to you via my writing that I'm a person who sometimes oversleeps, who tends toward compulsiveness, or who has made manifold though not fatal mistakes in his life. I'd rather not reveal these things, at least not here. (I'm working through them elsewhere.) Of course sometimes my prose unwittingly does communicate features of my personality that I am not proud of (e.g., compulsiveness, now that I think of it). But as I imagine the archaeologically constructible face I want you to see, I need to decide what that psychic mug shot should be like.

For example, I expect that many of you will be students—so I need to sound authoritative, "teacherly," in my claims, in my way of expression ("psychic mug shot"? Well, antically teacherly). I need to be someone who speaks from experience. At the same time, I want to make this readable and interesting to you—I don't want to sound stuffy or old-fashioned or hidebound, though I know that I run this risk. Some of my audience will also be teachers, and for teachers, I also want to sound as though I know my material, but an added feature comes into play here: teachers will likely be familiar, to an extent, with much of what I'm suggesting. So there has to be something original about it, or else they won't be interested. I need to keep in mind that teachers want a new, insightful, useful, teachable angle on material that they are already "inward with," that is, understand in a very thorough way. And finally, I expect a "general audience" might read this and might want something different from the previous groups. What they want I'm not completely sure, but I need to realize (as I write) that the personality I convey has to be one that can talk to people outside of the classroom or professor's office. It needs to be someone who might engage you in conversation on an airplane, at a cocktail party, at a fund-raiser, during intermission at a play, or even in casual talk at the post office.

This projected self, in rhetorical theory referred to as "ethos," permeates and informs the writing that you will do. The ethos needs to be someone that your audience will respond to immediately, the imaginary self that speaks in place of you, as your proxy, as maybe your "best" self; it needs to have a voice and personality that your audience will not only trust but also like.

MOTIVES

Behind both the imagining of the audience and the imagining of the ideal self you want to project to that audience, however, lies one very important issue: What are all of you—all of us—here for? Why are you writing, and why does an audience pay you any heed? In some ways, for teachers and students this question seems simple to answer: you are here to do the assignment, and the teacher, paid to read it, does so dutifully, or is supposed to. Yet this isn't really quite enough. You can't really write an assignment that says, "I am doing this because I have to. I want to complete this assignment, even though I would much rather be outside on the beach. I really want this to take only a few more hours." Nor could someone applying for a grant write, "I really just want the grant money. I need that grant money, so I can live comfortably and do what I want to do. My purpose here is to get that money." At the same time, I as teacher (as an audience grading a student's paper) cannot write, "I have to read this paper and I have. Now I have read it. There. It's read. I really wish I could be out on the beach rather than reading papers." I mean, these things might sometimes be true, but we have to look a little deeper for the motive and purpose behind writing—or, for that matter, behind being an audience.

Actually many motives inform both writing and reading. Certainly some of them are intellectual in nature. For example, sometimes writers need to convey information that readers need to hear. If someone will meet your plane when you fly to the Coast next week, you probably need to convey flight information to him or her. Or the audience might want entertainment. They want to be amused. Perhaps your audience wants to be inspired in some way. Or your audience could want knowledge. They might want, by contrast, merely to assess you, the writer (if you're writing a letter of application). Note that these motives can blend and blur somewhat, but writers need to imagine, as they project and infer their audience, what primary purpose their writing will serve.

Other motives, such as the desire just to finish what you are writing or reading—what might be called ulterior motives—clearly vie with the more explicit, more intellectual ones, but you need, I think, to hold those ulterior ones in abeyance while you try to envision an audience of people who want to be there, who want to hear what you say. Think of yourself and your audience as inhabiting a magical, imaginary, ideal space, one in which you both are interested only in ideas. At the same time, you need to imagine yourself as getting fulfillment from the act of writing itself, and to see your imaginary space and time as not subject to the problems surrounding writing or the petty irritations of daily life. Of course, eventually the world will intrude on both writer and audience—the calls of human biology, of tight schedules, of competing claims on one's consciousness. The phone, the door, the newly arrived instant message, your back, your wrists, your ischial tuberosities. But for a brief time, try to imagine that you inhabit a universe of intellect and ideas rather than bodies and things, and that your audience dwells in that universe with you.

Therefore, as you write, you must in some ways serve two (imagined, projected) masters: first, the conception you have of your audience, what they are like, what they are looking for; and second, the conception that you have of your own purpose, and of what kind of personality or character you want to project. In what follows, I want to examine the two principal variables that writers need to consider with respect to this dual construction, namely, the degree of "friendliness" (or unfriendliness) of a perceived audience; and the audience's level of specialization.

WRITING FOR A GENERAL AUDIENCE, SYMPATHETIC OR HOSTILE

When you don't really know that much about your audience, other than that it's not composed solely of specialists, you face significant challenges. You don't really know what they expect, nor do you know how various that audience's makeup might actually be. For example, there might be some specialists among the audience, but perhaps they do not make up the majority. Some of your audience might be more attentive than others. And levels of education will vary as well. But despite the apparently heterogeneous nature of the audience, which will present various difficulties, its degree of friendliness or hostility often emerges; and this in fact might be more useful than other kinds of knowledge as a gauge of how to direct your ideas, how to give certain emphases to and organize your argument.

Presenting ideas to a friendly audience—"preaching to the choir"—is generally not problematic. Thus many textbooks focus more on how you can present an argument to the opposite—a hostile audience. These ideas might initially strike you as largely irrelevant here, if you are a student, since your instructors are specialists, and to an extent you are as well, and thus they will not generally be hostile to the topics that you write about.

But sometimes the situation will arise—how do you persuade the audience who you know will vehemently disagree with you from the outset? How do you present a persuasive argument when you think that your audience's position is flat-out wrongheaded or misguided, and when you know for certain that they will take the same position with respect to what you offer?

First, you need to realize that such writing entails risk. Most people, including professors, do not want to be confronted in this manner. If you must do so, try to acknowledge very early in the paper that you know you are presenting an oppositional view, but that you think that position has some validity and needs to be expressed. And you should take very seriously the stating of what you perceive to be your audience's values, attempting to phrase them in as exact and fair a manner as possible. Finally, keep in mind that it will be very difficult to persuade your audience. You probably won't make someone change a deeply held belief, even if your paper is tightly argued and very well written. However, if you can get your audience to pause in the face of something challenging their belief, then you have to a large extent succeeded. Of course the audience might be only demurring before rejecting your idea, but that's OK: it's the hesitation that signals success.

The most important strategy to gain this pause, to forestall the outright rejection, consists in respecting your (hostile) audience. If your audience feels its viewpoint has at least been considered, they will be slightly more open to ideas that run directly counter to their own. Remember that in disagreeing with someone, you probably don't want to suggest that the person is stupid, doesn't deserve to be in the workforce, should be locked in an insane asylum or transformed into Soylent Green. Let me give you an example of an "oppositional" paper that failed to work for the very reason that the writer clearly did not respect his audience. In one class I taught, I asked students to write a proposal that argued for some change in the university, and to specify the audience to whom that proposal was directed. A student, let us call him Jim B., wrote an essay that proposed all required writing classes be discontinued and replaced with additional requirements in physical education. This does not on the face of it seem totally unreasonable, but the audience Jim B. specified (namely, me) was a person who had for many years taught required writing classes at that university. Jim B. argued that writing was a valueless skill, would never be used in his life or career ("all of my writing will be done by a low level functionary similar to a writing professor—a secretary or speechwriter," he wrote), while by contrast physical fitness should be a lifelong commitment and concern.

I think Jim B. (though capturing an idea about writing that many people in the general public assuredly share) had confused the idea of in-your-face confrontation with that of academic argument. Indeed, he was seeking not so much to persuade as to demean his audience, hardly the kind of strategy that led to success for him on that particular assignment, but perhaps the kind of thing that fulfilled some other need—which other I will leave to your imagination. Needless to say, the audience did not feel as though Jim B. really had much respect or consideration for him, and it seems likely that Jim B. hardly thought about that audience at all, except in a fleeting, occasional, and contemptuous way. He probably still despises me. But we in the class discussed his paper, since he openly disagreed with my evaluation of it, and his classmates in fact pointed out that he had disregarded one of the principal ideas in the course, specifically, knowing the audience.

Back to the more usual case—presenting ideas that fundamentally accord with or complement those being expressed by your instructor, your class, and your texts—let me offer this. You can be critical; you need not take for granted that any article or story or lecture is the final word or even the most accurate account of an issue. Yet you should look for subtleties and nuances in the given topic or subject, things that struck you yet were not discussed by the texts, class, or teacher. You should seek some insights that others do not have, or might not be sensitive to, or have overlooked. I don't adhere to the notion "Strive for mediocrity," take the safe, middling pathway that shows you know the material and have a solid sense of the subject matter. You do need this solid sense of mastery, I hasten to add; it's just not sufficient. You should challenge yourself to go to another stage of sophistication. Find your own individual ideas, distinguish them from those garnered elsewhere, and formulate an original and insightful response to the assignment.

WRITING FOR THE SPECIALIST AUDIENCE

In classroom situations your audience will likely be a specialist. He or she will be very willing to engage your ideas and will try to look at them in a favorable light—basically, a friendly specialist audience. In classes that require writing, the audience (i.e., the instructor) will surely value a sophisticated and carefully reasoned interpretation, an original approach, precise language use, grammatical accuracy, spelling correctness, a reasonable tone, fully developed and coherent paragraphs, a logical structure, and a clear argumentative line: all these have been traditionally valued and honored in classroom situations. But it would behoove you to determine even more specifically how best to reach this audience, not only in terms of how much you need to restate or defer to his or her views, but also in terms of preferred critical approaches, political slant, or argumentative strategies.

In terms of content, most instructors look for complexity, lucidity, and depth of insight. They want (though you might not initially believe this) *to learn something new* from reading an essay. They want their understanding of an issue, an idea, or a text broadened or complicated in some interesting way. They want a new angle on an old problem. They want knowledge. Of course this creates difficulties for you, since in fact they are usually very knowledgeable about—are typically specialists in—the very topic your paper examines. But believe it or not, a genuinely new approach, a new insight, quite often emerges in student essays, and it always earns professors' respect, perhaps to the extent that it gives them pause, making them reflect on issues about which their ideas might have stabilized or solidified.

At the same time that the specialized audience wants knowledge, though, they want a range of reference and language appropriate to the subject. A biologist, for example, would have little difficulty with the following language, found in a paper from the journal *Animal Behaviour*: "The square roots of the recorded duration of immobility values were taken to lessen the effect of the outliers on the mean for each test" (Gould and Arduino 922). Nor would a philosopher or historian balk at how Andreas Huyssen, a professor at Columbia University, expresses himself in his book *Present Pasts*: "As fundamentally contingent categories of historically rooted perception, time and space are always bound up with each other in complex ways, and the intensity of border-crossing memory discourses that characterize so much of contemporary culture in so many different parts of the world today proves the point" (12). Yet a general audience would, I think, find both of these sentences difficult, obscure, jargon-clotted.

Conversely, writing for the specialized audiences that both Gould and Huyssen project actually requires these writers to use certain language ("outliers," "immobility values," "border-crossing memory discourses") that others in the field will readily understand. In addition, the two professors use the passive voice ("were taken," "are always bound up with"), which natural and social scientists tend to favor. Using more conversational or ordinary language would require them to take a lot longer to get their point across and might even undermine their own credibility as specialists.

What makes writing for a specialist audience in some ways easy, though, is that that audience tends to be homogeneous and predictable. You know more or less the range of reference it needs. You as writer will also be able to predict the kind of language required in a given field. James Gould writes appositely about the distinguishing features of scientific writing:

> The dependence on rhetoric and Style is assumed to be minimal, and great suspicion attaches to papers that make overuse of the power of words. Students typically describe the style of published papers as cut and dried at best, and deliberately boring and obscure at worst. Ideally, our students should learn to make judicious use of rhetoric . . . but they should also understand what sorts of assignments they are likely to encounter in science courses that may actually punish rhetorical skill in the (let's hope mistaken) belief that the writer is being frivolous in the august presence of Scientific Endeavor. ("Science Writing")

That is, there are certain conventions that attach to scientific or indeed to any specialized form of discourse, and the specialist speaking to other specialists must heed these conventions.

Carl Becker, as noted above, calls these conventions a shared "climate of opinion," while the philosopher Frank Cioffi labels them "we-discourse": "'We-discourse' is for 'us'; and contrasts with 'they-discourse,' which is about 'them,'" he has suggested. I prefer the term "discourse environment." As you become more specialized in an area, you come to inhabit a certain discourse environment, and you learn how that discourse operates within that environment.

Inconveniently enough, though, we must move through multiple discourse environments, a fact that sometimes makes it difficult to navigate our lives. For example, the average person encounters wildly different discourse environments on a daily basis: the auto repair shop, an on-line chat room, the gym, a real estate agency, or a lawyer's office. In order to understand how each operates, or make some headway in getting what you want in each, you have to at least temporarily modify what you might think of as your "natural" discourse. For students, who have to both inhabit and write within many discourse environments, the task becomes even more challenging: since writing provides ocular evidence of a slipup, it highlights flaws in their mastery of the discourse environment. And the student's specialist discourse environments are all quite discrete, and sometimes even in competition with one another: you might have courses in history, English, political science, business, and biology, each of which has its own discourse environment, and each of which you need intimately to understand in order to write intelligibly or successfully.

Of course, you have a straightforward purpose in writing for a specialized audience: problems emerge in any field, and the specialist solves a given problem or problems, showing other specialists why his or her solution compels more attention and credibility than other, previously proposed ones—why it's an important problem, and how his or her solution is correct. Your audience might be hostile toward you in the sense that you disagree with some long-established principle in the field. Or they might object to the way that you present your claims. But writing for a specialist audience to a large extent exempts you from having to worry about that audience's hostility: if you write for them, even if you disagree with some widely shared tenets, you still occupy the position of an insider—someone in the same discourse environment—who wants to advance knowledge in or credibility of the field. Michael Moore, for example, in his movie *Bowling for Columbine* sought to increase his credibility with Charlton Heston by starting off (somewhat meretriciously, I'll admit) by showing Heston his National Rifle Association membership card. Moore did this to demonstrate that he was in favor of gun ownership and the sporting use of guns. He demonstrated himself to be part of the same discourse environment. And this action allowed him access to Heston's goodwill, at least until he started browbeating the elderly actor.

This is not to say that internecine disputes never develop within a field—disputes about value, importance, significance, or interpretation. Moore has a major conflict with Heston about guns, even though both men to an extent inhabit a rather specialist discourse environment. These disputes can end up fracturing the discourse environment into separate, hostile camps, such that one addressing the other must in fact face a hostile audience, people who see the specialized area in very different terms. This is, I think, a somewhat unusual situation, one you may not often encounter; in general it is the most difficult situation in which to make headway. Since your audience and you share so much of a discourse environment to begin with, the rift typically becomes acrimonious, even personal, and there's not much hope of bridging it.

Let me be clear, though, about the specialist audience. In order to gain entrance to it, you must inhabit its discourse environment, at least temporarily. As Gould suggests above, this involves using certain vocabulary, linguistic constructions, and conventions. But it also involves a certain assumption of shared values. Often it is this very assumption that splits apart when a specialist audience fractures into competing factions. Figuring out these values of your specialist audience, though, is very important, since in fact most of the writing you do will be for specialist audiences. Indeed, many problems people face with argumentative writing stem from the fact that they are actually addressing a specialist audience—whose values they don't really know—and treading into an alien discourse environment without knowing it. To an extent, this was the error Jim B. made: he was writing for someone who had for many years been involved with shaping and evaluating university curricula; hence when he proposed axing the writing requirement, he was inadvertently moving into the field of a specialist.

He might have been more cautious had he been writing in another discourse environment, one more explicitly specialist. I think most readers would agree that James Gould's and Andreas Huyssen's prose suggests a high level of specialization, and to write within that genre requires considerable training and expertise. Most people therefore foray only with great caution into biology or philosophy of history, since these fields require for entrance a specific modification of conversational English. However, some discourse environments subtly camouflage themselves. The following quite engaging sections from Arnold Weinstein's book *A Scream Goes through the House* do not at first blush appear specialist in nature:

I would argue that Proust's massive *Recherche du temps perdu* is our premier exemplar for actually rendering the twists and turns that mourning may entail. (304)

And a few paragraphs later,

There are two major deaths in Proust's book: first that of the grandmother, and then that of Albertine. They are handled differently. Proust depicts the grandmother's actual experience of sickness and dying in extraordinary detail. (306)

Nothing arcane or unusual here, or one wouldn't think so. Weinstein is merely recounting some details of the deaths as they are depicted in Marcel Proust's novel. And readers would think, too, that they could easily replicate this prose style, engage this writer in debate, or enter this discourse environment.

But in fact—and you need not just take my word for this—literary criticism has emerged as an enormously complex and difficult field, perhaps made more so by the fact that many examples often cited as exemplary use relatively conversational, accessible prose. The reader enters it, feels comfortable, and then, turned writer, tries to replicate the everyday, easily understood quality of the prose. Yet that quality is only a sporadic and surface feature of literary criticism's discourse environment. Weinstein himself abandons his conversational style quite often, reverting to language that is as esoteric as Huyssen's, as specialist as Gould's. For example, here is how he concludes his section on Proust:

By literalizing issues of discontinuity and oblivion, by arguing that the human subject is reborn and remade via forgetting, by proposing that every "I" is a serial "we" (that should bear a new name each time), Proust suggests that every life-in-time is an incessant, kaleidoscopic affair of death and alteration. (321)

Excerpting this is somewhat unfair, as the sentences I have quoted are only snippets of a larger argument, but suffice it to say that the discourse environment implicit in Weinstein's conclusion has a far richer and more complex makeup than you might at first have thought, and if as a writer you want to enter that discourse environment, you will need as much training as you'd need were you to enter that of Huyssen or Gould.

"THE SOUL SELECTS HER OWN SOCIETY"

Admittedly, you won't fully and finally know your audience for any of your writing. You'll have an idea of who they are, what their tastes and proclivities might be, and their level of specialization or sympathy with your position. But you generally won't know them that well. At the same time, though, you will need to convince them of something, argue for something of value to you and to them. In some ways this is an odd, even unnatural situation, brought about by the invention of movable type, the printing press, the computer. But as you imagine this audience, try also to do a little investigative work. Try to get a greater idea of what it is that they are like. What do they expect from your writing? Might you ask them what they expect? Look for models they have praised or dispraised. To what degree is this audience open to change? How much will they tolerate, even encourage, originality of form or content, experimentation in your work? To what degree will they want you to agree with them, and to what degree can you differentiate your position from theirs and still hold their attention or gain their respect?

All of these questions need to be paramount in your mind both before you start conceiving your ideas for a written work and as you write them out, for in an important sense you actively create an audience as you write. You create in a single reader some feelings with respect to you and your work; and in a larger group of potential readers or listeners, your work ends up "selecting its own society."

Who will be part of that society? Who will end up listening to you? I propose that your ultimate success as a writer has at its base two audience-related factors: First, to what degree does the urgency of your purpose coincide with your audience's feeling that that purpose is urgent too? I'll ask this in other terms. What motivates your writing, what problem are you solving, what important issues have you identified, what areas of ambiguity or uncertainty does your writing aim to clear up? And second, have you successfully convinced your audience that you're the one who's capable of solving this urgent problem? How, once you have done the work of audience-assessment, can you make that audience validate your voice and accept, or at least take into consideration, what you've discovered? You're in the discourse environment: now what? You need, in short, to come up with something to say—and to say to that particular audience. How you do this is the topic of the next chapter.

3

Prewriting and the Writing Process

INVENTION: STRATEGIES FOR GETTING STARTED

As I have said earlier, good writing typically emerges as the result of a process: writing, rewriting, invention, outlining, drafting; going over that draft; revising it, rewriting it, recasting it, polishing it; then repeating this, perhaps again and again. Good writing, the theory goes, must be constructed over time, like a tennis stroke or golf swing. It finds perfection only gradually, with many small modifications and improvements made over a relatively long period.

A book such as this one can give you a few dozen suggestions, perhaps, about writing, but at some point your success will depend on a very simple issue: how do you come up with a good idea? In fact, how do you arrive at the very best idea? Oftentimes, handily, the instructor will provide you with a list of possible topics, but sometimes none of these topics will appeal to you. And sometimes, the assignment will require you to invent a good topic on your own and write about that. Often the assignment will focus on a specific text or texts. Or sometimes the paper assigned might focus on a theme rather than a text. But on many occasions, you will probably have trouble coming up with something to write about. You might think, for example, that nothing you can say will be "good enough" for an expert in the field to read . . . or you might have no real opinions on any of the material you have to write a paper about . . . or everything you come up with seems obvious. What to do?

Ask yourself the following base-level, almost primitive questions: "Is there anything in the text (or topic of the course) that has bothered me?" "Did I like anything I read? Why or why not?" If the answers to these are negative, then ask more general questions: "What am I interested in?" "What's my major going to be?" "What are my career goals?" "What kinds of things do I do for fun?" "How are things going in my other classes?" "Has the drop/add period ended?"

Such interrogation seeks to discover—or perhaps reveal—an area of *emotional response* to the material that you need to write about. That emotional response must drive or give fuel to any written assignment. Why did you have that strong response? Did something in the text itself spark it? What do you think of as valuable, worth striving for, in society? Were you sensitized to some area of the text that, perhaps, others would ignore or pass over? Alternatively, why did you have little or no emotional response? Do you feel that the issues of the text have been bruited about so much that you've reached your level of satiety? Do you in general feel emotionless about your work, your reading, or your life? Do you find yourself merely doing what you are told and taking no pleasure in it? Are you seeing a therapist? I don't mean this facetiously: writing involves genuine emotional commitment and a considerable degree of self-knowledge.

After deciding on the kind of writing you need to do (see chapter 1)—and after some soul-searching or self-analysis—you might try a few possible gambits to come up with a paper topic or area of exploration:

- *Feelings.* Look for your emotional response to an issue/text/situation. This is the best place to begin. What is it that you *felt* when you encountered what you're writing about? David Bleich, a professor and literary critic, has advocated that we write out a statement whenever an element of the work or subject inspires some powerful emotional response. For example, if a work begins with a reference to a broken elbow, you might write about how you once had a broken elbow and the major effect that had on the way you perceived your own physicality. Or a work might have some reference to the idea of marriage and fortune, and you might have a specific strong feeling about "marrying for money," or have an interesting piece of advice that you've heard regarding this practice. Even small things might spark an intense response—for example, you might find yourself responding keenly to a description of a particular kind of automobile, game, or kiss. After you have compiled this list of things that you have had a response to, you need to think about how they might affect and effect your interpretation as a whole: seeing those things that had resonance within you allows you to figure out what you are actually responding to and to separate out the idiosyncratic, individual element from that which might interest a larger audience. But most of all it gets you going, gets you thinking and reacting to the subject matter. At this point in the composing process, that's most important.

- *Aporia.* This is a rhetorical term meaning "moment of doubt." Recent literary theory (particularly the approach called deconstruction) has employed this term quite extensively. When you read a text—a novel, essay, short story, what-have-you—where do your assumptions about its form, theme, language, or characters get called into question or become problematic? Typically, we look for patterns in a work, and we argue that those patterns are meaningful. (See chapter 1.) Where does the work defy your attempts at making sense of it? And is that defiance intentional or unintentional on the part of the author? If intentional, what is the artistic/argumentative strategy the author uses? If unintentional, do you have any explanation for this apparent blindness on the author's part?

- *Disjunction.* Similar to the above, disjunction occurs when things do not fit together well, or when they seem improperly, illogically, or irreconcilably joined. Look for the places in the text—or in the society from which that text emerged—where there are splits and breaks, and use this as a starting point for an essay examining this "lack of fit." Perhaps the most difficult feature of this strategy is limiting the number of disjunctions you examine, since so many seem to be proliferating in our society that we seem to face an almost infinite regress.

- *Nachgeschichte.* German for "after-story" (we have no such word in English)—this is an extension from the known into the unknown. In some way, it is the prediction of a future based on what we know about the past. What if a certain text's premises or ideas could be extrapolated? How might they appear in an extended, or future, version? What elements in the story allow us to infer what follows the story proper, that is, the events of "And they lived happily ever after"? What does a text imply will happen in the long term? And is this something that we should fear or feel good about?

- *Backstory or Vorgeschichte.*   The backstory or as-yet-unwritten "before-story" is what the text implies (and the reader to an extent infers) about what happened prior to the events of the story proper. Looking at the text, which typically gives multiple clues, and also using your imagination, try to figure out what the backstory would be like, either for a certain character or for a group or society. This is sometimes especially interesting when you examine the situations of minor characters, which leads to . . .

- *Parallel tale.*   Many times minor characters will appear in a novel, a play, or a film, and do some piece of dramatic business and then depart. What if you were to look at the story as seen from their point of view? What if you were to look at history through the eyes of a minor figure, maybe someone whose viewpoint is rarely seen? For example, in *Rosencrantz and Guildenstern Are Dead*, his rewrite of *Hamlet*, Tom Stoppard tells the story from the perspective of two minor characters in. Try something similar. Focusing on the minuscule figures, try to see through their eyes the majuscule events and characters of a novel, a play, or even history. Alternatively, you could comment on what the literary theorist Gerald Prince terms the "disnarrated" portions of a narrative: "all the events that *do not* happen but, nonetheless, are referred to (in a negative or hypothetical mode) by the narrative text" (qtd. by Kafalenos 3). Such an exercise could lead to an interpretation of a story, a news event, or a theory somewhat different from anything you had previously conceived.

- *Penumbral suspicions.*   You might have certain unclassifiable feelings or intuitions about a work or subject, things that seem not fully logical or definable but exist as whiffs and traces, decided but near-indetectable hoverings. You might just play around with the subject, toying with its ideas and implications. You don't have to commit to any argumentative statement about it, just yet, so feel free to follow hunches, feelings, guesses. . . . Sometimes this leads to a really interesting insight.

In general, you want to be able to figure out not only the most obvious solution or answer to a given problem or topic but also one that has the quality of a new insight. Two classic (but by no means outdated) books on creativity, *Conceptual Blockbusting* by James Adams, and *Lateral Thinking* by Edward de Bono, might change the way you think. They both argue that you need to back up and question all your assumptions, question your whole project or enterprise, question how it is that you arrived at the judgments you have arrived at, and perhaps discover a different path or solution. For that matter, you could discover you want no path at all or that the answer lies in multiple solutions rather than just one.

In addition, you might look for secondary sources. See what other people have had to say about the same text or about the same or a similar problem. You can surf the Net for a general and rather undifferentiated series of wide-ranging responses (some excellent, some awful, most somewhere in between). Or you can do work at the library, using on-line and hard-copy databases to help you find relevant books and articles. Of course your paper might not be a "research" paper per se, but often reading others' ideas will give you a point of departure, will supply you with some of the key issues in what might be an ongoing debate—what I have called the "dialectical discourse"—or might even give you the material for a counterargument or two in your own essay. Reading secondary material often helps to sharpen your own point of view.

IMPORTANT NOTE!

When consulting or drawing from secondary sources, take especial care. You must scrupulously credit the author of the piece you are using if you employ any *ideas, phrases, or sentences from his or her work*. Even if you paraphrase that person's ideas, you must give a source and page reference.

WRITER'S BLOCK

Overcoming writer's block can sometimes be done through rather "mechanical" means. For example, Peter Elbow in his book *Writing without Teachers* invents the term "freewrite" to describe a process of composition that will help you come up with ideas. Unlike its historical forebear, automatic writing, which was writing done without conscious effort of the will, freewriting consists of writing whatever comes to your mind: in some real sense you are trying to capture on the page your own stream of consciousness. Only one rule: you cannot stop to think about or revise what you write—open the tap of your consciousness and let it flow through your pen. So keep that pen on the page. If you can't think of what to write, just write, "I can't think of what to write. I can't think of what to write. I can't think of what to write." This gets tiresome very soon, so generally you end up thinking of something more interesting. You can time yourself—doing this for, say, ten minutes is probably a good start— or you can just freewrite until you come up with something that looks to you like a good idea.

Keep in mind, though, that a freewrite does not a paper make. Free association is not usually enough for a paper. While you might be able to rescue a few sentences or perhaps a paragraph from a ten-minute freewrite, you should probably use a freewrite just as a way to generate ideas, to generate heat if not always a great deal of light. But where there is heat, light will probably follow—at least, that's the general sequence of events.

You can make a freewrite more useful, however, by "focusing" it—go back to what you have freewritten and find the very best idea within it; now freewrite on that idea. Alternatively, you could find four or five interesting or surprising phrases in what you've freewritten and use those as a basis for another freewrite. You might also find that sharing freewriting with others makes for an interesting and productive brainstorming session. Read aloud what you have written, and maybe offer commentary to one another as well. One of my friends even had the guests freewrite at his wedding—and share with the group what they had written!

A "newrite" (or "New-Write"), an exercise I have invented that intends to do more or less the same thing as the freewrite, lets you take your pen off the page. In this type of writing, you consciously attempt to write something different and, yes, even weird. Just write a paper or a paragraph that you know won't fulfill the assignment, but that self-consciously experiments with language use, point of view, genre. For example, write without using any "to be" verbs. (This *is* hard!) Avoid the letters *a* and *i*. Pretend that you are someone from the distant future reading these texts or taking this course. See the issues from the point of view of a gigantic, toothless dragon hand-puppet named Smok—or one that can change sizes at will. Invent a new language to describe various things that seem to you nondescribable, or invent a new emotion that you felt emerge in you after having read something. Use drawings, pictograms, or hieroglyphics to get your idea across. Draw out your idea on a piece of paper, and then use transparencies to draw out modifications to it, overlaying each transparency on top of the original. Translate your ideas into a musical score, inventing (if you need to) a personal system of notation.

This, too, often succeeds in getting some ideas going, but do keep in mind, again, that like a freewrite, a newrite itself will almost certainly not stand as an appropriate response to most assignments. Now and then you can use a newrite-like paper in a course, but for the most part, such a gambit is risky, like the "hostile audience" one described above. Ideally, the "newrite" will get you thinking in different directions and perhaps will open up a way to reconsider the text or topic under consideration. On the whole these invention strategies should give you ways to begin rather than serve as ends in themselves, but beginning is often the most difficult part of writing an essay.

Once you've decided what to do, though, once you have some ideas, you've officially begun: now what? Maybe figure out a sequence you'd like to use. Which ideas should come first, second, third? I suggest that you make up an outline.

Many experienced writers do not work from outlines, will do very little revising or rewriting, and will publish essentially first drafts of their work. Many of my colleagues have told me—somewhat conspiratorially—that they never use an outline and do little by way of prewriting or, for that matter, rewriting. I hasten to add, however, that most of these writers can do this only in areas where they are already expert and therefore have all-but-completely composed their writings in their heads. And they are also experienced writers whose writing production devices are as grooved as the motor skills of a professional athlete.

You might write without an outline or draft yourself. You might feel an inspiration, then sit down at the keyboard and pound out what is essentially a first draft but which superbly represents an organized version of your thoughts and ideas on an issue. On the other hand, you might have to go through something similar to the writing steps I have mentioned above and elaborate below. Obviously there are as many ways to compose as there are writers, and individual writers will often use varying methods themselves. With each writing task, you will help yourself discover and refine your own "writing production device." Don't feel as if you should settle on a single process of writing your papers. Feel free to experiment. I will offer a fairly reliable pattern of composition, but I do so with the proviso that I don't always use this pattern myself and that many other professionals use a much abridged—or much more anarchic—form of it. Still, the stages outlined are probably those that most writers go through either in their heads or on paper, and you would do well to at least consider these as you prepare your work.

THE PROCESS OF WRITING

Reflecting

Once you have your topic, have thought about your response to it, and after you have done some freewriting—but before you actually begin to draft an essay—spend some time again, in the ways I have suggested above, analyzing the audience, the assignment, the materials that the assignment covers, and your own motivations for writing. For example, if you have decided to write about a theme in a certain novel, you might want to reread and review your notes on that novel and the sections of the novel that you will probably discuss. (This is easier than writing, by the way!) If you have an assigned topic, you need to go over that assignment quite carefully, making sure that you understand it fully. If you don't, you might contact your instructor to ask for clarification and amplification. At this point, you need to raise those "base-level questions": what audience do you have for this piece of writing—what does the audience know about your subject? You might also examine your own reasons for writing on this particular subject and topic: Are you likely to be biased about it? Do you have some special qualification for writing on this topic? What brought you to it? These issues you might think about rather than actually discuss in writing, but they will have a major influence on the way your essay takes shape.

At this stage, I think about the topic and make a list of all the points worth making. This slightly haphazard collection of ideas has no particular length limitation but usually has no more than ten or fifteen points. Make these points as succinctly as possible, but *in sentence form*. I urge you to put them in this form, because in any shorthand version their impact can be lost or forgotten as the writing process continues. For example, I might write (of *The Scarlet Letter* on the topic of role-playing), "Dimmesdale becomes a better and more passionate preacher as a result of having sinned," rather than, say, "Dimmesdale's sin vs. preaching ability," though this latter phrase might seem to capture the gist of the sentence. I don't look, by the way, for any startling or great insight just yet—rather, I just compile ideas that seem to me relevant at the time. I might use them as major points or perhaps just as evidence in support of a thesis. Only the writing itself will reveal how they might function.

◉

Outlining

After composing this list of points, I try to group them into logical clusters. Which several ideas might belong or be discussed together? How can I take these ten ideas (say), all of which I consider important, and classify or arrange them? As you might imagine, thus begins the anlage of an outline, but it's still only embryonic. I cluster my ideas into groups based on their interconnections, similarities, or family resemblance, I continue thinking about the ideas themselves, the topic, the subject, and I often think of additional ideas. (In fact, at any stage in the writing process, I am open to and seek out new ideas—new evidence, new points, new examples, new counterexamples.)

Now I try to find the point or question—what might be called the overridingly important question or problem that organizes or subsumes the others. Is there one major question the answer to which will be the point that I am making here? Is one of them a stronger, more argumentative, more striking and original point than the others? Is there an "alpha male (or female)" point? Can any of the ideas be turned into such a point? If I can find something like this, then I have discovered a tentative or provisional thesis—or one answer to the large question. I can abandon this point, or revise it if I wish, but I'm striving at this early stage of writing to find something that will organize my ideas. The tentative thesis should accomplish this.

Next, I compose the outline itself. Earlier, I've mentioned colleagues who do not outline. When they tell me that they do not outline, I always think to myself, "They may not outline on paper, but they have an outline in their head." Like chess masters who can think twenty moves in advance, such writers don't need to take notes: they see their argument as a whole and can even perceive its component parts. Perhaps because I don't play chess, I find it easier to write the component parts down and tentatively establish the order in which I think they should appear.

Now you can compose an elaborated outline, one that reiterates much of the thought process that went into coming up with the thesis. I freewrite a summary of the points I would like to make in each of the sections. Some of the language here will likely appear in the final draft, I have discovered, but much of it I will abandon. I want at this stage to see whether I actually have something to say about my topic's various aspects, points, or subpoints, that is, about the ideas my outline has isolated. Can I defend all of these ideas? Do they all seem mutually exclusive—or do I find myself simply repeating the same point in different words? If so, I eliminate the duplication. Have I addressed the possible cons? How might a reader take issue with my arguments and ideas? Have I thought of all possible, reasonable objections?

Drafting

Drafting comes next. With my elaborated outline on the screen or next to me, I fill in each paragraph. The idea is not necessarily to develop a completely full paragraph but to get my ideas on the page as fully as I can at the moment. Again, I worry not so much about phrasing or absolute perfection as about just roughing out a version of the essay. In this phase you will feel the excitement of creativity, the passion of expressing your ideas. Here is where the lightning bolt hits and you discover your real thesis—or you discover that your tentative thesis will probably work as your final thesis, what you really want to say. One of my professors said that this stage of the writing process resembles lust: it is unfettered, free, natural, full of excitement and discovery.

As you've probably discovered, most school and professional writing, done under some pressure of time, prevents us from pondering every stage or taking time to ponder each word or phrase. Sometimes writers have to simply push on and express themselves as best they can given the time constraints. One professional writer contends that every time you write something you know fails to fully represent your idea, you permanently damage your prose style. Hyperbole to be sure, but still this thought always hovers in the back of my mind while I compose, and whenever I write something I recognize as weak or slovenly, I immediately try to rewrite or rephrase.

After the draft, I recommend that you wait twenty-four to forty-eight hours. After a day or two, you will see your writing in a new light and will feel quite differently about some of the ideas you had. Certain sentences, embarrassingly, will fluoresce on the page, they are so glaringly ill-phrased, while others—ones that you can hardly remember having composed—might startle you with their brilliance. Just don't let their candlepower blind you to any larger problems.

Rewriting

Here begins the rewriting process. If the drafting stage resembled lust, this stage might embody love: here you must be careful, considerate, thoughtful—faithful to your idea. You need to evaluate your paper, first, as an entirety: does the whole argument make sense? Have you left out any crucial points or stages of argument? Overlooked any obvious and strong cons? How is the wording? Is it smooth, lucid, accurate? Does it sound right, even rhythmical, to your mind's ear? Can you make it better? Here you should work on the exact form of your thesis. Here, too, you should consider carefully how you have arranged the various elements of the paper: Could it be more logically organized? Are the paragraph breaks accurate? Could you develop some ideas more or eliminate others that seem weak, repetitious, or lacking in originality?

Going Public

Usually, now it is best to share the paper with someone whose opinions you trust, someone who can offer intelligent and constructive criticism. You need to remember that another person will see things in your paper that you do not, and another person will also fail to see things perfectly obvious to you (and hence require rephrasing or more explanation). Try to take into account every one of your editor's suggestions, while still retaining fidelity to your original work. *Don't allow that editor to rewrite your work, though. That's your job.* Sometimes the comments will be about word choice or phrasing. Sometimes the editorial remarks will be much more far-reaching. But whatever the case, take them into account, and, provided that your reader has done a scrupulous job, this will immeasurably improve your work.

Remember, though, that no paper ever really reaches perfection. In some sense we don't finish our papers; rather, we set them loose and say goodbye. Indeed, when I look back at some published work of my own, I always feel an impulse to revise, and I cringe at the awkwardness of the phrasing or the triteness of some metaphors. I console myself with the notion that writing can always be improved, yet the time at our disposal is always finite. To come up with as good a work as possible, though, make sure you allow yourself the time to compose it with care and plan it in as carefully sequenced a manner as possible—if not the one outlined above, then something similar of your own devising. I will examine this writing process in more detail later on (see chaps. 7–8), but here I have been trying to emphasize how important it is to see writing as process, not just as some magical or genetic gift.

4

The Thesis

WHAT IS A THESIS, ANYWAY?

The thesis stands out as the most important sentence or sentence group in your essay. It might be helpful to think of it as the DNA of your essay, the compact, coded sentence that predicts the body. The thesis is an interpretation, an angle, an insight, an optic on, a perceptive view of, an analytical slant on, an evaluative synthesis of . . . *something*—a text, an issue, a conflict. It explains *the most important issue*, the one most in need of explanation. The thesis makes up the core material that would remain, if you had to boil your paper down to just twenty or thirty or forty words, if you had to distill it into its concentrated essence.

Because it makes up such an important component of the essay, the thesis should be something you spend considerable time and energy formulating, revising, and polishing. Some writers suggest that you start with only a provisional thesis and write the paper on the basis of it, modifying the thesis as you come to know its ins and outs. Writing in the *Chronicle Review*, University of Wisconsin English professor Heather Dubrow quotes the architect Louis I. Kahn, whose ideas about a building can be nicely applied to a thesis. "When you have all the answers about a building before you start building it, your answers are not true. The building gives you answers as it grows and becomes itself" (B13). Indeed, when formulating a thesis, you need to realize it will inevitably change as you write your paper; it will become more complex; it will present problems that you had not been able to foresee; it will evolve. You need to leave room for these possibilities.

Another way to see the thesis is as an insight you've arrived at (about the topic) only after a lot of thought. It's a conclusion. The paper, then, explains the thought process you went through to arrive at the thesis, at the same time that it displays this very process. This recursive nature of writing can sometimes be daunting, though, since as you write the paper, you will—unfortunately—often discover flaws in the thought process you used to arrive at the thesis.

Indeed, sometimes you will find that what is really original about your paper does not emerge until after you have written five pages' worth of thoughts on a provisional thesis. Of course once you have made this discovery, you'll need to go back to the beginning and start anew! (No one promised that writing was going to be easy; in fact, quite the opposite.) In a textbook on writing, the poet Donald Hall suggests you automatically reject the first four or five thesis statements that you think of, as these will be ones that would be obvious to everyone. This is an interesting idea, and one that I always allow to hover in my consciousness, but I should add that sometimes you will indeed come upon an excellent thesis right away. When this happens, I think you will know it. It's unusual, but it happens now and then: each writing situation has its own structure, its own series of problems, and its own unique solutions. As I mentioned earlier, there's no single right way to compose.

Writing is hard work, and good writing, while it occasionally springs magically or bewilderingly from your frontal lobes, will more often be the result of revision, reflection, and many hours' anguished labor. "Labor" is the right word, for indeed writing does resemble giving birth to something very new.

PLACEMENT OF THESIS

Where should you place your thesis? Many textbook writers suggest that a thesis can go anywhere, really—at the beginning, middle, or end of the paper; in fact, the whole paper can be a thesis.

Well, true enough. Such a suggestion is theoretically correct. But it fails to give enough direction. I suggest that you place your thesis near the beginning of the essay. It should probably not be at the very beginning—for the reader needs to be prepared for your idea about a given issue, and probably should know a little about the general subject and topic that you deal with. I recommend placing the thesis at the end of your introduction. This is a safe, albeit conservative positioning of it. Again, though you can experiment with placement of the thesis, putting it earlier or later, this could generate confusion: your reader might not follow what you are arguing for, or think you are arguing something else. Worse, your reader might be bored and ask, "What point are you trying to make?"

WORDING

Work on the wording of your thesis. Say clearly what you mean. Make the thesis forceful in its impact. Make it live in the reader's memory. Make it roll off the tongue, slide off the pen, clatter beautifully off the keyboard—or at least appear to have. Avoid using "to be" verbs and passive constructions. We all know the difficulty of coming up with a thesis that seems perfectly honed and smooth, but the effort is worth it. Avoid the clunkiness of structures such as "My thesis is that . . ." or "I intend to prove the thesis that . . ." Such verbal constructions might seem to patronize the reader or might be perceived as padding. Also your thesis should be evident without your having to signpost it. Don't discuss what you are going to do. Just do it.

Sometimes writers of argument feel they don't want to reveal their main idea right away. Thinking that they need to "save" something for the paper proper, they cultivate a coyness. This is no place for coyness. Reveal your main idea. "There are several ways in which the two novels differ," for example, is a vague, overly general, overly coy thesis. What are the ways that the novels differ, why are the contrasts important, and why should anyone bother to read an essay about them? Let's improve on it some: "The two novels differ in that the quest in *Cold Mountain*, while ending 'unhappily,' nonetheless enlarges the main characters' sense of love—for one another, for what they are doing; while the quest in *The Painted Bird*, though one that the protagonist survives, demolishes his and the reader's sense of hope for the individual, the world, for all mankind." You might have to define what you mean by "love" or "hope"—key thesis-linked terms—but this thesis is a great deal more specific and more argumentative: indeed, if your thesis is to live, it will live in its detail, its specificity.

Here is another thesis that could use some tuning up: "If we are going to continue accomplishing in this practice, action should be taken to diminish the increasingly unanswered demand for human organs." I have a couple of problems with this thesis. First, "continue accomplishing in this practice" sounds odd. This sentence was generated by a native speaker of English, so there's no excuse for such an unnatural, awkward formulation. Second, it uses the passive, which makes the thesis too vague: "action should be taken," it asserts, but I ask, "by whom"? And finally, what kind of action does the writer advocate? It's necessary to specify in the thesis. Here's a revised version: "Demand for donated organs will always exceed the supply of those available for transplant; thus while setting up a system for organ donation and transplant, we need to maintain a balance between egalitarian, democratic principles and medical need." Notice, again, that a number of the key terms need to be defined, but the thesis is a good deal more specific, and its argument is relatively clearly stated.

THE ARGUMENTATIVE THESIS

An argumentative thesis is provocative, interesting, striking—so much so that it catches the reader up short. Yet it's a balancing act, too, a kind of oxymoron, in that it needs to be full of competing opposites: it must be counterintuitive but reasonable; controversial but not an old debate; complex but graspable; creative but grounded in a shared reality. It should be evocative without being vague, clear and specific yet not a blueprint for a paper, nuanced but not ambiguous.

The argumentative thesis is not just a verbal fabrication, a manufactured piece of prose that fits a prescribed set of technical specifications. It's more than an utterance, a notion, a conception, or a proposition; it's almost a philosophy in that it represents a mode of thought, a kind of discourse, a way of dealing with the world, or, in our situation, with texts of various kinds.

To further capture the elusive construct of an argumentative thesis, I offer an idea from T. S. Eliot in his essay on Dante. Eliot writes about "genuine" poetry—and I think this also applies to the argumentative thesis—that it "can communicate before it is understood" (206). Indeed, to be argumentative, a thesis must convey to its audience something complex, interesting and new—"make it new"— prior to the point at which an audience fully understands it. The paper that emerges from such a thesis will give the fuller explanation, it is to be hoped, but it will be that paper's burden not only to make understood what could not initially be communicated but also to reveal why it could not be communicated instantly. If, by contrast, the thesis is totally comprehensible at the outset, there is probably something wrong with it, and the paper that follows will, typically, be predictable and ho-hum, as it strenuously argues for something that most readers would accept without proof. Of course it needs to be totally apprehensible and clear, but the genuinely new idea cannot be fully communicable at its first introduction.

"FORETHOUGHT" REVISITED IN LIGHT OF ARGUMENT

How do you generate actively argumentative thesis statements? In the last thirty years or so, we've been emphasizing the process of writing, and writers have suggested that that process—prewriting, freewriting, clustering, outlining, gathering evidence, drafting, rewriting—has as much (or maybe more) importance as the product, namely, the finished essay. One interesting way of expressing this is from the writer Lee Stringer, who in a public lecture at Powell's Books in Portland, Oregon, in July 2004 told an audience that writing is not just about construction but about "exploration" and "exacavation."

In general, though, not enough emphasis has been placed on what one might term "forethought" about the paper's idea or thesis. Going back to Eliot, one might ask what it is that a paper's thesis communicates prior to its being understood, and part of my answer is, it communicates some of the writer's forethought. Learning what this forethought consists of can help you generate more complex, more rotund, more fresh and new thesis statements, and better papers, and can help you understand the mode of thought that writing papers such as these both teaches and requires. Elaborating on the ideas of the previous chapter, I want to propose four areas of possible forethought, though I do so only with the proviso that this is by no means an exhaustive list.

1. "Argument" implies that more than one party is involved. And people cannot be intelligent all by themselves. So there must be an audience: what is it like? Clearly, college essays are not written for a

universal audience. Indeed, it is quite a narrow, even parochial audience: a person professionally involved with the topic, who has read a lot of material about it, and who has doubtless repeatedly read the text or texts under discussion. As I said above, this is a specialist audience—and a sympathetic one. Yet this audience needs a lot to be surprised or enlightened. Indeed, this audience longs for surprise, is parched for enlightenment. This audience does not want, for example, simplistic answers to rather obvious questions. This audience does not want a thesis he or she has read before, many—or even a few—times.

2. Forethought also needs to consider the competition: possible as well as actual competing explanations/individuals need to be looked at, imagined, or at least provisionally constructed. Just as when I decide to write a scholarly article on, say, a poet named H.D., I turn to the articles that have already appeared about her (and about imagist poetry, about early twentieth-century American poetry, about women's poetry, among others) in order to determine the context for what I might write; just as I look at and read other articles in journals I want to publish in to see the kinds of approaches being used, the level of documentation, the affiliations of the authors, the length and style of the essays, so, too, you must look to your "competition"—namely, fellow students. Of course this is in a way a more difficult task than mine, since you don't typically have access to a whole set of essays. You need in fact to infer the kinds of things that scholars can more easily discern about competition. A knowledge of the competition forms an important element of forethought—and constitutes a furthering of the notion of audience, for as the audience reads the multiple responses in a class or in a journal, that audience's expectations change: its patience with certain kinds of ideas diminishes, just as its longing for others (or maybe just for unfamiliar ones) likely becomes more acute. Of course this can be intimidating too—but after you have finished being intimidated by the writing of your peers, and after they've finished being intimidated by aspects of yours that you probably didn't even think about, then maybe you can all sit down to do something better still.

3. Forethought also involves determining your relation to the assignment. What does the assignment really call for? Is it looking for

reiteration of the ideas of the course, or is it looking for some inventive, original idea? Is it requiring you to show that you've grasped certain concepts, or that you can handle a certain technical vocabulary being taught? To what extent is the assignment actually just testing whether you've "gotten" the ideas of, say, four or five key texts? To what extent is the assignment about the text, and to what extent is the text supposed to be used only as a pretext? Often, the argumentativeness of a thesis hinges on certain unspoken guidelines, which, not too surprisingly, vary from course to course.

4. Last piece of forethought, but in some ways the prime mover: You need to grapple with your own response to a work or works, or to a series of ideas under scrutiny in a class. If your reaction is muted or nonexistent, then why write anything? (When I was a freshman, I never even considered the option of telling a professor that the provided paper topics all seemed boring to me. But I should have done so when that was the case, and teachers should encourage students to take that initiative.) If you have generated a thesis you are certain is correct, then why argue for that thesis? This connects both with Louis I. Kahn's idea about a building and also with the notion of "negative capability": John Keats's idea that writers should be willing to inhabit realms of abstraction and nonclarity for relatively long periods of time before responding to things.

I want to suggest that inhabiting those realms is sometimes valuable precisely insofar as it does not have conclusive results. "The only means of strengthening the intellect," Keats declares in a letter he wrote to George and Georgiana Keats in September 1819, "is to make up one's mind about nothing—to let the mind be a thoroughfare for all thought" (515). Indeed, forethought about one's own various responses to a work suggests that writers run down many uncharted thoroughfares and byways and endure blunting up against the walls that close some of them off. Of course, blunting up against things is not a lot of fun. Keats offers Shakespeare as the example of a person "capable of being in uncertainties, mysteries, doubts, without any irritable reaching after fact and reason" (Letter to George and Thomas Keats, 21, 27 December 1817, 370). This is not necessarily a state of bliss or contentment, but it might be one from which emerges something of value. You have to learn to look for areas of dissonance, of nonfit, of possibly contradictory interpretations and ambiguities—Keats's "uncertainties, mysteries, doubts"—within a work, rather than looking only for overriding and obvious themes and problems everyone would notice.

THE "PSEUDO-THESIS"

What happens when you do not engage in this relatively extended forethought? You tend to generate the pseudo-thesis (or perhaps that would be soo-DOTH-esis). Note that these statements seriously attempt a thesis and are generally written quite clearly, such that the reader has a good idea of what the writer means. What I'm saying is that they're not grammatically confused or garbled. They are pseudo-theses in that they don't really advance any new idea or provide a genuinely creative insight or imagining. I am not going to discuss here the compacted or elliptical thesis, which is mysterious, vague, and ultimately meaningless: such a thesis represents a failure of language rather than one of thought. Nor will I consider the "dead-horse thesis," which appears to be argumentative but in fact is just taking an already established side in an old, never-to-be-resolved debate ("Abortion should be made a crime because x, y, or z . . ."), because this kind of thesis is uncommon in text-based analyses, such as the ones I will look at here. But do keep in mind that certain issues, such as abortion, gun control, animal experimentation, and the like, invite such thesis construction: it's very difficult to have an original response to these issues anymore. They're the equivalent of television commercials you've seen a hundred times.

Text-based papers, then, often generate pseudo-theses such as the following:

1. A description of research or summary of the texts
2. A blueprint for a paper that follows
3. A too easily conceded thesis, labeled variously the "okey-dokey thesis," the "reasonable person" thesis, the "ho-hum" thesis, or the "so what?" thesis
4. A madcap or lunatic invention that everyone, including the author, knows to be zany and inappropriate, and that never attempts to offer anything but that very zaniness

Interestingly, all of these misinterpretations of the idea of a thesis stem from a misunderstanding of what the audience wants or expects. The first, the summarizer, thinks that the audience wants only "proof" that the student writer has read a text and knows some or all of its main features. The second, the blueprinter, feels that the audience, living in a hopelessly chaotic world, wants orderliness, organization, a plan or road map, really anything that will stave off ever-encroaching anarchy. The third, the reasonable person, thinks all that's called for is a true and accurate statement that basically everyone will agree with, and since that's always worked in the past, why shouldn't it here? The fourth has the misguided notion that all the audience is looking for is creativity—unharnessed, unspancelled, unleashed.

Each of these positions naturally and even logically generates a pseudo-argument to back up the thesis. Not too much careful forethought goes into these. And I want to mention as a caveat or disclaimer that I don't mean to disparage the generic student-responses that I will be discussing. Indeed, these students are merely attempting to reconcile the quite alien notion of writing a paper for a university class with what they have previously been taught. They don't differ that much from you.

To help illustrate some of these ideas about theses, I want to look at some thesis statements about a poem entitled "The Pool." It is quite brief, so I think you can take it all in and more or less figure out what's going on. Written by a poet who called herself H.D., Hilda Doolittle or Hilda Aldington, this poem originally appeared in 1915.

> Are you alive?
> I touch you.
> You quiver like a sea-fish.
> I cover you with my net.
> What are you—banded one?

I choose this not only because I like it but because it was chosen by I. A. Richards in *Principles of Literary Criticism* as his first example in a chapter entitled "Badness in Poetry." He labels it an "instance of defective communication" (199). Ouch.

Pseudo-thesis: Summary

Here are some sample student responses to this poem. "How can I come up with something new and exciting or even interesting about this?" the first student asks in near exasperation. This student generally writes a summary or description of the text. A thesis from him or her might run, "'The Pool' is about someone who encounters a pool of water, who touches it, and watches, surprised, at the effects of having touched it." This is often the "I must defer to the genius of others" position, which does have something to recommend it. But it's too timid. It shies from any real interpretation. Actually, the genuine problem is a misconception of the assignment: the student thinks assignments are just trying to get him or her to provide proof that the work or book has been read.

Pseudo-thesis: Blueprint

The second objection is less passive in its aggressiveness. "But this was the way we were taught," a student, David B., told my class. "My whole high school English department taught the same idea—that the thesis was a kind of 'road map' for the rest of the essay. What's wrong with that?" Indeed, what is wrong with it? I concede that probably in high school it's not a bad idea to hold up this particular ideal. I might do so myself. Why? The blueprint thesis—I take the term from Richard Marius—does force novice writers to come up with some kind of organizing principle. It does urge on them some kind of unifying structure. But in university-level classes, we want more than evidence of organization. You are no longer novices, especially if you've read this far! I think David B. was probably trained to write what we unaffectionately call the five-paragraph essay, namely, an introduction with a three-pronged thesis, each point of which is developed in its own brief paragraph, and then a conclusion in paragraph five.

Blueprint theses also have a tendency to turn Procrustean. Procrustes is a figure from Greek myth: he lived in a hut in the woods, and when travelers stopped at his house, he would offer them a bed to sleep in. Little did they know that if they were too tall for the bed, he would cut them down to fit, and if too short, they would be subject to stretching by their host. (Procrustes also apparently had other ways of dispatching unwitting wanderers, but we won't get into those.) My point here is that when you have a blueprint, you tend to modify the evidence so that it fits the blueprint perfectly. Such modification is Procrustean—or, in a word, fatal. You need in your papers to be more open to possibilities of things that don't fit, and you need not only to deal with them but actively to seek them out. Blueprints offer only a plan that will be followed to the letter.

A blueprint thesis for "The Pool" might look like this. "In her poem 'The Pool,' H.D. (Hilda Doolittle or Hilda Aldington) depicts an individual who addresses nature—represented by a pool of water—disrupts it briefly, and then marvels at the changes she has wrought." Now, this does have something to recommend it. There is the start of an analysis here, and it's slightly more than just a summary as well. This student has a much better idea of how to fill up a paper (probably five paragraphs too), than the previous summerupper. One hopes that the blueprint builder will in fact come up with an argument. Sometimes they do. The student has found something to generalize about (pool suggests nature) and has found a narrative, a sense of change undergone by the poem's speaker. There is even a "marveling" going on.

It's a start, but the tightly controlled blueprint argument will probably prevent much change or growth of thesis—it's too tidy, this thesis; it leaves no room for surprise, discovery, and excitement. It's exactly what Kahn is alluding to when he talks about having all the answers to a building before you build it. The blueprint contains all the main points of a paper—on page 1. Again, it might be a good idea in secondary education, but I don't recommend it; in fact, it's really only a form of elaborated outlining.

Pseudo-thesis: "Okey-Dokey"

Creators of the "okey-dokey" or the third kind of pseudo-thesis feel not so much betrayed by their previous education as suspicious of what I'm offering in its place. "Why do I have to come up with what you call an 'argumentative thesis'?" (usually accompanied by air-quotes). "I can find plenty of good, solid evidence to back up a thesis, and then you say that's not argumentative. Or I can come up with a thesis that doesn't have much potential support, and I can invent b.s. to back it up. Is that what you want?" A student named Scott G. asked me this, and yes, he really used the term "b.s." Here is my response to Scott G. "If you can find plenty of good, solid evidence for a thesis, then probably others can too. Probably that thesis is just a bit too obvious, too easy to support. As for coming up with a thesis that you can find only b.s. to back up—well, I can't recommend that, either. These are not the only two choices; it's not an either/or situation. You need to find a subtle, complex thesis that you can back up with evidence that's not b.s. The evidence for it should also be 'good' and 'solid,' but you have to argue for its goodness, prove its solidity."

Scott G. and many others are arguing for what I term the "reasonable person thesis." It might be called the "oh-so-reasonable person thesis," now that I think of it, or the too-easily-conceded thesis, as well as the "okey-dokey thesis." Here's an example of a thesis in this genre: "'The Pool' shows the difficulty of connecting with nature and the impossibility of knowing how one's intervention into natural events will affect them and us." OK. In fact, okey-dokey.

Many times you will be tempted, I think, to look for a very reasonable middle ground. There are perhaps two quite radically opposed positions, neither of which might seem suitable, so why not split the difference and argue for an intermediate position? It does seem a reasonable gambit. Maybe, though, it's a bit too reasonable, a "reasonable person" gambit. And the paper that will emerge from this rhetorical tactic generally is so reasonable that it puts the reader to sleep.

One more example, though I could give you many more from what seems to me a too oft-tapped resource of rhetorical strategies: "The natural language of the poem mirrors the naturalness of the pool of water." This kind of thesis suggests that the paper's argument won't matter. Again, it's a reasonable enough statement, but in short, if I weren't being paid to read the paper that follows these pseudo-theses, I'd be off to the gym.

Pseudo-thesis: Zany

The final genre of pseudo-argument, at least that I want to offer right now, grows out of a kind of madcap pseudo-thesis. "You wanted something argumentative, didn't you?" students who come up with such pseudo-theses typically ask. In a newspaper column, the humorist Dave Barry suggested that the best way to write papers in college writing courses was to make the most outlandish comparisons possible. He said that as soon as he did this, he started getting high grades. For example, he said that he compared Herman Melville's *Moby-Dick* to the Republic of Ireland.

Here are some zany thesis statements about H.D.'s poem. "The Pool" is about a tiger lying in its own pool of blood. It's about a pregnant woman touching her swollen belly. It's about swimming laps and watching the lane lines painted on the bottom of the pool. As one tires, the lines become hazy, confusing. I know that feeling of lines becoming hazy. These are explanations that I have actually seen offered. Here, too, each writer has misconstrued audience, purpose, and relation to subject matter but, even worse, has in some sense cut the cord that grounds his or her explanation to the text itself. Your papers and the interpretations offered therein are not versions of patients' responses to inkblots: they must be constructs that others— an audience—can be swayed to finally perceive as sound explanations, not merely private reactions that one either sees or does not, depending on mood, personality, receptivity, and the like. In short, these pseudo-theses emerge from the idea that a thesis needs only to be asserted. In fact, it has to be proven. And that's the hard part.

A version of the zany thesis is what I term the "wampyjogged thesis"—namely, the verbal construction that is so dense and/or metaphorically expressed that it *sounds* complex, elaborate, and smart, but in fact is, at worst, just plain b.s., to use Scott G.'s term. or at best, okey-dokey. I've written some of these myself, so I sympathize with the impulse. "H.D.'s poem recounts the unknowability of the natural world, suggesting that when one submits to it, the mind, reduced to near-autistic cerebration, attains to reptile-status." This sounds pretty highfalutin, but the writer is only arguing that the speaker has a somewhat simplistic or childlike response to the depicted world. Ho hum. Or another: "'The Pool,' with its staccato imagery suggestive of the trench warfare that surrounded H.D. herself, makes words into weapons with which the newly armed woman of the world can engage nature red in tooth and claw, or in all its pervasive, embryonic wetness." This writer, alluding to Tennyson, has greater confidence, but I just don't know what her point is. Words are weapons? Is this an allusion to Amiri Baraka? I'm just not sure. Both of these thesis statements seem impressive at first, but they sound new only because they're couched in such ornate language. Ornate language doesn't constitute an argument; it's just a zany writing style used to disguise the fact that the writer has no real argument.

SOME ACTUAL ARGUMENTS

What, then, is a solidly argumentative—and provable—thesis about "The Pool"? Actually, this is an amazingly difficult poem. In fact, it seems to me that coming up with a genuinely argumentative thesis about it is an excellent exercise. Richards's thesis is a strong one, namely, that the poem lacks any emotional content. But that doesn't seem likely to be something a student working on only "The Pool" would generate, for its understanding depends on the context set up by the entire book. Here is Richards:

> Not the brevity only of the Vehicle, but its simplicity, make it ineffective. The sacrifice of metre in free verse needs, in almost all cases, to be compensated by length. The loss of so much of the formal structure leads otherwise to tenuousness and ambiguity. Even when, as here, the original experience is presumably slight, tenuous and fleeting, the mere correspondence of matter to form is insufficient. The experience invoked in the reader is not sufficiently specific. A poet may, it is true, make an unlimited demand upon the reader, and the greatest poets make the greatest claim, but the demand must be proportional to the poet's own contribution. The reader here supplies too much of the poem. Had the poet said only "I went and poked about rocklings, and caught the pool itself," the reader, who converts what is printed above into a poem, would still have been able to construct an experience of equal value; for what results is almost independent of the author. (200)

In short, Richards finds the poem too easily paraphrasable, and the paraphrase—as well as the poem—is about a fundamentally exiguous experience. I disagree; and I disagree with his paraphrase. In fact I think his argument is ridiculous But it is an argument.

It seems to me that a useful way of thinking about how to come up with an argumentative thesis is to think of a major, overriding, important—and ultimately unanswerable—question about the work or issue. Richards seems to be asking, "Why is it that this poem does not excite any response in me?" and he comes up with the idea above regarding the absence of a significant experience behind H.D.'s poem.

Here is an excellent student response to the poem, one that taught me something about H.D. and her transgressiveness. The curious thing about Nina B.'s response, in fact, is that it assumes H.D. to be male, an assumption that seems relatively reasonable. And the student's thesis suggests that the poem's speaker manifests a very typically male attitude toward the pool itself:

> By entitling his poem "The Pool," H.D. thrusts [an] image of human interference upon readers. The poem itself, however, does not limit itself to discussion of a pool, but has a broader, more generalized focus. Building on this allusion to human tampering, H.D. explores the instinctive, human response to any encounter with "the other." When faced with some foreign entity that defies comprehension, be it an element of the natural world or a member of an alien race, humans reveal a need to draw this entity into their respective sphere of control. Through attempts at classification or physical exploitation, man betrays an intolerance for the unknown, which is grounded in a fear of overthrow; to avoid domination, humans dominate. In "The Pool," brief though it may be, H.D. depicts some encounter with "the other" and uses it to exemplify the human need to suppress, coupled with an inherent unconcern for the object of subjugation.

Nina B. has developed a highly argumentative position, even though—or maybe because—she mistook the author for male. The idea of dominating so as not to be dominated, and the lack of consideration for the object being dominated, take on a different slant if one assumes a male speaker as opposed to a female one; H.D.'s poem indeed reveals itself as a highly "gendered" statement. Maybe

Richards actually resented the poem and the poet because H.D. was a woman adopting a male point of view? It seems that taking an argumentative stance can often lead to sudden, unexpected insights.

Let me offer my own interpretation, expanding on the arguments offered by some of the student writers I cited above. I posed the question "What seems odd and special about the consciousness depicted by this poem?" Here's a provisional answer:

> H.D.'s 1915 poem "The Pool" invites the reader into its five short lines, but their apparent simplicity soon gives way to multiple levels of evocativeness. The poem explores the difficulty of defining the ever escalating blurs of boundary line between the "me" and the "not me"—or between the self and the other—as the self attempts to impinge on that other. It shows how forays beyond the self result in confusion, loss of control, and possibly even remorse. "The Pool" questions one's most basic assumptions about life and the world by showing how human agency can have unpredictable, unrecognizable, even frightening, ramifications. In fact, the poem dramatizes how the effort to make even a tiny impact on the world beyond the self is doomed from the start; it's a shaky unbalancing of some unknown equilibrium, a tentative tendril sent out to some vast unknown organism. The poem depicts a consciousness almost psychopathically ill-equipped to cope with the world, and this inability to cope emerges, paradoxically, out of a terribly heightened sensitivity, not just to change, but to nature and to experience itself.

I don't know whether I'm entirely happy with this, but it seems to me that the thesis does have an argumentative edge, blunt at present, but still palpable. I think many people might object to the idea of the speaker's being called a psychopath, and also to the notion that this psychopathology is evidenced or maybe caused by a heightened appreciation of nature.

ARGUMENT AND UNCERTAINTY

But the point is, finally, that I'm not sure. I don't know how this will play out. I had to think about the poem for a long time to come up with this, to be sure, but I would need to proceed by subjecting it to various kinds of counterarguments, to multiple "tests," some of which would necessarily involve, at least for me, a close look at other works by H.D., other literary-critical responses to her oeuvre, and the work being done on imagist poetry right now. In short, I would need to project a context, infer an audience, and also reexamine my own interpretation of the poem. I'd have to do a little more by way of forethought.

THE Δ-THESIS

And as I imposed on my thesis pressure from actual counterarguments offered by other critics, as well as from ones I might anticipate, as I brought more evidence to bear both for my thesis and against it, I would notice the thesis beginning to mutate or change, so much so that by the end of the paper, I could not simply reiterate my thesis but would actually have come to a new point, an enhanced version of the thesis, an idea I could not have started with but might now assert because I have been putting my thesis under pressure for five or eight or eighteen pages. The thesis has evolved, has become the equivalent of a second, a changed, thesis, the "Δ-Thesis" or "ΔT." I'll go even further. If you've actively and creatively supported your thesis, if you've genuinely sought out and engaged counterarguments, and at the end you repeat your thesis exactly as it was initially formulated, it will have acquired a new, different meaning. What it was initially communicating is now understood, or better understood. In your ΔT, you should explain and reflect on that new idea.

We have a familiar word for ΔT—a conclusion. And while such an evolution of the thesis is a desideratum, any conclusion is ultimately never "right," or "definitive," or "final." It is not incontrovertible. Eliot says that poetry communicates before it is understood; a thesis should do the same, but by the end of an essay generated by that thesis, an approach to understanding should also have emerged. And that's OK; that's the point.

Only approaching understanding? Yes. It seems to me that knowledge in humanistic discourse is always only asymptotic: it approaches a truth but never actually touches it. As the philosopher

Frank Ramsey remarks, "meaning is mainly potential" (1); that is, the search for it opens up types of understanding that lead to new, often interesting questions, which then open outward to more questions, rather than answering them and shutting down discussion. We don't really ever discover "the" truth—"the the"—what or how a poem means, for example; there's no "Aha!" experience by which all aporias and perplexities of a work are suddenly resolved.

What you're doing consists of asking progressively more difficult questions and not being satisfied with the answers you come up with. Finally, you will arrive at a question and at an answer that you know most people aren't going to accept, at least not initially, but it's one that you deeply believe, and you want to show how you arrived at it. That's your thesis. You develop this idea as you show your thought process. You know that what you write represents only a series of successive approximations of a truth. And after you've demonstrated that thought process—you've laid it out in the entire paper—your conclusion shows something novel. It's not so much that you've been unable to solve or answer all problems. Rather, the thesis, now that you've explored and explained it, opens up new areas on inquiry (if it's an argumentative these), raises still more questions. In fact, one can start with a paper's conclusion and use that as a thesis (I recommend you try this, by the way) or use someone else's conclusion and develop that idea. By the end of a paper, you might rightly ask, looking at your own lines on the page, "What are you—banded one?" or maybe, "Are you alive?"

5

Saying Something New: Ways toward Creativity

"How do you actually come up with something new, though?" People ask me this all the time. I don't actually have the secret; I also struggle to come up with something new. The plain fact is it's not easy. I suggested above that you use certain strategies, such as looking for a moment of doubt, or running down "penumbral suspicions," or trying to analyze your feelings with respect to a topic. But many times, while these strategies help a writer to get words on the page, they don't do much to guarantee that those words crackle, spark, or even smolder with originality.

The novelist and scientist Thomas McMahon suggests that ideas just come in, as if from nowhere. "As far as I can tell, ideas always show up . . . absolutely free. And very often, in a nearly final form" (qtd. by A. Becker 10). But I don't really think most people have the confidence even to recognize a good idea if one appears before us. Theories of verbal creativity—sometimes called "invention theories"—have filled many volumes. I would like to very briefly delineate a few that might help you generate something original and striking. Ironically, these strategies themselves are not highly original, and I gleaned them over the course of years of teaching. Bear in mind that sometimes originality will not compel your audience, though; they might be looking for something else entirely. In that case, you should probably just skip this section.

But let's say that your assignment or area requires a genuine imaginativeness; you do not want to just repeat what's been said before, but instead want to come up with something new. My suggestion, in brief form, can be summarized as "Defining the Assignment in a New Way."

One thing I do want to offer by way of a caveat: sometimes people look for writing shortcuts—templates or tricks that they can use and that will allow them to circumvent the arduous process of writing, re-vising, writing, revising, and then writing some more. No such short-cuts exist. Writing is simply hard work. Even McMahon contends that testing ideas always requires hard work. Though ideas just emerge, he claims, "What you do have to do is test them, with your education or with your experience, to see whether they're any good. You can go to school or grow old learning how to test ideas. That takes hard work. But no one can teach you how to get them. They come for nothing" (120). While I like McMahon's emphasis on test-ing the ideas—developing them in some useful way—I think his own natural creativity might not be the norm. Ideas don't always "come for nothing," and in fact the hard part for most of us is to get those ideas that for him were so abundant or various.

So how do you define the assignment or task in a novel way, a way that will generate ideas? One of the most striking examples that James Adams uses in his book *Conceptual Blockbusting*, which I mention above, involves solving the nine-dot problem. Imagine nine dots laid out in a 3 × 3 grid. The task is to connect them all with four or fewer lines but without removing your pencil from the page.

•   •   •

•   •   •

•   •   •

Solving this typically involves going outside the actual grid a couple of times. Most people think that they must not move their pencil be-yond the box created by the dots. But the instructions do not specify this limitation. It might be that this puzzle was the model for the by now somewhat trite expression "thinking outside the box."

To generalize the idea, then, one needs to determine what artifi-cial, or self-imposed boundaries stand as barricades to creative solu-tions. More interesting solutions Adams suggests redefine the task in increasingly "outside the box" manners. For example, one person suggested taking the piece of paper and crumpling it into a ball, then driving the pencil through that. Another suggested really huge dots and small spaces between them, so that a broad pencil would intersect them all. And my favorite example: lay the grid flat on the ground, and draw a single line through the top row of dots. Continue on around the earth, and then pass through the second row of dots. One more circumnavigation of the planet, and the third row of dots is connected, and all this with just one line! I know that the solution implies a globe-wrapping piece of paper and in general lacks practicability, but I can only applaud the way that it redefines the whole assignment, evaporating various constraints (not only of the nine-dot grid but of the conventional page or pencil, or of the need for visas in order to get into all the countries one would have to gain entrance to on the way). Breaking the page rule could allow you to extend the idea even further, drawing an infinitely long line in our universe (which apparently is finite)—eventually that line will intersect every point of space, including the nine dots.

How might this apply to writing? I have four suggestions, though of course these are by no means exhaustive:

1. Let's start with that "zany" pseudo-thesis. Offer a solution that you know is zany or outlandish, but here's the difference between what I suggest here and a pseudo-thesis: take it seriously enough to try to make it work. "Trying to make it work" is the key here—zaniness is not an end in itself; rather, you need to use zaniness to provide you with a new angle.
2. Explore contradictory feelings or evidence. Most of the time, we just gloss over contradictions—we are looking for patterns that make sense, and contradictions we more or less minimize. Actually seeking out those contradictions can often open up a topic.
3. Bring in ideas and structures from another, apparently unrelated discipline.
4. Invent a new form by which to express yourself, or modify your own writing in some curious, special way.
5. Do research on the issue, seeking points of disagreement among scholars.

Let me explain the first four of these tactics. The fifth I discuss in greater detail in chapter 9. Keep in mind that I'm not importuning you to be "different" just for the sake of being different. But using tactics such as these might well lead you to new, interesting insights or discoveries.

ZANY AND RANDOM THOUGHTS

Ernest Hemingway would write out his stories and be pleased sometimes when he could not read a word but would misinterpret what it said; often that would lead him to some new angle on the narrative. For example, let's say that in the sentence above I were to reread and misconstrue one word, "pleased." Maybe I would misread this as "teased" or "plural" or "pheasant" (people who have seen my handwriting would know these are not themselves improbable misreadings!). "Pheasant" and "teased" do not help much. Oh, but I typed, "does nit help much." Perhaps "nits" are relevant here? You know, as in "picking nits"? Makes me wonder how much a single sentence relies on every small detail, every nit that a nitpicker would pick. Or a peck of pickled peppers. But I digress.

How about "plural" instead of "pleased"? This suggests that Hemingway was not singular but plural. Well, that's in itself interesting for a couple of reasons. First, Hemingway has much more than just a single side to his prose. Many people work under the impression that he wrote all simple sentences and very plain stories that displayed no emotion on the part of the narrator. This is certainly not the case. He had several styles in his repertoire. And he would often use very complex sentences. He also wrote some poetry. Consider this poem of Hemingway's, "The Earnest Liberal's Lament":

> I know monks
> Masturbate at night
> That pet cats screw
> That some girls bite.
> And yet, Oh Lord,
> What can I do
> To set things right?
>
> (Biblioctopus.com)

Well, this seems very nontypical Hemingway! This is not the disinterested, affectless recorder of atrocities, no, not at all.

Hemingway's plurality also emerges from his having so many imitators. It strikes me, now that I think of it, that the whole "minimalist" school of American writers—Raymond Carver, Frederick Barthelme, Joan Didion, among others—all owe considerable allegiance to Hemingway. Then, too, people who preceded Hemingway (I'm thinking of Sherwood Anderson in particular, but to a lesser extent Willa Cather and Stephen Crane) formed and provided literary models for Hemingway; they pluralized in some manner the Hemingway form.

Now I'm not sure how much these spin-offs from a misreading of a word in a line really help me to get my point across or give me insights about how to generate new ideas. But here's a suggestion: pluralize yourself. How would you be different if you had grown up poor rather than rich or rich rather than poor, or middle-class rather than either of the preceding? How would you respond if faced with a much younger version of yourself? Or with a much older version of yourself? Or how about if you were faced with a version of yourself who had committed a terrible crime, or had gone into some legitimate field very different from your chosen one, or had grown up to be six feet ten inches tall—or three feet ten inches, or some height (or weight) very different from your own? Pluralize yourself as a different religion, ethnicity, gender—or as someone with none of these things, if that's possible. Suddenly you find that you have a new angle on the writing, a new set of filters through which you view the whole enterprise.

CONTRADICTORY FEELINGS OR EVIDENCE

In a course I teach about medical narratives, one student, Jessica C., decided that she wanted to write an essay about the pain that we as readers sometimes feel in relation to stories. She noticed that in fact the pain of sick or dying characters in some stories didn't bother her all that much, but in other stories the pain really disturbed her. This, to her, was a contradiction. Why was she sympathetic, or even empathetic, when she read some stories, but when she read others, the plight of suffering characters didn't move her? Such a problem led to an interesting paper, which also employed the application of ideas from another field. I will get to that in a minute.

Another example of contradictory feelings. Let's say you want to examine some aspect of consumer desire in the United States. This topic I think most people can understand and work with, since most Americans are expert consumers. Does a contradiction exist in the idea of "consumer desire"? It seems to me that perhaps one does. We as consumers certainly have desires—we want to buy something or maybe a lot of things—but at the same time we have fears: those things won't be affordable, won't be available, won't live up to our expectations, will hurt us in some weird and unforeseeable way, will lead us to have to buy even more things, will require incredibly heavy maintenance, or will mark us in some way as perhaps politically aligned with the repressive regime of the country where the product was made, or as an advocate of child labor, the exploitation of political prisoners, or the brutal murder of baby seals, crocodiles, minks, or rain forest flora and fauna. So suddenly a paper about consumer desire, once the contradictions hovering around it emerge, becomes really rather complex and possibly compelling.

But let's take it to another stage of contradiction. Let's examine consumer desirelessness, rather than just consumer desire. The phenomenon of walking around malls or driving through shopping districts, or for that matter browsing on the Internet, palls for many consumers—to the point at which they may lose all desire. They may find themselves suddenly flooded with so many choices, none apparently better than the rest, that they find themselves not just unable to make a choice but entirely indifferent, stunned numb by overchoice. Looking at that feeling might lead to the exploration of the myth that our heavily consumer-based society wants us to believe, namely, that some products out there will fulfill us, that will make our lives complete where they are now fragmentary, that will make us happy, successful, sexy, beautiful, young, and smart. At what point in a consumer's experience does this myth break down? What must happen? Is it only a matter of age, income bracket, experience? It seems to me that these are some interesting questions you might explore in an essay.

IDEAS OR STRUCTURES FROM ANOTHER DISCIPLINE

Back to Jessica C., who examined the pain of various fictional characters—she did indeed invent a provocative problem that drove forward her thesis, but I also want to cite her way of exploring this question, since it exemplifies the strategy of looking outside the discipline. After having done quite a lot of reading in and around the whole issue of feeling pain, she kept on noticing references to Elisabeth Kübler-Ross, whose work examined the social/psychological states of the dying. As background, here's a brief overview of Kübler-Ross's ideas: "Her influential *On Death and Dying* (1969) mapped out a five-stage framework to explain the experience of dying patients, which progressed through denial, anger, bargaining with God, depression, and acceptance" (*Columbia* 1558). Jessica thought that this five-stage experience might somehow mirror the empathetic experience of death, that is, how a reader feels when she or he reads the story of a dying character. She further suggested that if a narrative in some sense allowed or forced the reader to go through all five stages of the process, then that work was not so difficult to endure, and it did not disturb the reader. By contrast, if for some reason one or more of the stages were truncated, the reader's felt experience was painful. Of course I realize that this interpretation sees Kübler-Ross's ideas as somehow apodictic—absolute truth—but just the same, Jessica's application of the five stages of dying to the reader of stories about dying seems to me a creative, striking connection.

A version of bringing a structure from another discipline, the comparison-contrast often helps generate new ideas. I don't recommend totally antic comparisons such as the one Dave Barry suggested (*Moby-Dick* and the Republic of Ireland), but I do encourage you to look beyond the obvious, the relatively or reasonably similar. For example, a paper about, say, sport-utility vehicles (SUVs) might compare Hummers with BMWs and Mercedes Geländewagens. Or Range Rovers and Toyota Land Cruisers. There are lots of possibilities, but I would suggest that going outside the SUV class might be more interesting. Comparing an SUV to a car is relatively often done, so perhaps you could compare an SUV to a tank? Or to a boat? For some reason these also strike me as too obvious, too limiting. Maybe an SUV could be compared to some sort of animal? Again, too literalist, is it? SUVs are really very much like elephants (large, lumbering, etc.). But what about dinosaurs? Maybe the SUV as a reincarnation of the extinct dinosaur would lead to new insights. Some are heavily armored, like the stegosaurus; others are relatively small but aggressive, like an al-

losaurus; some seem to take to water, as did others of the ancient reptiles. And still others amaze us with their gigantic proportions.

I'm not sure this would get us far, but maybe an expansion to other
forms would be better; let's forget about modes of transport or things
that literally move outside the human body, switching our focus to
things that move, or were thought to have moved, inside that body.
We can then compare the SUV one of the four humors—black
bile (anger), yellow bile (depression), blood (liveliness), or phlegm
(lethargy). These were thought in ancient times to dwell within each
person; the idea was to seek a balance. Could our vehicles be catego-
rized along these same lines? If so, then the SUV might be said to represent blood (liveliness), but I'd argue that this is a masquerade form,
and in fact it more often really is one of the other three humors.
Again, I don't think this works, quite, since the categories of humors
fail to map onto SUVs. But maybe it would be more useful to think
of SUVs and vehicles on our roads in general as resembling the flood
of various components of blood in our circulatory systems. Cars
might be the plasma that flows around everything; trucks the red
blood cells, carrying oxygen and nutrients, that is, needed materials;
the police cars, the white blood cells; motorcycles, invading bacteria
. . . and SUVs would be, what? Cancer. Uncontrolled growth.

Now I don't think many people would find imaginative the idea
that an SUV is just a metastatic version of a car, but that comparison
might give some insight to the topic in general, and to the motives of
people who buy SUVs, to the purpose of such vehicles on the roads,
to the results of having so many of them. You are trying to expand
your mode of thought about an issue or idea, and I think the comparison might have that effect. Of course, if you are a great lover of
SUVs, you might take a different angle or paint anti-SUV commenta-
tors as absurd because they liken your favorite vehicle to a tumor.

But why stop with SUVs or single them out, really? Why not try
to see all motor vehicles as cancerous? Wouldn't that be a more honest
appraisal? And if these vehicles are the cancer, then what do we do to
cure it? As you can see, this kind of comparison-contrast brings to
light some genuinely fundamental issues—can or ought we as a society do without automotive transport? Is our system of transportation
killing us slowly or even rather rapidly? And what would the alternatives be? Are the car-dependent culture and its gradual erosion of our

planet as inevitable as are cancers to organisms that have evolved through a process of mutation? Suddenly the topic has opened outward, maybe itself metastasizing too wildly. But using this last-mentioned metaphor might lead to ideas about "curing" the problem afflicting the planet, through removal of the worst part of the problem, or perhaps through some version of chemotherapy, like controlling the chemicals that these cars emit.

INVENTING NEW FORMS

Since most of you are trying to write "formal" essays, reinventing the form of an essay has certain risks. You will probably need to ascertain to what extent your audience is willing to look at "new versions" of the essay or argument, and to what extent they want the more or less standard form described above. Hence you might view this section on invention of new forms as being only instrumentally valuable. It might lead you to an insight or idea about a subject, and then you could write out that idea in a more traditional format.

Let's say in a political theory class you have to write a paper about John Rawls's "veil of ignorance." Rawls, a modern political philosopher, proposed that inequalities in the distribution of wealth and power are not all evil or negative in a given society, just so long as the interests of the least fortunate are kept in mind. He invented the term "veil of ignorance" to suggest that when designing a society, we have to imagine the designers working as if they were veiled from knowing their own status, education, or even racial or gender identity, a situation that would likely allow for the creation of a society that granted considerable rights to the worst off—since the persons designing it understand that they could be those very people. Your paper analyzing Rawls's position will have to draw on *Theory of Justice* (1971) as well as on secondary sources. It might be that you have a prompt to answer, such as "Using Rawls's 'veil of ignorance' idea, propose how a society might implement this technique and restructure its system of equality."

You might feel somewhat stymied at this point. You will probably have read some political philosophy, but you won't really know from what angle to build a society along the lines that Rawls suggests, nor will you be able even to envision such a system, since Rawls's idea was more of a thought experiment than a proposal he wanted to implement. After all, people cannot be stripped of their identities or knowledge of themselves—and if they could, would we want to listen to them, especially if it were somehow up to them how to distribute the wealth and power in a given society?

Maybe, since you feel stymied, you should try to invent a new form. You might consider writing a brief play or short story, for example, in which the society you imagine could exist. People might be given drugs, say, to make them unaware of who they were. Or such drugs could be put in the water supply or air, and the whole populace could be polled about a new organizational system. Or perhaps there could be some element of sabotage, or a small group, getting wind of what was going to happen, could invest in gas masks, lots of bottled spring water, and canned goods, and use their advantage to skew the results. What would human reaction be to such a system as the veil of ignorance? Your play or short story could analyze that. From there, you might in fact come up with something original as a thesis to a paper about the topic.

Alternatively, you might conduct a series of interviews with friends, family, teachers, or strangers. You might ask them questions about social inequality, about what they conceive of as an ideal society, and about what they would do were they placed in a situation such that they did not know their own status when making decisions. These interviews could well form the basis for a paper about Rawls.

Such tactics would require you to write two pieces, though—an exploratory one, and then a final copy (which itself might have multiple drafts). Could you just use some other form that would serve as the final version? Perhaps you could set up Rawls in conversation with several other political philosophers—Aristotle, Rousseau, Locke, Marx—and, using their own words, create a scene in which they discuss their ideas. Again, you will need to ascertain whether your audience is willing to accept such a deviation from the standard argument, but if they are, such an approach might well prove to be refreshing. And it might lead to new insights about the philosophy itself.

*   *   *

Will any of these strategies lead you to new ideas? I'm not sure. But they all have one thing in common: they all require you to think about the assignment or task—the invention of ideas in writing—in some new way. Many times, I have seen students engage in self-censorship, stopping the elaboration of a thought because they feel it doesn't fit the assignment exactly, or it will move them into tangential or eccentric realms, or it will be too controversial and will generate dispute or controversy. Don't worry so much about "getting along," mimicking a party line, or fitting into a mold. Rather, think about your writing in the exact opposite terms: You want to stir things up. You want to generate debate.

Again, you need to respect your audience and keep in mind what it wants. Yet while you need to respect the interests and requirements that any audience (inferred or actual) imposes, you don't want to be in the position of being beholden to that audience. Sometimes when I speak with students about their writing, they say, "But what do YOU want?" seeming to suggest they need a set of explicit instructions that they can follow as if they were assembling a new electronic device. They will follow my guidance, do in their writing whatever it is that I want them to do. You need to discard and replace this model. What I really want is for you to think for yourself, for you to come up with an original idea that I didn't think of, imply, or program you with. Writing requires belief in yourself as a person who can generate ideas that are original, striking, creative—and at the same time fit the assignment. You need somehow to have the emotional independence to feel that you really can come up with something intellectually solid, original, and defensible, rather than kowtowing to a perceived audience's prejudices or preconceptions. You have to remember that most audiences don't want a catechism or a recitation of their own views. They would prefer something that expands their range of knowledge, challenges them, makes them flex and tax their minds.

6

Paragraph Design

Let's back up a little. You have some ideas for what you want to write, but before you commit yourself to paper, you wonder, what kind of paragraphs should I use? There seem to be all kinds of paragraphs in the textual universe surrounding us. Which are best? How can I find the right kinds of paragraphs to advance my ideas?

A kind of paper in miniature, complete with its own thesis statement, "body," and conclusion, the paragraph is the unit that carries forward a single stage in an argument. I know some writing teachers hate this analogy, perhaps because it too severely delimits the possible forms a paragraph can take. But regardless, it is crucial to craft each paragraph such that it both makes sense on its own and fits into the entirety of the paper. So as you compose, you must keep both of these notions in mind: how to organize the mini-paper of the paragraph, and how that mini-paper fits into or advances the entire paper, the larger argument.

TOPIC SENTENCES

The "thesis" of the paragraph is often called the "topic sentence," but perhaps a better name for it is the occasionally used "controlling idea." It controls or determines the rest of the paragraph. It is the most important single point of the paragraph, the essence to which the paragraph might be reduced. Usually, but not always, this is the first sentence of the paragraph. Such a positioning is a safe one, though sometimes writers will opt for a closing sentence as a topic sentence, or will have a topic sentence in the middle of a paragraph. Some writers refer to and recommend the "hinge-structure," a structure in which the paragraph finds its true direction about halfway through. John Muir, in a 1920 essay entitled "Save the Redwoods," uses a hinge-structure for his conclusion:

Any fool can destroy trees. They cannot defend themselves or run away. And few destroyers of trees ever plant any; nor can planting avail much toward restoring our grand aboriginal giants. It took more than three thousand years to make some of the oldest of the Sequoias, trees that are still standing in perfect strength and beauty, waving and singing in the mighty forests of the Sierra. Through all the eventful centuries since Christ's time, and long before that, God has cared for these trees, saved them from drought, disease, avalanches, and a thousand storms; but he cannot save them from sawmills and fools; this is left to the American people. The news from Washington is encouraging. On March third the House passed a bill providing for the Government acquisition of the Calaveras giants. The danger these Sequoias have been in will do good far beyond the boundaries of the Calaveras Grove, in saving other groves and forests, and quickening interest in forest affairs in general. While the iron of public sentiment is hot let us strike hard. In particular, a reservation or national park of the only other species of Sequoia, the *sempervivens*, or redwood, hardly less wonderful than the *gigantean*, should be quickly secured. It will have to be acquired by gift or purchase, for the Government has sold every section of the entire redwood belt from the Oregon boundary to below Santa Cruz. (831)

Notice that in this longish (ten-sentence) paragraph, the fifth sentence ("Through all the eventful centuries . . .") acts as a hinge. The first four sentences (about fools who kill mighty trees) serve to capture the reader's imagination and indignation, but it soon becomes clear that the paragraph does not really examine the fool who destroys trees; it instead offers a suggestion that the only ones who can now save the giant trees are the American people.

Muir uses this format, I think, because his previous paragraph concluded with a discussion of how we are the guardians of the trees in our country, asserting that "the American people are equal to this trust . . . as soon as they see it and understand it" (830). To follow that sentiment with the idea of the fifth sentence above, which ends, "this is left to the American people," might have struck Muir as being redundant or repetitious, so he restructured his final paragraph, opening it instead with a brief, pithy, almost epigrammatic sentence, "Any fool can destroy trees." Indeed, his use of the hinge structure makes his concluding paragraph overall far more powerful.

As always, the rules here will bend as you push against their limits; feel free to experiment with the placement of topic sentences. My own preference is for an initial-sentence placement, with the "hinge-structure" a close second. Sometimes alternative placements can add interest to a paragraph (and paper), offering the reader a little more variety than would a repeated structure. I strongly recommend that you do place a topic sentence somewhere in the paragraph, however; allowing your controlling idea to remain implicit or deploying the entire paragraph as its own topic sentence both strike me as risky strategies, more apt to confuse the reader than to enlighten or engage.

Succeeding sentences make up the paragraph's "body," and the final sentence, the paragraph's conclusion. One advantage to seeing paragraphs this way comes from the analogy to the parts of a paper: just as the thesis of a paper must be different from its conclusion, so a topic sentence must not be merely repeated at the end of a paragraph. A paragraph must "go" somewhere. It represents, specifically, a stage in your argument. For example, the following paragraph starts well, but I wrote it to illustrate a specific kind of paragraph problem that I have encountered surprisingly often. It goes in a circle. (This is a narrative, but the same principles apply in expository prose.)

> It was a textbook example of a frightening house. The windows banged as if of their own accord. Shrill voices and shrieks that almost exceeded the power of the human ear to grasp emerged from the house's eaves. Bats flew in and out of the windows. And oddly shrouded forms, what could be just wisps of smoke or play of light from shadow and moonbeam, seemed to float behind the partially broken or cracked and cobwebbed windowpanes. It was a textbook example of a frightening house.

The paragraph has some good supportive details, but it needs to give more of a sense of progress. For example, it could end, "'Yes,' he thought, 'it's true that you never can go home again,'" or, "Indeed, Hollywood movie sets do their best to embody rather than avoid cliché." Perhaps, "He couldn't believe that his grandmother had lived here her whole life." Something is needed to "conclude" the paragraph, to lead the reader in some clear direction, to help the reader figure out what argument is being advanced.

C. T. Winchester provides us with an interesting example of how a paragraph develops and changes; it's an expository prose paragraph that "goes somewhere":

> It is evident, from these considerations, that poetry can never be translated. Its finer and subtler essence always escapes in the process. Dependent for its individual poetic quality, in every instance, upon the inexplicable power of language, that quality is lost the moment the language is changed. The intellectual content of a poem, the outlines of its imagery, its more vague and general emotional effects—these may be transferred to another tongue. The translator may be content with these, and win the praise of what is called fidelity; or, if he be himself a poet, he may weave the thought and imagery of his author into a new poem of his own which shall run parallel with the original and have perhaps a similar charm. But in either case his work is seen to be something very different from the poem he has attempted to translate. (245)

Winchester actually has a two-sentence "topic sentence" in this paragraph, but it's clear that he has a definite argumentative edge here ("poetry can never be translated"). Over the course of his paragraph, though, he takes two small counterarguments into account: the poem's general emotional effects can be "transferred to another tongue"; and, provided that the translator is a poet, a new poem can be created that will "run parallel with the original and have perhaps a similar charm." And yet by the paragraph's end, Winchester has made it clear that such transference to a new language or such a creation of a new poem still differs too much from the original. So he has backed away some from his topic sentence's declaration that poetry can never be translated. It can be translated, ultimately, but neither faithfully nor well. One of the nice things about Winchester's paragraph, though, is that it uses a topic sentence early in the paragraph, thus allowing the reader to grasp readily what idea is going to be developed.

TRANSITIONS AND "THE OOZE"

An additional advantage to early placement of the topic sentence is that it will reveal when an essay has made a transition to a new stage. Not only is the paper moving to a new stage (as the paragraph break suggests), but, the topic sentence proclaims, *this is* that new stage. When writers bury their topic sentence in the middle of paragraphs, there seems to be no dividing point between one paragraph (or idea) and another. The paragraphs seem to ooze one into the next. Such a construction makes the whole paper seem a little hard to grasp, a bit inchoate and muddy. I strongly recommend avoiding the "ooze," or if you must place your topic sentences somewhere other than the beginning, do so only occasionally.

Sometimes the "oozing" quality emerges because students have been taught that they need to prepare the reader for the next paragraph by having an introduction to that paragraph's idea at the end of the paragraph before it. This is a mistake. Yes, you do need to make a smooth transition from one paragraph to the next, and at the same time the last sentence of a given paragraph makes a concluding point to that paragraph. So it's quite an important sentence. But it's more important as a conclusion to a unit of thought than as a transitional device. A signal of a new idea or of a new phase of thought, a different subject or perspective, should not displace or constitute that concluding sentence.

Your transitional device should be in the topic sentence of the paragraph, which at once signals a new idea and ties it in to the previous one. You need to make sure that this topic sentence obviously marks a change in direction. To anchor it to the previous paragraph, you should probably repeat some key idea, phrase, word (or even sentence structure) from the end of the preceding paragraph as you introduce the new topic of the new paragraph. Thus the topic sentence does double duty: it logically ties the new topic to the previous paragraph's yet at the same time introduces something clearly demarcated as new. It's sort of like a New Year's Eve or birthday party—a link to the past but a trumpeting of the new.

A topic sentence can on occasion "control" more than one paragraph, I should point out, especially in situations in which the writer suggests a classification and each element of the classification requires a fair amount of support. But on the whole it is best to use a topic sentence for each paragraph. You are writing, for the most part, to communicate your ideas, and typically the most straightforward method of presentation will be the best. Just keep in mind that variation, while it can raise the interest level of an essay, can also muddle your meaning, so when you do attempt any kind of innovation, you need to be especially careful that meaning isn't being sacrificed on the altar of novelty.

PARAGRAPH DEVELOPMENT: THE USE OF EVIDENCE

How do you fill up the paragraph? What goes after the topic sentence? The general idea is that the paragraph "proves" or "supports" the topic sentence: it offers details, examples, incidents, logical arguments, or narrative—in a word, evidence—that elaborates on and explains the idea of the topic sentence. Paragraphs need to be developed just as arguments are developed in the paper proper, and as with papers, there are many methods of development. Typically, these methods are delineated as classification, cause-effect, definition, description, process, comparison-contrast, example, or a combination of these. Instead of trying to decide which of these to use in developing each of your paragraphs, it would be best simply to keep in mind that you need to expand, explore, and explain—even exploit—your topic sentence. Some modes will be more useful in some situations than others, but in all cases, you need to offer more than just a topic sentence and a reiteration of that sentence. Like the thesis, the topic sentence must be more than merely asserted: you need to prove it.

You prove it through the use of evidence. For some reason, much discussion of writing has taken on a legalistic tone—"marshaling evidence," "providing warrants," "making a case"—though the writing that you do will probably not be used in court papers. Evidence consists of what you fill up your paragraphs with. Often thought to be the heart of argument (as Emerson remarks, "Hug your facts"), evidence usually consists of the material you have discovered or assembled that makes you believe what you believe. It does consist of facts, quotations, statistics, definitions—specifically, the material that you use to support your thesis, or to support some subpoint of your thesis. It can also be the material that you have discovered that helps to defeat a counterargument.

The key is this: you must find evidence that your audience will see as not only true but also somehow representative. You have to be "fair" in the selection process that you've used to uncover it, and you have to be fair as well in presenting a balanced picture of the evidence that you use. It need not necessarily be always novel or different; you can draw on material that has already been brought to light. But you may want to frame that evidence in such a way that it has a new impact. In short, you need to make the evidence work to advance your argument, thesis, or idea.

There is no set length for a paragraph. A paragraph of one sentence can be fully developed; a paragraph of ten sentences can be underdeveloped. But what's the ideal length? I have hedged for so long in an attempt to answer this question that now I just give a suggestion. Probably the safest length for a paragraph in a student essay is six to nine sentences. Paragraphs of fewer than six sentences probably lack development; those of ten or more can typically be broken somewhere, and each resultant paragraph developed more fully. But keep in mind that some paragraphs with fewer than six or more than nine sentences will be fine; these numerical limits represent only a very general suggestion. Your instructors will probably never count the number of sentences per paragraph. It is your goal to make sure, though, that the development of your paragraph sufficiently explains the idea of its topic sentence. (This paragraph has nine sentences, not counting this one: just made it!)

PARAGRAPH COHERENCE AND COHESIVENESS

One of the most difficult aspects of writing consists of disciplining yourself to discuss, within a paragraph, only the issues of the topic sentence. This concept is known as paragraph unity or coherence. A coherent paragraph limits itself to the points needed to prove the topic sentence, expanding on those as much as necessary to explain them but not so much as to stray into what might be a new topic for another paragraph.

A final idea to bear in mind when you construct your paragraphs relates to how the sentences lead one into another. If the sentences connect smoothly and logically, that is, if their transitions allow them to flow into one another without a choppy or staccato effect, then the paragraph can be considered cohesive.

One of the ways to think about this concept is to envision it in terms of new information and old information. A topic sentence, as I suggested above, has to link up to the previous paragraph—so it repeats some idea, word, or structure from that previous paragraph, what might be considered "old" information. It adds something to this "old" information, however: something "new" (thus justifying the start of a new paragraph). This kind of cohesion carries on into the paragraph itself, where new information is best introduced if it is preceded by, or introduced by, old information. As an example, the following two sentences seem to lack cohesion (the example is one that Professor Donald W. Cummings introduced me to):

> When we were on vacation, we came upon a bear. A forest ranger we encountered told us that someone had evidently shot the bear.

While these are not by any means terrible sentences, between the two the reader has to pause too long, I think, to figure out the consecutiveness of thought. It seems to me an example of what might be viewed as follows:

> New information$_1$ [NI$_1$](vacation, bear). New information$_2$ [NI$_2$](ranger, shooting), old information [OI] or NI$_1$ (bear).

Or, in short form,

> NI$_1$. NI$_2$, OI [NI$_1$].

The new information is followed by more new information, which is confusing.

Ideally, the sentences should be joined in this fashion: NI$_1$. OI, [NI$_1$] NI$_2$. This might be done in any of a number of ways, but the most logical might be the following:

When we were on vacation, we came upon a bear. The animal, we later found out from a forest ranger, had evidently been shot.

When the details are presented in this manner, the weakness of the whole universe of information being conveyed also becomes more pronounced. Had they come upon a wounded bear, a dead bear, or a bear that was healthy and would be shot later in the day? In short, the writer will be more likely to clear up the sequence of events if an "NI_1. OI, NI_2" format is followed:

When we were on vacation, we encountered a bear that looked a little weak. Its weakness, we later discovered from a ranger, was caused by the bear's having been shot earlier that week.

The format of this sentence is

NI_1 (vacation, bear, weakness of bear). OI (bear's weakness), NI_2 (ranger), OI (weak bear, cause of this) NI_3 (shooting earlier in week).

The important cohesive links, then, are the OI ("bear's weakness") between the two sentences, and the OI ("weak bear—cause of this") between the main verb and its agent. Notice, too, that the two pieces of old information, the linking OIs, are rather similar to each other, thus making the cohesiveness even greater.

Here are examples of some breakdowns in cohesion. The first is from an essay by Robert Lipsyte entitled "Athletes Offer Straight Talk about Cancer." Lipsyte is writing about Lance Armstrong, the great cyclist:

Armstrong, of course, is the most celebrated drug-taker in sports: the chemotherapy treatment that burned out the testicular cancer that had reached his brain in 1996 was the first step toward his amazing three consecutive victories in the Tour, starting in 1999. It happens that EPO, or erythropoietin, the blood-enriching drug prescribed to boost his chemo-suppressed immune system, is also the banned drug of choice among world-class cyclists.

Lipsyte has omitted a connective between these two sentences, leaving the reader a little confused in the move from sentence one to sentence two. The first sentence describes Armstrong and the Tour de France, which Armstrong had at that time won three times. Then, with no real link, the second sentence starts discussing EPO. It would be relatively easy to segue more smoothly and with greater cohesion into that second sentence—simply by starting with OI (old information), but old information from early in the preceding sentence. Try reading the original with this sentence inserted between the first and second sentences: "Part of his chemotherapy involved taking EPO."

As you see, to avoid sounding repetitious, you don't always need to link one sentence to the tail end of the one before. Sometimes you should link a new sentence to the OI from the first portion of the one before. So instead of writing, "Janine worked in a savings bank as vice president. A vice president has a very important job. This job entails figuring out how to invest the bank's financial resources," You might write something such as the following:

> Janine worked in a savings bank as vice president. She had, in fact, a very important job, as she had to figure out how to invest the bank's financial resources.

Notice that the second sentence goes back to the beginning of the first sentence (to "Janine worked"), not to its ending.

Here is a more elaborated example that I have made up, linking the beginning of each sentence to the end of the one before, and you can see that the writing sounds immature and repetitious. It's an exaggeration of what I often encounter in both professional and student writing, but it's only a slight exaggeration:

> Many commentators have noted the importance of the novel, *Flatland. Flatland*, the creation of Edwin Abbott, remains one of the few examples of mathematical science fiction. Mathematical science fiction, that is, science fiction that concerns themes from mathematics, such as dimensionality, can usually also function as an allegory. A typical allegory that critics have seen at work in Abbott's novel revolves around the plight

of an individual who, armed with some special information or some great insight into the universe, faces a disbelieving society. The disbelieving society, in the case of *Flatland*, is, of course, the two-dimensional inhabitants of the world, who do not realize (as the protagonist does) that there is a third dimension. The third dimension remains mysterious and even inexplicable to them, as they lack the conceptual apparatus to understand anything outside of their own two dimensions. Their own two dimensions limit them from seeing another dimension, which would be similar to people who were prevented by their own prejudices and predispositions from seeing the "truth" of a given situation. A given situation, indeed, can have more than one "truth," however; perhaps Abbott's idea was just to suggest that surface appearance might be only one of a multitude of possible "truths."

This is clearly connection with a vengeance; it cries for something like variety. It seems to me, though, that there are enough ideas in this paragraph that it can be rather easily revised into something that resembles mature prose.

More typically, though, disconnectedness poses a greater and more often encountered problem. It sometimes represents a pathological problem. Consider this letter that Jonathan Franzen quotes in his essay "My Father's Brain":

> We got your letter a couple of days ago and were pleased to see how well you were doing in school, particularly in math. It is important to write well, as the ability to exchange ideas will govern the use that one country can make of another country's ideas.
>
> Most of your nearest relatives are good writers, and thereby took the load off me. I should have learned better how to write, but it is so easy to say, Let Mom do it.
>
> I know that my writing will not be easy to read, but I have a problem with the nerves in my legs and tremors in my hands. In looking at what I have written, I expect you will have difficulty to understand, but with a little luck, I may keep up with you.
>
> We have had a change in the weather from cold and wet to

dry with fair blue skies. I hope it stays this way. Keep up the good work.

This letter was written by a man who had Alzheimer's disease. Yet it is not so very different from many paragraphs that one encounters in writing by people who are not evidently suffering from a degenerative condition of the brain. The general point is this: work on making your sentences tie into each other so that the interstices are neither glaringly obvious nor artificially stitched close. The "stitching" of your paragraph should be neither whipstitch big and sloppy nor so tight that every seam shows.

Consider by way of contrast some writing from a medical text, the *Merck Manual*. I had been stung by a bee and went to the manual for information. The author of the entry seems to have found himself in some trouble because he clearly had a very limited space and had to convey an enormous amount of information. Here's what he has written:

> Insects that sting are members of the order Hymenoptera of the class Insecta. There are two major subgroups: apids (honeybees, bumblebees) and vespids (wasps, yellow jackets, hornets). The fire ant is a nonwinged member of Hymenoptera. Apids are docile and usually do not sting unless provoked. The stinger of the honeybee has multiple barbs, which usually detach after a sting. The venom of apids contains phospholipase A_2, hyaluronase, apamin, melittin, and kinins. Vespids have few barbs and can inflict multiple stings. Vespid venom contains phospholipase, hyaluronase, and a protein termed antigen 5. Yellow jackets are the major cause of allergic reactions to insect stings in the USA. (Beers and Berkow 2650)

Where is the topic sentence of this paragraph? Is it really about Hymenoptera, various stingers, venom, or allergies? In such an information-rich paragraph, the reader needs more guidance, more direction as to what's important, what less so. Let me offer a rewrite:

> Stinging insects (the order Hymenoptera of the class Insecta) contain three major subgroups: apids (honeybees, bumblebees), vespids (wasps, yellow jackets, hornets), and ants—all of which have slightly different habits and venoms. Apids,

typically docile and not stinging unless provoked, nonetheless sometimes do so, and the stinger of one apid, the honeybee, has multiple barbs, which usually detach after a sting. Their venom contains phospholipase A_2, hyaluronase, apamin, melittin, and kinins. By contrast, vespids such as yellow jackets, which cause the majority of allergic reactions to insect stings in the USA, have few barbs but can inflict multiple stings; their venom contains phospholipase, hyaluronase, and antigen 5, a protein.

I combined the first three sentences into one topic sentence and tried to include within it some clue as to what the rest of the paragraph would cover. "By contrast" offers a transitional element to help guide the reader. The original author, after a brief mention of the fire ant, seems to have left it alone: that seems to me a good idea too.

If given a little more space, the author could have written three paragraphs rather than one, and his topic sentences could have been as follows:

1. A large and diverse order of the animal kingdom, Hymenoptera includes all the common stinging insects.
2. Among Hymenoptera, the insects' stinging habits vary, as do the nature of the stingers and the chemical makeup of the venom.
3. Humans can have allergic reactions to any of these venoms, but the yellow jacket causes the most widespread problem.

The original paragraph contains at least three major idea clusters, and packing them all into one paragraph is probably not the most efficient way to convey all the information. Indeed, that strategy works against the author: his paragraph structure breaks down, and the ideas become obscured.

With each paragraph, remember, you need to ask yourself, what is the point I'm trying to make here? How does it fit into my larger argument, yet how does it make sense within its limited confines? Your idea first has to work in its own paragraph, has to be lucid and well-developed enough to make sense on its own, before it can function as part of a larger whole.

7

Developing an Argument

THE ELEMENTS OF THE ESSAY

Most argumentative essays have a similar organization, which is often called a "structure" or "shape." While I don't want to strait-jacket you with a fixed form, I do want to suggest that certain elements of the essay are essential:

1. Title
2. Introduction and thesis
3. Body
4. Conclusion

Most, that is, include a title; an introduction of some kind, which includes a thesis statement (or a "claim"); support for that thesis (examples, evidence, elaboration, classification, qualification, distinction, definition, division), as well as "con" arguments that the paper addresses in some way, either refuting them or incorporating them into the thesis; and a conclusion (what I have termed a Δ thesis). I want to emphasize here that argumentative essays have an interconnectedness: just as a sentence is not merely a heap of words, an essay isn't merely a piling up of elements. Its separate parts must work in unison with one another. We can identify the thesis, or the evidence, and the conclusion, but these elements are successful only insofar as they are part of a whole.

Another way of thinking about paper structure could be one that used "thesis" in some form to describe each part. While this is atypical, let me present the idea at least provisionally. (Note that you need not include all of these elements. One or two of those with an asterisk might be omitted.)

Introduction	[Pre-Thesis]
Thesis	
Background information	[Arche-Thesis]
Support	[Sub-Thesis]
*Counterargument₁	[Counter-Thesis]
Support	[Sub-Thesis]
*Counterargument₂	[Counter-Sub-Thesis]
Summary of argument	[Syn-Thesis]
*Counterargument₃	[Counter-Syn-Thesis]
Support	[Sub-Thesis]
Conclusion	[Neo-Thesis]

You can probably imagine why this particular nomenclature will never catch on, but it does give the idea of how a paper has to have all of its parts interconnected.

INDIVIDUAL PARTS OF THE ESSAY

At the same time that you conceive of the paper as an entirety, you should consider the component parts of its argument: the title, the introduction, the body, and the conclusion. I'll address the first three of these components here; I reserve my detailed discussion of conclusions for the next chapter.

Title

Your paper needs to be titled. The title should answer the question "What is this paper going to be about?" It should describe the paper's content. Make the title brief and descriptive. It should invite the reader in. Try not to hide what the paper will discuss or examine; try not to be obscure or playful or punning or condescending.

The punning title, for example, of a paper on Henry David Thoreau's work *Walden*, "Thoreau-Up," is both too childish and too mocking: it does not suggest a serious or analytical essay is likely to follow. I don't think the writer has given us enough information to transform this into a good title, but here's an attempt: "The Lack of Economy in Thoreau's *Walden*"; "How Thoreau's Works Were Made Trite by 1960s Popular Culture"; or even something as simple as "Is

Thoreau Overrated?" In a similar vein, one of my fellow students entitled his paper on *Paradise Lost*, "*Paradise Lost*: A Loser," a title impressive only in its failure. A more effective title, one implying a more balanced, scholarly analysis, might be "Narrative Discontinuities in *Paradise Lost*." Another title (which I encountered in a graduate seminar on the works of Henry James), "Why Henry James Does Not Quite Cut It as a Novelist," also does not work, I feel, largely because of the dismissive tone it sets up, which places the reader (in this case, the professor who assigned the work by Henry James) on the defensive. "Does Not Cut It," I feel obliged to add, does not itself stylistically "cut it" as appropriate formal English.

Remember that since the title is the first piece of information encountered, it not only gives the initial clue as to what the paper will be about, but also conveys your tone, your relation to the subject matter. A good title should be informative, concise, and straightforward. In scholarly essays, it's best not to use a title that angers, offends, or assaults the reader—unless that is your intention and you are self-consciously writing a broadside, diatribe, or screed: not typical assignments, I hasten to point out. Strive more for *captatio benevolentiae*: self-consciously capturing the goodwill of the audience, getting them on your side before they have read your paper.

Introduction, and the Thesis Therein

A tension exists between the title you have chosen and the first words of your essay. You have given your reader two new pieces of information, and he or she must process them both. Hence there should not be too great a disjunction between these two elements. Your introduction should probably expand on some of the ideas of the title, but most of all it must continue to invite the reader inside: it must be engaging and interesting. Some people call it a "hook"; this is a crass expression of the same idea. I would not recommend a long first sentence, for example, as that could be off-putting or confusing. An excellent first sentence comes from Scott Sanders's essay on the lack of character development in science fiction, "Invisible Men and Women: The Disappearance of Character in Science Fiction." He writes, "Science fiction is the home of invisible men and women." This more or less repeats the idea of his title, but it does so in an engaging and interesting manner. Notice, for example, the double entendre. Try to excite your readers' interest and imagination; give them credit for being smart and observant.

As you proceed into the introduction, keep in mind that it needs to continue presenting information to the reader, basic background material, such as the subject, topic, and thesis of your paper. The subject is usually the thing—book, poem, principle, idea—being analyzed; the topic is some aspect of the subject; the thesis is an argumentative "take" on the topic. For example, in a paper called "Public Secrets: Confession in *The Scarlet Letter*," your subject might be Nathaniel Hawthorne's novel, *The Scarlet Letter*; your topic might be the public confession of sin in the novel; and your thesis might be the following:

> While Hawthorne's characters and narrator claim that the best way to live one's life is to confess openly to one's sins and shortcomings, the dramatic structure of the novel suggests that such a confession is not only impossible but also self-destructive and counterproductive; for those who confess are ostracized by society, and those who harbor secrets discover that doing so gives them power and effectuality.

Notice the complexity of this statement. And note, too, that you might not agree with it right away. Don't be afraid of the possibility of counterexamples (e.g., in this case, Hester Prynne's power even though she confesses): you will address these in the course of the essay.

Here's another good thesis on the novel, this by University of California English professor David Van Leer:

> Everywhere in the tales, the philosophical assumptions of Hawthorne's narrators are as important as the moral judgments they make. So, in *The Scarlet Letter*, a narration that at times seems indecisive—an intellectual cacophony—is itself part of the book's characterization of the problem. (5758)

This is an imaginative look at the novel, taking something that might be construed as a negative feature of its art, something defective in its composition, and suggesting that it contributes to the novel's success.

In addition, your introduction needs to set up something of the context for your discussion. It needs to suggest why your topic or subject is really worth writing about. Is it something that has recently been in the public eye? Is it something that is controversial and potentially explosive? Is it something that automatically would interest any reader—and if so, in what way? You don't want your essays to be merely dry academic exercises; instead, you want them somehow to elicit a recognition of their importance, immediacy, even drama. What brought you to write about this? And if there are many articles or essays about the same topic, what kinds of issues do they offer as the crucial ones that you will reconsider? You need to set your ideas within a field of discourse and at the same time distinguish your insight, angle, or interpretation from those that have preceded it. Yours is not a disembodied voice discussing some recondite issue that interests no one. No. Your voice has importance; your topic, immediacy. And your thesis about the topic will offer something new and controversial.

Most introductions are rewritten several times, in fact often after the rest of the essay has been finished. So while it's nice to draft a satisfying opening paragraph, you probably shouldn't spend a great deal of time on it in the first draft or two since you will return to it repeatedly. But in the end, you do ultimately need to get the introduction just right: it needs to be precisely composed and well balanced. Extra time spent on it will inevitably be well spent.

Body of Essay

The body forms the bulk of your paper. In the body, you will attempt to prove your thesis, use evidence to support its controversial assertions, and deal with possible counterarguments. The body must actually present the evidence and do the arguing. Such evidence might include relevant facts that you have encountered in books or articles, quotations from the text that you might be analyzing, logical inferences of various kinds, or explanations of what you mean. Many writing courses use the following terminology: your thesis is a kind of "*claim*," and to support your claim, you must provide in the paper various "*warrants*." More plainly, the idea is that you must do more than just assert: you must convince; you must persuade.

Some portions of the body will explain in detail what exactly you mean. These sections might be called "elaborations" of your thesis. They give more examples, provide more detailed definitions of various important terms (ones that are ambiguous, politically charged, or technical, for example), and flesh out the thesis. Such sections should probably come fairly early in the paper, for they still essentially set the groundwork ("arche-thetic," as I term it above). But you might have various sections in the paper (which might be titled separately, in fact), and each of these sections might well call for significant elaboration. Very often you will need to define certain important terms—such as ones that you use in a special way, for example. It's up to you to figure out what terms are being used in ways that your audience might not grasp intuitively—and then explain those terms. Indeed, many arguments hinge on just such definitions: an essay about abortion, if it defines human life as existing from the moment of conception, predetermines its argument: in this case, it's the very definition of key terms that must be argued for most strenuously.

Evidence should appear in other sections of the body. This will typically be in the form of quotations or references from a variety of sources. Keep in mind that such presentation of evidence is done only to support and develop your thesis; it should not be offered as truth in and of itself. Oftentimes students will suggest an idea and then quote an authority who, in print, says essentially the same thing. A strategy such as this does not prove your assertion to be true. Instead it suggests that you are lacking in originality and invest complete credence in an external source. A better strategy involves differentiating, if ever so slightly, your own position from that of the person you are quoting. (It probably will be different, but if you find that you cannot do this—that is, if someone already came up with the exact idea you have—you probably need to find a new idea or develop it in a different direction.) Present evidence only insofar as it functions as part of your argument. You should evaluate and comment on that evidence in order to clarify and expand your own position.

Extension of your thesis will also be a part of the body. Your aim is not to elaborate on or give evidence for only a single idea but also to expand, complicate, and extend your thesis to cover other, related areas, ones that your reader might not have been able to predict. You want to surprise the reader. Going in slightly unexpected directions can keep your reader engaged with your ideas and at the same time can be a way to demonstrate, hone, and clarify your thesis. Remember that throughout the essay, your thesis must grow and evolve, sometimes in ways that you yourself might not have been able to predict or anticipate.

But at the same time the evolution represents a logical progression of thought. If you discuss, say, three books or essays, you don't want your discussion of each to repeat the same ideas or analytical pattern; rather, you want to arrange the paper so that each discussion builds on what went before. The points you make about the second text emerge from points you made about the first, and the points you make about the third text could not be made without the foundational analysis of the first two.

The topic sentence in each paragraph typically advances the thesis to a new stage. At the same time, the topic sentence must do the work of controlling the ideas of its own paragraph. Hence you should very carefully think about and clearly phrase your topic sentences. A reader should get a clear conception of your argument by reading the introduction, the topic sentence of each paragraph, and your conclusion. Such a schematic reading won't capture all the complexity of your argument, nor will it allow the reader to see all the evidence that you use, but it should give a relatively complete notion of your paper's shape. And sometimes, the topic sentence of a paragraph might relate more directly to the preceding paragraph than to the thesis, but since the preceding paragraph is closely linked to the thesis, the overall organization makes sense.

DEVELOPMENT OF AN ARGUMENTATIVE ESSAY

I have been beleaguering students for decades with the idea of an argumentative thesis. But you resist. It's understandable: for the most part you don't really believe that a good argumentative thesis will "solve the problem" of producing a paper since you quite pragmatically see papers in quantitative terms. A thesis is one sentence, which is easy enough to write; why all the hassle over just one sentence? What's more worrisome is filling up the following five or ten or however many pages. Thus I have been trying to adopt a two-pronged approach. I'm striving now to present development in such a way that it bolsters the idea of an argument, so that in fact you will be able to develop your essay if and only if you have an argument. Describing development in a certain way might, I'm hoping, encourage or even compel an argumentative approach.

Essay as Dialogue

I'd like to suggest that envisioning the entire paper as a kind of dialogue—as a series of provisional answers to imagined questions—might demonstrate the attractiveness and appeal of written argument. I want to use some slightly recondite concepts to delineate this dialectical conception: *erotesis* and *prolepsis*. Specifically, I'm proposing that you propel your argument forward erotetically, by opening up a wide variety and a large number of questions of all kinds. Yet in order to rein in and organize this interrogative proliferation, you also need to employ forethought about what your audience is like. Specifically, I propose this forethought consist largely of prolepsis—or anticipation—inferring what kind of questions, and even exactly what questions, might interest the audience.

I first encountered the term *erotesis*, hijacked from classical rhetoric, and used in what I think is probably an eccentric but nonetheless a valuable manner, in *The Philosophy of Horror, or Paradoxes of the Heart,* by the philosopher Noël Carroll. (Typically *erotesis* refers to questions that imply strong affirmation or denial [Lanham 46.]) The kind of frightening, engrossing, breathless horror story that most of us are familiar with is, in Carroll's terms, "erotetic narrative." Such narratives, he suggests, use the rhetorical figure of erotesis—questioning or interrogating for rhetorical effect—in order to draw the reader in, in order to make the narrative frightening, engrossing, and breathless. Carroll writes,

> Popular novels are often called "page-turners" in honor of the way they keep their readers obsessively entranced. As well, it is commonly thought that this is a function of the heavy emphasis that they place on narrative. The erotetic model of narration, applied to popular fictions, suggests . . . the nature of the connection between the page-turning phenomenon and

the kind of narration being employed in popular fiction: viz.,
the reader is turning pages to find out answers to the questions that have been saliently posed. (132)

Such a narrative asks questions for which the reader needs answers,
and the reader reads on, must read on, is compelled to read on, will
read on even if a bear were to start chomping on his or her leg—
because the reader must get those answers.

But in some sense the questions do depend—even in Carroll's
model—on a certain kind of audience, an audience sensitive to the
questions being raised. While erotesis moves the narrative forward,
prolepsis places limits on the erotesis such that the audience's point
of view, interests, and predilections are taken into account. It's an interactive dialectic in horror stories, but Carroll has also suggested
that erotesis and prolepsis drive many popular television shows and
movies. And I think the two concepts at once complicate and clarify
what we mean by development of an academic essay.

The Example-Supportable Assertion and the Pseudo-Thesis

Such advice markedly varies from standard advice, which might be
that after presenting a thesis, a paper should probably clarify what
that thesis means, following up with examples of the claim put
forth. I'm not suggesting that this structure is entirely wrongheaded.
One does want to make a claim of some sort and then back up that
claim. This claim needs evidence of some kind—some support,
some examples—which makes up the bulk of the paper.

But a problem emerges with the suggestion that only "examples"
can prove or support a thesis, because examples can be used to support a pseudo-thesis as well as a genuinely argumentative thesis.
Thus many writers, using examples to support their pseudo-theses,
automatically think they are doing the right thing. In fact, examples
provide a great deal of (the wrong kind of) comfort: examples nicely
fill up pages. I'm not suggesting that we throw out the idea of the
"example," which is obviously a staple of scholarship, something we
use all the time in our writing—I'm using examples here; this whole
section is an example. Rather, the example can be dangerous to rely
on as the primary method of development of a thesis or, especially,

as the principle behind development. You can too easily think that if you can find examples of what you mean, you have done the right thing. In fact, generalizations for which examples can be readily found are frequently boring and simplistic ones, while generalizations of the greatest value are most often ones for which examples are not immediately available.

Theses/Pseudo-Theses about "The Pool"

Let us return to "The Pool" by H.D., partly because the "examples" it seems to provide are so sparse.

> Are you alive?
> I touch you.
> You quiver like a sea-fish.
> I cover you with my net.
> What are you—banded one?

As I mentioned in chapter 4, a zany but interesting pseudo-thesis about this poem emerged from my class, and it might be useful to look at it in a little more detail. Its writer felt his idea was nicely "supportable" by "examples": " 'The Pool' is a poem about someone touching a tiger lying in a pool of its own blood." "Are you alive?" the speaker asks the hapless beast. "I touch you": yes, we can touch the tiger because it's dead or dying, and everyone would naturally want to do this (I suppose). "You quiver like a sea-fish": indeed, the animal is probably not quite dead yet, quivers at our touch. "I cover you with my net": better throw the net over it anyway, just in case, since tigers, especially if wounded, can be dangerous (this line in the poem, by the way, more or less prevents the zebra-lying-in-a-pool-of-its-own-blood reading). "What are you—banded one?" What can we make of such a powerful (banded/striped) beast laid low, deprived of its energy or life; what is it now, but a hunk of organic matter? Note that each of the line readings derives from and gives an example of what the writer meant by the thesis statement. There's even the implicit con argument (you wanted con arguments, didn't you?) about the zebra. If you want, we can go so far as to throw one in about the striped sea bass.

Now, what's wrong with this reading? I'm afraid that writing how the poem depicts a dying tiger causes the poem to die as well. But let's suspend disbelief. If one wants to see the poem as being about a dying tiger—well, OK, I'll run with that for the nonce. Why is *that* interpretation significant? What does it tell us all about tigers, dying, an encounter with death, the wildness of nondomesticable animals, the jungle, our relationship to the beasts? Can we generalize to talk about humans' relation to nature? Maybe it's about the death of a "tiger of a person"? In short, might we make this into a defensible interpretation of the poem? I think many students grew up with the idea that literature, especially poetry, has at its core some hidden meaning or secret message that the teacher knows but is withholding. And the point of a paper is just to uncover that secret meaning, give examples from the poem to support it, and get the A (or at least a B). It's the very idea of examples (to support that "secret meaning") that allowed this kind of paper to be spawned.

It might just be that example-supportable assertions are not necessarily the right place to begin. Example-supportable assertions, I'm suggesting, tend to be too easy and tend to invite summary, often resulting in the "dying tiger trap." But on the other hand, assertions that are not example-supportable might seem too airy, too unsubstantiated or inferential, to be really grasped. So we can't abandon the idea of the example altogether. But it seems to me that to get you to make the startling or insightful inference, I need to show you that you must do more than merely give examples of what you mean.

The Development of Your Essay

Let's look in more detail at what erotesis and prolepsis can provide in addition to or in place of the example-supportable assertion. An erotesis generator and a prolepsis sensor, taken together, might be said to constitute a kind of demon—a heuristic similar to Maxwell's Demon, which James Clerk Maxwell (in a markedly different context) proposed as being able to group fast-moving molecules on one side of a dual-chambered vessel and slow-moving ones on the other (hence apparently refuting the second law of thermodynamics). Out of a sense of good taste I propose that we *not* call our demon "Cioffi's Demon." Instead, substituting the everyday terms "question" for "erotesis" and "expectation" for "prolepsis," I suggest that an "ever-questioning, anticipation-sensing" demon might be useful. If you want to give it a name, call it the "Development Demon." Like Maxwell's Demon, this entity also has two major roles: (1) imagining manifold, multifarious questions; and (2) anticipating what the audience would conceive of as useful questions.

Using this Development Demon might help show you how your writing must do more than just reflect and chart your interpretation, thoughts, insights, ideas, or the like. Besides doing these things, your papers must also take, in some real sense, a second essayistic journey: you must also subject your thesis to the machinations of the Demon, namely, to constant questioning of all kinds, and to a parallel conscious anticipation of an imagined audience response, in order to see not only how much of the thesis survives the ordeal but also how it has been changed—developed, enlarged, enhanced—by the experience.

This Demon, I should point out, is an androgynous entity. I am reminded of Virginia Woolf's somewhat aphoristic statement in *A Room of One's Own*: "Some collaboration has to take place in the mind between the woman and the man before the art of creation can be accomplished. Some marriage of opposites has to be consummated" (136). The Demon, then, must be something that does not take a position either exclusively male or exclusively female. Its questionings, its forecastings, must come from an as-if-sexless, as-if-two-gendered, entity. Its ever-questioning stance must "embrace multitudes."

Of course academic papers are supposed to be not just posing rhetorical questions but asserting things. True enough. But I want to persuade you that if your assertions are not calibrated to an audience's interests and wonderings, readers tend to ignore them as irrelevant or obvious. And if assertions are thus calibrated, then suddenly they become suffused with importance and significance.

An essay composed as I'm suggesting would not have to reproduce the actual questions—these would remain tacit—but it would answer them as if they were being asked by an imagined, an inferred audience: the audience anticipated by the Development Demon. A version of the "reader over your shoulder," to use the title of a book by Robert Graves and Alan Hodge, this entity functions as an invisible and slightly prickly but relatively willing-to-be-persuaded interlocutor. It isn't out to hurt your feelings or belittle or demean you; it aims, rather, to help you discover something akin to truth. This entity really wants to know something about the topic or subject, is a being driven purely by curiosity, by a craving for idea. It is this entity's questions and anticipations and the writer's answers to them that drive the paper forward. In some way the Development Demon is an ideal version of the professor reading the paper, but in fact it should form part of your consciousness, should be an imaginative projection that guides you as writer through the composing process.

What Kinds of Questions?

A large question, typically unspoken, precedes a thesis. I want to call this a "macro-question," a term coined by Noël Carroll, "a means for organizing whole narratives" (135). This is the big question that really produces the whole paper. Wayne Booth calls this a "problem"; Gordon Harvey, a "motive." In any event, it resembles the question in a reader's mind after the first page of a whodunit. Who, exactly, has done it? In a horror story, What is the monster like? Or, How do we stop it? The need to find out the answer gives velocity to a narrative that follows. Of course, Carroll's ideas apply to narrative and not specifically to the expository, argumentative essay. But I think we might present the argument essay as a kind of narrative, for in some sense it is a narrative of a thought process, of a kind of verbal contest with a perceived but often largely inferred audience.

How do we come up with the macro-question? What activity should you engage in before formulating it? It seems to me that there are a variety of options, when the subject is literature, and the options would vary somewhat in the case of an argument about a political issue, a historical event, or some other topic. But in terms of textual analysis papers, I suggest that before writing at all, you try to generate a wide variety of other questions, opening gambits—ones somewhat similar to the "discussion questions" teachers sometimes prepare for a seminar or class. These typically look for areas of confusion, dissonance, nonfit, bafflement, perplexity—for things about the text or the reading experience that are enigmatic and worth exploring. Do any details of the text-world not make sense? Are there any striking changes in characters' personalities—

especially between the beginning and the end of the work? Are there areas of especial intensity in the story, places where the author seems to be working extra hard, or stepping out of one voice into another? Are the various themes the work touches on handled in what seems an odd or interesting, a provocative or controversial manner? What does the work seem to be suggesting about them? Are there curious or startling patterns—of imagery, for example? And finally, though I know this cannot be an exhaustive list, how does the work make you, the reader, feel? Do you have any strong emotions, or especially any conflicting emotions? Why so? Can they be connected to something about the text?

These opening-gambit questions can even be contextual: Why was this text assigned? Were you in a particularly bad or good mood when you read it? What in the world could (insert the name of a person) see in this? I don't recommend that you mechanically go through this list one question at a time, but rather that you use it as a way to open up possibilities about the issue or text, identify questions that might help you formulate a macro-question, and, perhaps most important, figure out just what you really feel about a work, how you have internalized it, what you think is "going on" in it—what questions it leaves unanswered, evocative; what lingers with you like a pleasant aftertaste or, for that matter, a noxious eluate.

From your opening-gambit questions you should choose a macro-question, or create one that's a composite, perhaps, of several questions, an activity that the Development Demon should assist you in. What's the audience like? What might interest them? What is really "new" here, really "original"? What might be worthwhile and interesting to explore in a whole paper? Admittedly, there's a bit of magic here—well, I've already invoked a magical entity!—and we have to concede that the writer's experience helps make the Demon more capable of making a good judgment. But in general, a viable macro-question has to be one that compels the interest and enthusiasm of both the writer and the inferred audience. And it's probably best to generate a lot of opening questions, ones of all stripes and shapes and sizes. Some of the thought behind these questions might go into the introduction. But the most important of the questions generated would function as or help make up the macro-question, which would then be answered, at least provisionally, by the thesis.

A macro-question has the effect of not only providing impetus for the thesis but also of subsuming the whole argument—it does this by sparking still more questions. My thesis, "'The Pool' is about the clash of feminine and masculine ways of seeing the not-me," might have been an answer to the macro-question "What is the tension in this apparently tensionless poem?" and it leads to still further questioning—what Carroll calls "micro-questions." "Micro-questions," Carroll suggests, "organize the small-scale events of the plot, even as they carry forward the macro-question in the story" (136). In the case of academic argument essays, I think these micro-questions fall into four major categories. First, they call for clarification: What do you mean? (in my idiolect, "Huh?"). Second, they can call for development, contextualizing ("And—?"), or even, *though not exclusively*, examples ("F'r'instance?"). Third, they can ask why something is significant or important ("So?"). Finally, the micro-question can be an actual objection to some stage of an argument ("What?" or "What about *x*?").

With respect to my thesis about "The Pool"'s being a clash of feminine and masculine ways of seeing the "not-me," here are some micro-questions that could follow: "What is the feminine way of seeing the 'not-me'? What is the masculine way?" (Clarification). "What is a 'not-me,' anyhow?" (Clarification). "The phrase is Emerson's. Significant?" (Contextualizing). "What do 'touching' and 'covering with a net' suggest?" (Development). "Why would feminine and masculine necessarily be in conflict?" (Development). "What is the importance of this tension or conflict?" (Significance). "What kind of consciousness does the speaker of the poem embody—is it hermaphroditic?" (Significance). "How does that consciousness accord with a more traditional lyric poem's? Is this a poem about lyric poetry?" (Contextualizing, Significance). It seems to me that all of these questions would provide a paper that differed a great deal from one driven by example alone because—and this should be no surprise—their answers would have to be argued for rather than merely asserted or produced as evidentiary.

Some micro-questions are always available, to a certain extent, for a writer of an argumentative essay. Such micro-questions might well achieve the status of macro-question, though this is something you might have to decide only after you have done quite a bit of writing.

The extent to which you use these will vary, depending on the way that you have assessed your audience's interests and background, but here are the standard ones:

1. What is the background on the issue under scrutiny? Typically this micro-question will be posed (tacitly) and answered toward the beginning of the essay. It might be necessary for the reader who is unfamiliar with the issues being discussed.
2. Why does this issue have importance? Again, this would be an early micro-question, though it might also appear throughout the essay. As your argument develops, new aspects of an issue emerge. And these issues could well have an importance that the reader would not be sensitive to or aware of at the opening of the essay.
3. Are your major thesis-driving concepts sufficiently precise and well defined?
4. Is the evidence you are using being handled fairly? Do you represent it accurately? Do you understand it?
5. What are some positions that others have taken, or solutions that others have offered? Typically, this kind of micro-question is posed and explored in a research paper. If no research is necessary, however, the writer might pose hypothetical other positions, and this leads into the most important micro-question, namely . . .
6. What arguments might be deployed against yours?

The Counterargument; Infeeling

Generated by the Development Demon in its crankiest incarnation, this last micro-question—audience objection—genuinely drives forward a paper's development. Strong objections—commonly called counterarguments—must be raised and dealt with. John Stuart Mill discusses this notion in *On Liberty* (1859), and he is worth quoting at length. Mill contends that

> when we turn to subjects infinitely more complicated, to morals, religion, politics, social relations, and the business of life, three-fourths of the arguments for every disputed opin-

ion consist in dispelling the appearances which favor some opinion different from it. The greatest orator, save one, of antiquity, has left it on record that he always studied his adversary's case with as great, if not with still greater, intensity than even his own. (35)

Interestingly, Mill suggests that 75 percent of an argued opinion should deal with counterarguments, but typically in my classes, despite my emphasis on the counterargument, the papers submitted rarely spend more than a paragraph on the counterargument—and when that much is included, it's a rarity.

Why is the counterargument such an alien concept? Students ask me all the time, "Why bring up arguments against your own?" Or "Isn't bringing up these arguments just going to be prejudiced anyway?" a question that I think means something like, "Isn't inventing counterarguments a false contrivance, since you are bringing them up in order to dismiss them in the end?" If you have presented the paper's development, though, as emerging through erotesis and prolepsis, some of these objections can be easily headed off. You have anticipated what the audience needs by way of explanation, elaboration, and significance, and you have also anticipated what kinds of objections they might raise. Alternative explanations, possible objections from an inferred audience, are welcome, not necessarily hostile, since looking at them might help you further interrogate the issue raised by the argumentative thesis.

But you need more than to merely "look at" counterarguments or give them a passing nod. You need to engage them in a deep and serious manner. Mill writes,

> Nor is it enough that he should hear the arguments of adversaries from his own teachers, presented as they state them, and accompanied by what they offer as refutations. That is not the way to do justice to the arguments or bring them into real contact with his own mind. He must be able to hear them from persons who actually believe them, who defend them in earnest and do their very utmost for them. He must know them in their most plausible and persuasive form; he must feel the whole force of the difficulty which the true view of the subject has to encounter and dispose of, else he will

never really possess himself of the portion of truth which meets and removes the difficulty. (35)

Indeed, I suggest that the way you "know them in their most plausible and persuasive form" is to empathize with your opposition, attempting perhaps to inhabit its consciousness. This mental-emotional extension of self also informs (though to a lesser degree) the conception of audience throughout the whole paper. I had first thought to describe this by using the German word *Einfühlung*, which was translated as "empathy" after Theodore Lipps and others proposed using it in reference to aesthetic and philosophical issues in the late nineteenth century. But *Einfühlung* carries some contradictory or mismatched philosophical baggage (Chismar). Let me introduce a word that seems to convey better what I mean, and that might be a more adequate translation of *Einfühlung*: "infeeling." I think this is the concept I am trying to get across—you have to strive for infeeling your opponents' positions, trying to experience and to an extent even become those positions.

The advantage of "infeeling" over "empathy" is that with "infeeling" there exists a possibility that the writer will in fact turn around and side with the opposition, will take some material, some perspective, some insight, some ideology from the "other side." With empathy, there always seems to exist a sharp split between the me and the "other": one puts oneself in another's shoes, but only temporarily, only contemplatively. Like empathy, infeeling requires an extension of self, but unlike empathy, this extension of self can result in a modification of self, or at least of one's ideas. Infeeling is bidirectional, is done not just for comprehension of another's state or position, but for the purpose of allowing that state or position to influence, undermine, even dement one's own.

What if no actual opposition exists? In this case, you either lack an argumentative thesis, or you need to invent an opposition. As Mill remarks, "So essential is this discipline to a real understanding of moral and human subjects that, if opponents of all-important truths do not exist, it is indispensable to imagine them and supply them with the strongest arguments which the most skillful devil's advocate can conjure up" (36). In short, your argument needs to be imaginative in the sense that it has an originality and individuality to it, but it also must be imaginative in that you need to imagine an opposition if none exists. Through the work of the Development Demon—an interrogative, anticipatory mode of thought, really—as well as through the act of infeeling with a perceived opposition, you should, over the course of the essay, arrive at a new idea, one that represents an evolution of the thesis, a three-dimensionalizing of its initial configuration. More than just making explicit what the paper has implied, the conclusion enables you to ask a macro-question about that newly explicit notion. It is a widening outward—a familiar idea—but it is also a kind of "second thesis" to the paper: one animated by the Development Demon's metaphoric stretching of the original.

Looking closely and infeelingly at the opposition not only complicates the argument, allowing for a conclusion that advances the original thesis, but also lends credibility to the writer's ethos, which appears the more trustworthy for its willingness to address opposing viewpoints, its readiness to abandon apparently adamantine positions, its willingness to negotiate multiple truths. Such a rhetorical strategy helps differentiate the idea of academic argument from ugly dispute or verbal altercation: indeed, you can't infeel with a person you're arguing with or about to punch in the jaw.

8

Different Structures, Novel Organizational Principles

THE ANTIARGUMENT STANCE

One of the major problems with teaching argument has emerged only in the last few years: students do not want to argue very much. You might see argument as a bit antisocial, really, whether we are talking about actual arguments or academic ones. I received an email early this term from a student, G.M., who contends that the whole basis for argument is rebarbative—at least to his generation. Here's an excerpt of what he writes in response to my ideas about the argumentative essay:

> In my lifetime I have not seen anything so polarizing as war and thus I have not *felt* the amount of momentary certainty that many past generations have. I do not want to hurt anyone's *feeling* with my ideas. . . . Even in writing this short idea, I try to remove much of its abrasive qualities from the final draft. . . . Violence is on another level . . . , for I do not believe in war, but confrontation's very redeemable qualities are normally overlooked. . . . (My emphasis)

A cri de coeur, to be sure, which ends "thank you for being there on paper, with your essay, and in person, as a teacher." In my response to G.M., I suggested that he needs to differentiate between actual pacifism and intellectual pacifism, and that by deciding to be a university student, he has perforce renounced the intellectual variant.

But his point still stands. An aggressiveness suffuses academic argument; it's one of those competitive intellectual endeavors like debating or playing chess. Certainly, these are fine, admirable activities, but I just don't want to be involved with people who do them. I want to relax with my friends and colleagues. But with respect to writing academic essays, it may ultimately be impossible to throw out the whole idea of conflict, because we are dealing with a phenomenon that presumes a disrupted equilibrium of sorts, a disruption that engenders the very writing of the essay. Perhaps seeing the essay in the terms I am suggesting—questioning, anticipating, infeeling—will diminish its inherently aggressive ontology, for the terms I propose imply reflection, rumination, and conciliation, even though they in fact allow for mano a mano with ideas.

But G.M. at least wanted to engage in debate. That very willingness suggests I've won him over. But what if you are not so much unwilling to assume the aggressive stance of argumentative discourse as unable to understand the whole genre—or you've opted to go into fields that do not require discursive writing? Some of you are specific about your inability to write in this manner: "I've always been bad at English," you might confess. "I've always hated writing." You may well have essentialized yourself as a weak writer, and classes requiring papers do not, shall we say, make up the bulk of your schedule. Some of you might be skeptical of the entire enterprise: "I have had only one English teacher mention the idea of the 'argumentative thesis.' I am unfamiliar with its principles, which conflict with the scientific-evidence-based writing that I am used to." I have been trying to demystify the writing process as much as possible, but for many of you, it still has too much magic, too much subjectivity.

SUBJECTIVE KNOWLEDGE

There, I've said it. It's subjective knowledge. It's also a matter of being able to manipulate subjective discourse. I mean, how do you really know what questions are important ones? How do you project an audience or for that matter its feelings? Yet some people seem to be able to perform these psi-power-like mental feats—and they seem to have been able to do so all through grade school and high school, and in college. It comes naturally to them; just as some people have perfect pitch, so some seem to have the aptitude for this kind of discourse. Others are tone-deaf. What help is there for those who—either innately or through personal preference—are tone-deaf to the music of argument?

If you are one of these students—the unwilling (G.M.), the incapable, the skeptical—I think you need to do two things. First, you need to reconceptualize the kind of enterprise or endeavor a college paper represents. You need to use various forethought-provoking, predrafting exercises to generate ideas about the audience; questions about the issue, idea, or text; counterarguments, a ΔT. You need to get feedback on how your questions seem to work. You need to internalize the notion that good writing requires rewriting.

Now, I'm not sure how the terms I have introduced will interest or excite you, but I think you should envision them within a larger context of how we create and advance humanistic knowledge: asking questions, tentatively answering them; proposing ideas, imagining how an audience will respond; asking new questions. Indeed, the process has a cyclical snake-with-a-tail-in-its-mouth quality. It may even seem redundant. But it's a fertile redundancy.

SAYING SOMETHING NEW, TAKE TWO

Well, then—where does this not-too-terribly-redundantly bring us? We—your writing instructors—are trying to get you to look at problems, issues, ideas, or texts, and to articulate the complexity of your own response to them, to ask why, for example, they are interesting, provocative, important, urgently compelling, or the like. Yet we also want you to engage us as an audience, identifying intersections between elements of the issue and elements of the audience, just as we in the audience recognize these intersections. In a crucial sense, while the academic essay focuses on a subject, even more it's an attempt to modify the audience's perception of its previous relationship and response to that subject. We want you to tell us feelings and ideas that *we* had but didn't realize we had, or didn't realize the importance of. We want your papers to help us recall and reevaluate what was inchoate but nonetheless strongly felt about, for example, a social issue, a historical event, a literary text.

To put it in Aristotelian terms, we want an anagnorisis, a surprising recognition of some previously submerged, subarticulate response; we want something that will reorganize and explain the phenomenology of our own experience, the complexities of our own perceptions. Paradoxically, we as an audience initially resist that explanation, need to be talked, cajoled, seduced into accepting it—that's how far it is from our forebrain. And perhaps even more paradoxically, we can't say or tell just what we want explained because we don't know yet—if we could articulate what we wanted, it would be something we knew or suspected, hence not good enough. Tell me something I know but didn't know I knew—then talk me into it.

This might seem an impossible task. But keep in mind that writing is not merely the completion of a set series of tasks, a mechanical process anyone can teach or follow. No. We teach stages of a process, but it's the gestalt that matters most. We should really be trying to infect you with a longing, a curiosity, a desire to figure something out—a desire to explore a fundamentally unanswerable question. You may be attempting to discover "new knowledge," yet you are also trying to persuade an audience not only that what you've discovered is important, but that it logically connects with, complements, resuscitates, clarifies—makes somehow vivid or vital or special—what that audience knew before. For finally, here's what we really want: we want you to instruct us; we want you to tell us about our own experience.

THE CONCLUSION AS THREE-DIMENSIONAL THESIS: ΔT REVISITED

Student essays, when they fail, fail most often at the outset and the conclusion. Conclusions, in particular, present problems, perhaps because these sections are composed last and often show most clearly the effects of time pressure. But try not to let pressures of time prevent you from working on your conclusion, for the conclusion, read last, is the last to impress itself on your reader's brain and leaves the most lasting impression.

What should a conclusion be like? Your conclusion needs to be a final point. It is not just the last point in a series, but *the* final point that you want to make. Hence it is not just a summary of what you did, nor a dying gasp ("That's all, folks!"), nor some totally new topic or idea. Instead, it's the point that you can finally make after having argued your thesis for three or four or forty pages. It must therefore reflect the distance that your paper has traveled, showing how your thought has changed along the way.

One way of conceptualizing this might be to see the conclusion as a second thesis: an enhanced, fortified, complicated version of the original. It cannot be opposed to or undermine the original thesis—that would be counterproductive and confusing. But it must represent an evolution over the original. Remember that you have been arguing your position throughout the paper, looking not only at supportive evidence but also at counterarguments; hence your thesis will have changed somewhat. If you can imagine your thesis as a steel bar that you will support with evidence, think of how it might have deflected underneath the weight of the con arguments. In your conclusion, acknowledge how that thesis has changed. Ask yourself the implications of this change. You might even go back to the opening and look at your discussion of the context for your topic. In what way does the evolved thesis redefine the context of the issues you have been dealing with? Why is your new thesis important? What impact might it have?

Your conclusion must answer the most poignant micro-question that your imaginary reader will ask, namely, "*So what?*" Sometimes you will have to write several conclusions and really search hard for the best final point for your paper to present. What are the ramifications of all that you have argued? What does it imply? Writing, you have probably discovered, is hard work; come up with a conclusion that will justify the effort and thought and sweat that you put into the paper you have composed.

What should happen in a paper is that at the end your general idea has become more specific, as you've dealt with certain examples; in some way enlarged, as you have expanded its scope; and in some way modified, as your argument has offered complication and elaboration, and as you have dealt with counterarguments in various ways. Your conclusion connects to your original thesis but differs from it enough that it's fundamentally a second thesis. This I have referred to as a change in the thesis—a ΔT—and this can happen only when you begin with a complex, a three-dimensional, thesis, and then bring that somewhere interesting and new.

A ΔT can be too small or too large, however. If you have a very small ΔT, then perhaps you need to rethink your paper's structure and conclusion: are there implications of the thesis that you have perhaps overlooked? But if the change in the thesis is so great that you are taking an opposite position to that of your thesis, a position hostile to your opening thesis, then it's fairly clear that you need to start anew, as your fundamental relationship to the subject has evidently changed.

One student, Jelena M., objected to this conceptualization of a paper's structure because it implies a certain contrivance. She said, "If I really *believe* in my thesis, really *believe it's true*—you know, have thought about it just as you suggest—then what can I say in a conclusion except, 'There—that just shows you that my thesis is true!'" Well, OK. But here is my suggestion about the "proven" thesis. First, if you have a genuinely argumentative thesis, you will have dealt with con arguments, and to some of those, you probably should have conceded something. In addition, as you wrote, you probably discovered things about your thesis that you didn't know before. That should perhaps be reflected in the conclusion.

But Jelena M.'s objection raises an important issue: what you have to do in your conclusion, even if you have "proven" your thesis, involves more than just reiterating that thesis. Instead, what you have to do is step back some from your paper, look at it, and ask yourself another series of micro-questions: "Well, now that I have proven my thesis, what can I say about that? How can I take my thought to the next level? Are there any larger issues I might now address?" (These are specific instances of the "So what?" micro-question.) Concluding by answering those kinds of micro-questions virtually guarantees you an interesting ΔT.

Another student, Will L., had an interesting story to relate about how one of his previous writing teachers composed her essays. He said, "My teacher would essentially write her whole paper, and then, by the conclusion of the paper, would finally arrive at what she realized was the actual thesis." An interesting strategy, to be sure, if a somewhat uneconomical one, in terms of time (though as you know, I sometimes recommend it myself). But I think what happened with the teacher was simply that she used the initial writing of the paper as the necessary "forethought" that should precede creation of a thesis.

And that brings me to reiterate my final point about final points.

The academic argument paper's ideas do not appear on the page in the same chronological sequence in which they emerged as you wrote. That is, the sequence of ideas in your paper does not precisely replicate the thought process you went through, since you probably had to go through a lot of forethought, culling, winnowing, and predrafting in order to arrive at the thesis.

As I said earlier, your thesis, like Will's teacher's, is an *endpoint*—a *conclusion*. Oddly, though, in your paper, that thesis goes near the *beginning* of your essay. In the body of your essay, you essentially show (in organized, but abridged format!) the thought process you went through—including evidence you found that was significant, con arguments that were serious, and the like—in order to have arrived at your thesis.

But then, after you've finished showing that thought process, you can't just leave your reader flat. You have to reflect on the thesis and its proof. You have to come up with a statement you can now offer as a conclusion after having proved your thesis. What can you say now that you have written the paper? How are your thesis and its proof significant?

Here is the sequence I'm suggesting:

1. Begin with forethought, generation of ideas, trying out of provisional theses.
2. Consider evidence in support of the thesis.
3. Consider con arguments, or evidence against the thesis.
4. Pin down an idea about what the thesis should really be.
5. Now, begin writing, using that thesis.
6. Tell the reader, in the body of the paper, what you did in order to arrive at that thesis. That is, show highlights of 1–3 above.
7. Bring in other, clarifying ideas (or con arguments or supportive evidence) you think of along the way but had not thought of prior to actually writing out the draft of the paper.
8. Look at what you have written, namely, your thesis and the thought process you went through to arrive at it (here recast as supportive evidence). Now think of its further implications: the ΔT or conclusion.

OTHER STRUCTURES/STRATEGIES: "CREATIVE NONFICTION"

Sometimes writers abandon the familiar shape of argument and, still staying in the general realm of nonfiction, find new ways of making their points. This is always a possibility, but it must be done with considerable caution. Abandoning the standard structure of argument can mean abandoning the genre altogether and attempting to make similar points using another genre, which itself has a very different set of conventions.

For example, sometimes a parody of an argumentative paper, presenting an outrageous position but using the elements of argument, makes the strongest statement. The most famous example of this must surely be Jonathan Swift's "A Modest Proposal" (1729), which mock-soberly argues that cannibalism (specifically, the eating of children) would end the famine in Ireland. Essentially, Swift takes on the point of view of a totally amoral individual. Another strikingly unusual and inhuman (though not inhumane) point of view informs Horace Miner's essay "Body Ritual among the Nacirema," which appeared in the professional journal *American Anthropologist* in 1965 and has been widely anthologized ever since. Miner describes what the reader eventually discovers is U.S. culture as if seen from the perspective of an anthropologist visiting from another planet. His essay demonstrates that even a careful and intelligent observer can make hilariously incorrect inferences when attempting to understand a very different culture.

But such examples are exceptional ones, and their rarity in some sense bolsters and proves the value of the standard-format argument. In fact, when I read works written in the same vein as Swift's or Miner's essays, I often long for a standard argumentative format. My own suggestion is that if you wish to use some alternative structure or format, discuss it with your instructor, giving both a detailed presentation of what you want to do and a rationale for it. Such a course of action might also lead you to the discovery that you can make your points even better, perhaps, using the standard format— which, I've been strenuously asserting, allows for a good deal of creativity within its familiar structure.

The genre of "creative nonfiction" or "the lyrical essay" has also emerged as an important one in the field of writing. There are workshops, journals, graduate programs, conferences, and annual anthologies dedicated to this type of writing, and you will almost certainly encounter essays of this genre in reading either for courses or for pleasure. Of the popular magazines, the *New Yorker*, *Harper's*, and the *Atlantic Monthly* all regularly publish essays of this kind.

Stylistically various, thematically diverse, and generically unclassifiable, these essays differ from fiction or poetry in a single regard: they ground themselves in actual facts and a shared, historically verifiable world. Here is a succinct one-paragraph description, by Robert Scholes and Carl Klaus, of this genre:

> In the narrative essay, the author becomes a narrator. But the narrative essay differs from the story itself in that it is built around a specific event or situation which has existed in time and space, and it presents itself as a kind of record of that event or situation. The story told in an essay may be highly personal, moving toward autobiography, or as impersonal as a journalistic "story" of current events. It may focus on a particular event or sequence of events; or it may concentrate on a place or person, becoming a travelogue or character sketch. But its essence lies in its telling us the "truth" about something which is itself actual or historical. The "truth" of this kind of essay includes not only accuracy with respect to factual data, but also depth of insight into the causes and meanings of events, the motives and values of the personages represented. (22)

Fiction, poetry, and drama project imagined worlds, which clearly relate to actuality, to the "real," but do not claim veridicality. The nonfiction essay does make such a claim.

There are few "rules" for this type of writing. Unlike the argument, which has a relatively conventional structure, including the elements I have enumerated above (thesis, development, conclusion, etc.), the "lyrical essay" may include whatever elements that the author feels are necessary to make a point. Perhaps that, ultimately, is the rule: the essay has to make a point, has to have something to say, regardless of how unusual its structure or strategy may be.

Let me offer one additional suggestion to you here: this kind of essay needs to convey a point, but it also has to allow for the possibility of other views. One of its notable practitioners, Philip Garrison, has said that it needs to demonstrate *strong but mixed feelings* about a given issue. If it shows only strong, "unmixed" feelings, then the reader might well feel excluded—as merely a witness to a prolonged tirade. If it shows weak and mixed feelings, or weak and unmixed feelings, then the reader is not likely to care. To put this into the terms introduced earlier on, this essay, despite its nontraditional form, must have something equivalent to a thesis—this might be the whole essay, or it might be implicit, or it might come as the last sentence. It also must accommodate counterarguments to the extent that it sees the thesis as not being the final, definitive word, or to the extent that it sees its own form (if you can imagine this) as not being necessarily the perfect vehicle for conveying its idea, or to the extent that its message, idea, thesis, what-have-you, ultimately resists codification and remains ambiguous, elusive, evanescent.

Many times these works take the form of narratives. Here is a story; it happened to me, or to someone I know. It really happened. But usually, interwoven with these narratives are expository sections that help convey the point or idea. Often more than one narrative appears, or a narrative is nested inside the main narrative. So despite their narrative appearance, these essays do more than tell a true story; they guide the reader somewhat toward an understanding. What resonates about this story? Why is it significant, not just to the author but to the reader as well? Creative nonfiction is a rich, complex, and capacious art form; hence it resists easy definition.

REWRITING

You may be asked to rewrite your essay. This is not a humiliation or a signal of failure. I am typically asked (by editors) to rewrite essays that I submit for publication. In fact, I am very grateful for editorial input, and I find that the essays and books I have had to rework tend to be far better than those works accepted as submitted.

First, you must attend to the issues that the instructor has highlighted on your pages. The simplest of these will be correcting typographical, spelling, form, and usage errors. If there are comma splices, repair them; if there are problems with form, consult the handbook or style guide used in the course; if there are comments you don't understand, ask your instructor. You might also work with a tutor to solidify some of your ideas about usage and form, and, additionally, regularly consult a handbook of usage.

Your paragraphs might need reordering, revision, or restructuring. Do the topic sentences seem to generate the ideas of the paragraphs? Do the paragraphs focus on the ideas of the topic sentences? If they do not, you need to rewrite. As Susan Bell, a longtime editor, remarks: "Organization and clarity do not dominate the writing process. At some point, though, a writer must pull coherence from confusion, illuminate what lives in shadow, shade what shines too brightly" (149). Once you have written an essay, often the way you should have written it becomes clear.

However, a rewrite does not stop there. You also need to consider problems with thesis, structure, and conclusion. Identify the paper's weaknesses, and decide how to revise these areas. Remember that you should preserve the good things about your paper while improving those areas that seem to be weak or incorrect. So don't throw away the whole paper and start over. Instead, examine what you have done, and think of ways to explore it more carefully, more deeply, and more persuasively.

You might want to figure out whether your argument is really the best one you can make, or your structure the best one that you can adopt. Take a look at your conclusion and compare it with your thesis. Do you see any development of that thesis? Is the conclusion something that you might start with rather than conclude with?

One of the most common problems I encounter is the absence of an argumentative thesis. Make sure that what you are trying to prove or argue for is something worth arguing for. I very often encounter the easily conceded thesis statement. If I concede your thesis, then the subsequent "proof" does not really seem necessary or important. Point up your thesis—either by adding a "because" clause or by looking for ways that you can individualize your idea. I suggest that you try also to see what other writers have said: check the Internet, library catalogs, and other resources to see whether your topic has been written about before. Sometimes this kind of contextualizing allows for much more complex views on an issue. If you use sources, be sure to acknowledge them.

As for improving the development of your argument, try to decide whether there are key issues you are overlooking, or key objections to your argument that you have just decided to ignore. You ignore these at your peril, for if the reader can easily come up with objections to your ideas, then the essay seems a little naive or one-sided. Remember John Stuart Mill's claim that 75 percent of your paper should consist of dealing with opposing views. He's engaging in hyperbole, I think, but strive for at least 25 percent. Too, if you have incorporated obviously weak or wobbly "con" arguments—arguments included only because they are easy to defeat and make your argument look good by comparison—you need to eliminate those "straw men" from your paper.

In addition, attempt to make your argument grow and evolve. As you develop your ideas through the use of examples, definitions, contextualizations, classifications, qualifications, and con arguments, you'll discover that the issues you deal with inevitably become much more complex, more slippery and ambiguous, than you had first thought. This ambiguity you need to address, even cultivate, rather than ignore or bypass.

Finally, look at the conclusion. Does it have a strong impact? Is it a worthwhile way to close your paper? Again, the conclusion, the last piece of writing that your reader will take in, has to demonstrate a new idea of some kind, not just a reiteration or rephrasing of your thesis. It has to *matter*. Make sure that the conclusion shows a distance traveled, what I have called a Δ-Thesis: it should not contradict your thesis, but it needs to somehow reflect your having argued for four or five or ten pages the issues that your thesis raised. Remember: it's your last chance in the essay, so make those final words resonate, ring, tintinnabulate in your reader's ears. Make that reader feel not just rewarded for having read your work but also a bit sorry that it's ended.

9

The Imaginative Research Paper

Why write a research paper, other than, say, it's been assigned to you? I want to suggest (realizing all the while that you are going to be slightly skeptical) that writing a research paper can be valuable in and of itself—that is, by its own merits—because it will help you discover things about the world, the culture, and yourself. As an undergraduate, I had several research paper assignments, and now, thirty-something years later, I can still remember the topics I wrote about, some of the sources I used, and some of the insights I gained. Herbert Aptheker, a famous historian who wrote about slavery in the United States, died just recently, and I felt sad because he had provided me with much to think about regarding the antebellum U.S. slave system. And when I read about riots and revolts in other countries, or about social unrest in our own country, I think of the "theory of relative deprivation" proposed by Ted Robert Gurr, which I discovered when writing about slave revolts in the U.S. and ancient Rome. In short, writing a research paper in college changes the way one processes knowledge and information, the way one views the past and the present. Ideally, it's an enriching and formative experience, and I mention my own in some detail because in fact I went on to study not history but literature, yet I still remember the history-related research that I did.

Specifically, what happens to you as you do research papers? Obviously, quite a lot, but I'd like to focus on one psychological transmutation that typically takes place: you become a splitter rather than a lumper. A splitter makes fine distinctions, classifies things with great care into many differing categories, and sharpens differences rather than leveling them out. By contrast, a lumper levels differences and highlights similarities. A lumper might look at a watch and say, "It's a wristwatch," while a splitter might say, "It's a late 1990s Audemars-Piguet tourbillion minute repeater—in platinum."

Of course, you might say, what's the difference? In this case the difference is that an average wristwatch costs fifteen dollars, while the Audemars-Piguet would run you about a quarter of a million. So the difference is $249,985, to be exact. Plus tax. But you wouldn't know this until—until when? Until you'd done some research, until you became "inward with the material." Indeed, people are rarely lumpers with respect to the things they really like. And the material in your course—well, you can be certain that's something about which your professor is a splitter extraordinaire.

INVENTION AND RESEARCH

Let me outline the basic pattern of a research paper. First, you will need to find a topic. Usually, you'll be writing within a given subject area or field—the one specified by your course, that is—which should help define your options some. Check with your professor, and/or reread several times the description of what you have to do for your paper, since you don't want to invest a lot of time doing the "wrong" thing. You might not really know what you want to write about. But that's OK. Part of the initial writing process involves discovering what's sufficiently interesting to you, and what has already been written on a given issue or problem.

That brings me to the next issue. Your motivation for writing the paper should probably revolve around solving a problem—answering a macro-question—of some kind. I have spoken before about the "dissonance" that often forms the impetus for a paper; similarly, when you do a research paper, you need to find something to talk about that's not been resolved or settled or talked to death. This problem needs to relate to the course, and, more explicitly, to the assignment.

In a way, this is the most interesting part of the research paper, because during this initial phase, you can basically read all sorts of material, even that which is only tangentially relevant to your topic. This is also the time for revisiting the course texts, going to Google and other search engines to see what range of materials the Internet has to offer, exploring the library's resources, talking with other students about their topics, and consulting with your professor and with librarians about possibilities for your research.

At this stage it is useful to photocopy or print out all the potentially useful sources you consult. This would be less useful for books than it would be for articles. Typically, after photocopying an article (or a book section), I will staple it into a manila folder, making sure to include a photocopy of the title page or pages that include the source's bibliographic information (author, title, journal or publisher, date, volume). I then annotate these sources, directly on the pages themselves, either using a highlighter or just underlining material.

(I hasten to add here parenthetically that this situation with photocopying, stapling, and reading of hard copy will likely change in the near future. First, almost everything ever published will eventually—soon—be available on the Web. Second, as a researcher, you will be able electronically to capture the material you need and place it in a working file on your hard drive or a portable storage device [whatever supersedes floppies, zip-drives, super-discs, and writable CDs]. Then, as you compose your paper, the research library of material you've discovered will be continuously available to you. You will be able to quickly search it, quote from it, and generate bibliographic entries. If I were in the prediction business, I'd say this will largely be in place by no later than 2010. But I'm not.)

I do not recommend that you copy quotations out onto note-cards. You might have been taught in previous courses or in high school that notecards were the preferred way to keep track of information during the research process, but photocopying is cheap and readily available now, and the Internet has made accessible much material that is easily printable. The fact is that if you use notecards to record material from sources (via direct quotation), there is the chance that you will mistranscribe it, be unable to read your handwriting, or—worse—think that the words you have written out are your own. (Several scholars have recently been accused, in widely publicized cases, of using others' words as their own. It seems to me most likely that they simply misread their own notes.) Using photocopied sources keeps it clear whose words are whose. Hence if you want to use notecards to organize your research materials, photocopy material and then paste that onto the notecards. The less longhand copying that you do, the better.

At this stage, too, as you search around on the Internet, you need to determine which on-line sources are credible and sound, and which are not. Here is a quick series of guidelines that I use. The first four concern "provenance," that is, where the site originated—and hence ask the questions "Who has authored this site and what is its purpose?"; the next five have more to do with the content and organization of the site itself:

1. In general, you need to figure out the contextual information that is quite clear when you are dealing with hard-copy resources but is often absent on Web pages. When you pick up a book, you can easily determine the author, title, publisher, and date of publication. You have a sense of the book's seriousness of purpose by its use of a bibliography, an index, and references. You might have a biographical blurb about the author, or even snippets of quotations from reviews of the book. These all suggest to you the level of its seriousness, and the degree to which it can be trusted as a source. With Web pages, a little more detective work is often required.

2. Now, is there an author? That is, do you know who has put the site together? If not, this is a bad sign, though it does not necessarily mean that you should discard the information from the site. You need to be careful, though, as to how much credence you place in it. If an author's name does appear, put that name into a search engine to see what other kinds of things the person is connected with.

3. Is this author connected with any institution of higher learning, or with a governmental agency, or with a church-related organization, or with a business of some kind? If academically or governmentally connected, the Web site has potential for being very good material. Some academic Web sites are promotional in nature, though, so be careful when using these for information. If the site is connected to a church or a business, the likelihood of its being good is somewhat lessened. (Some businesses have academic integrity, though: the *Encyclopaedia Britannica* and the *Oxford English Dictionary* are examples of creditable sources that are businesses. Similarly, the sites of major corporations tend to be reli-

able if inevitably somewhat tendentious. Church-related sites can also be helpful, but again, you need to attempt to evaluate them using some other (internal) criteria before automatically accepting what they are offering.)

4. If a site is connected to a group that has political aspirations, the site's integrity is problematic. In a like manner, propagandistic sites lack credibility.

5. What is the language of the site like? Are the words correctly spelled? Does the site use appropriate, fundamentally accurate grammar, spelling, punctuation? If not, the site's credibility suffers, to my mind. I would still scan through the site, however; a few spelling and usage errors do not necessarily constitute a fatal flaw. (However, be forewarned. I've noticed that on eBay, for example, those product descriptions that are most ill-spelled, ill-conceived, and illiterate have provided me with the most problems as a buyer. Admittedly that is anecdotal evidence, but it also strikes me as powerful. I know this is an ad hominem argument [see chapter 10], but sometimes ad hominem arguments are logically sound.)

6. Does the site seem to be current in its allusions, research materials, and the like? Often sites will remain for years on the Web but will never be updated or revised.

7. Are there "pop-ups" of any kind? These diminish a site's seriousness, I think, since the site is being used to generate income; still, it may be a solid reference tool. You also might check to see whether the site has implanted any "cookies" into your hard drive—a bad sign, if it has, since this suggests a commercial motivation for the site.

8. What banner ads appear on the site? These will tip you off somewhat to the kind of site you're visiting. The site's links are helpful in enabling you to figure out its value. And sometimes in fact the links will be more valuable than the site itself. If there is any pornography on the site, or any links to same, you should probably be cautious about using that site as a credible reference tool. If you are asked to provide your credit card number in order to access information on a site, do not do so:

there's a good chance the information you want will be available elsewhere, free.

9. Is the site a total put-on? A joke? Something pretending to be what it is not? There are an amazing number of such sites—the latest theories on *Hamlet*, for example, but offered by a twelve-year-old who's doing a research paper for her sixth-grade final project. (But bear in mind that this might be one sharp sixth grader, whose insights are genuine.) Obvious hoaxes, though, totally drain a Web site of credibility: the newly discovered short story by Franz Kafka, the real truth behind JFK's assassination, instructions for a do-it-yourself perpetual motion machine, advice for people who are abducted by creatures from another planet, how to deal with the relationships you had in your past lives. . . . The examples are almost literally endless, but the wilder the claims made by the site, the more likely that site is a sham.

10. Finally, though the site may be only a popularized account of an issue you are seriously exploring, or though it may be principally a vehicle for selling something, don't completely dismiss it. It may still contain some interesting ideas or give you an angle on your topic that you had not previously considered. However, just make sure that you investigate this angle much more thoroughly beyond this one site.

In addition to doing Web-based searches, you should also search the databases available at your library. For most topics, these are more valuable than the Web, because they contain material that is not (yet) available on-line. It is available, at present, only to institutions or individuals who subscribe to a given database. The companies putting together such databases (ProQuest, Lexis-Nexis, Medline, Ebsco, MLA International Bibliography, etc.) have hired people to scan in an amazing variety of articles from books, magazines, newspapers, and other periodicals; these are available (in fulltext or abstract-only format) to subscribers only. Most students, therefore, have access—via their university or college computer terminal—to a whole additional virtual library of information, which is almost always superior to the material available via the Internet: its provenance is clear and its authoritativeness as easy to verify as that of the hard-copy publication that the database reproduces or sends you to.

You will probably end up using databases to locate hard-copy material, such as journals and magazines (and books). Of course, you can also use the card catalog in your library (typically available on-line, now). These computer/Web-based resources will lead you to the old-fashioned books, newspapers, and magazines. And this is, at present, a good thing. In general, it is best to look for hard-copy resource materials because their provenance is more easily discoverable. Many teachers will in fact require that a sizable proportion of your sources be hard-copy materials.

Often, you'll find there's just an enormous amount of material on the subject you've chosen. Some students take this as a positive sign, choose five or six sources at random, and go from there. I, by contrast, see this surplus of information as indicative of a problem, namely, that your subject or topic is too broad. How can it be narrowed down? Is there some subtopic that you might look at? You need to become even more of a splitter here, if for no other reason than that you have to divide up the lump of material you've located.

Here are six ways to narrow down a topic:

1. Subdivide its content. If you are looking at, say, euthanasia, break it down into euthanasia for terminally ill infants (thus not having to deal with euthanasia for adults or animals, for example).
2. Subdivide by geographical scope. Look at euthanasia for terminally ill infants in Western Europe, say.
3. Narrow the time span. Look at what happened in just the last decade, or during the 1930s, perhaps.
4. Narrow by kinds of author. Look just at articles by medical doctors, perhaps, or just at accounts by parents of terminally ill infants.
5. Narrow by kind of source. You might look only at those articles that are not in mass circulation newspapers or periodicals, that is, only at articles in journals or in published books.

6. Narrow by language: you might choose to look only at English-language sources.

Yet keep in mind that even as you narrow your topic, you don't have to ignore material that could function as an overview. You should read some of this as well, since it will help you make better sense of the subtopic, the narrow area of research, that you are exploring.

DISCOVERY

As you read, annotate, and sort through the material you've gathered, look for some patterns: how do the various writers present the background, facts, issues, flashpoints, and their own positions? You are trying to get an overview of the issue, the topic, and even though you will have narrowed your topic down somewhat by this point, you will probably not have decided what you want to say. Don't push yourself yet to take a position. You are scanning what's out there; it's as if you are trying on for size various positions and perspectives and ideas. As you read and gather information, you will notice that your ideas become more complex as well as more informed.

Often, students will become very distressed at this stage of their research; they feel overwhelmed by the material and don't think there is enough time in the world for them to really understand the whole range of opinions and positions on a given topic. Everyone feels this at some point. Don't despair. You need not read every word of every article that you come across. In fact, you should really limit yourself to ascertaining the thesis statements—the main ideas—of the material that you encounter. In these initial stages, read broadly and selectively, rather than deeply or comprehensively. Get a sense of where the authors come down on a given issue, but don't try to capture or understand all the nuances of their arguments, not just yet.

In fact, 80–90 percent of what you read will not turn out to be material that you directly cite in your paper. But it is useful to have read it just the same: it gives you the equivalent of what stereo enthusiasts call "headroom"—an ability to perform at much higher levels than necessary. Used as a justification for the purchase of very powerful equipment (speakers, receivers), even though it might never be played at louder than living-room level, headroom is the gap between the maximum capacity of a piece of equipment and the typical requirement. For example, if a speaker is using only 10 percent of its capacity at any given time, it performs effortlessly and flawlessly. The same principle applies to your research; the more that you've done, the more "headroom" you have, the more easily you are able to handle the ideas and resources that you do cite. Having the 90 percent in abeyance, or not actively used, makes the 10 percent you do use more credible, more informed, more crisp, sharp, and solid.

Here's your goal at this point: you need to gather some information and sort out what is most important to you. That is, you need to flesh out some background and some details about the topic you're investigating. Another way to put this would be to say that you're trying to familiarize yourself with the range and terms of the arguments that have already been made. Or to use the language I am using here, you're trying to discover what sorts of macro- and micro-questions other writers and researchers are attempting to answer, and you're trying to decide which ones you might need to address in your paper. Remember that your paper should not merely summarize existing research or try to reproduce the range of opinions or insights on a given issue. That's called a "report," not a paper. You are instead trying to contribute to the universe of knowledge by saying something new. You want to generate original, imaginative ideas that differ in some ways from what you have read, for, finally, your idea is the most important one, not the ideas of the many authors you quote.

Essentially, what happens as you read widely is that you become inward with the topic, internalizing its issues and complexities. And this will be reflected in the next stage of writing, which involves moving from the position of an outsider viewing issues articulated by others to that of an insider who has something original to say about these very issues. In fact, you are ultimately trying to discover what it is that you feel about a given issue. Just as I read a student paper in order to discover what I really think, so you are doing research in order to determine your proclivities, inclinations, beliefs, and ideas. You'll find some authors you come to agree with and others that you think are flat-out wrong. Some will appear to you wrong in some places and right in others. But as you read—and this is the exciting thing about doing research on something you find interesting—you will discover that no one's position is the same as yours. Thus the more you read, the more you will clarify your idea of what it is that you really feel, and why you feel it. In many ways, doing a research paper is a discovery of self.

1984 ASTON MARTIN: "LOW-MILEAGE, PRISTINE—A ROLLING WORK OF ART"

You will find, also, that as your ideas become more informed, they will change—perhaps entirely! You might come to realize that your initial position was quite wrongheaded. There is nothing wrong with this; in fact, it happens all the time. Allow yourself to be open to the possibility of its happening to you. When I was doing research before buying a used car, I discovered some very striking things about the car I had wanted to buy. The low-mileage, perfect-condition Aston Martin Lagonda seemed a lot less attractive to me when I discovered that the electronics on the dashboard constantly failed (thus putting into question any mileage reading). I also discovered that there were at least three versions of this particular model, and only the latest (fuel-injected) version was desirable; the others were hard to start. The Web site I consulted, www.histomobile.com, revealed to me that the car was enormous—would barely fit in my garage. And www.fueleconomy.gov disclosed mileage information on this car: 10 mpg highway, 8 mpg city. Average mpg: 9. Even though Lagondanet (http://freespace.virgin.net/roger.ivett/library.html) had a positive write-up on the car, I found that only a little research made my position change quite radically.

So sometimes you will reverse a previously held position or idea. And in this case, it did not take much newly discovered information to discourage me from parting with $25,000 that I really don't have.

But, despite what might seem like lower stakes, writing about something requires more extensive and more in-depth research than deciding against buying a product. One can buy or decide not to on the basis of impulse. Research for a writing project must be done in a more deliberate manner. This Aston Martin is an interesting example, since a lot has been written on it, but it's very difficult material to locate. Automotive history is not really a "scholarly field," and research libraries will not typically have the very material you need to review. For example, Ebsco and ProQuest (search engines) did not turn up much beyond recent news stories about late model Aston Martins, the acquisition by Ford of Aston Martin, and the like. Nor did a search of the libraries at Princeton, Yale, the University of Pennsylvania, Dartmouth, Brown, or Cornell yield any material on Aston Martins.

So what to do? I decided to check www.bn.com. The Barnes and Noble site has a very extensive listing of books, both in and out of print, and its subject search engine is very useful. It turned up 171 hits for "Aston Martin" in books in print and 80 hits in out-of-print material. About 90 percent of these had nothing to do with Aston Martin automobiles (and were about Mazdas, Volvos, Jaguars—do you know why these turned up on the search?). But I did get 17 book titles that seemed to me promising. I would probably have to do an interlibrary loan request that had a wider reach than the Ivy League libraries. Or I could buy some of these books. I guess for people who can afford Aston Martins, this is only a minor expenditure, or maybe the first of many.

Before making any interlibrary loan requests or large purchases at Barnes and Noble, I turned to Google, which offered Lagondanet. This site, conveniently, has a bibliography, including not only these very hard-to-find books but also magazine articles that discuss the car. These too might be available via interlibrary loan, and I would certainly want to look at some of them. Again, though, since this material is "popular" in nature, it is going to be somewhat more difficult to find than, say, critiques of the early poetry of John Dryden.

Material on consumer goods is not available in academic libraries, because when you buy things, you are not usually attempting to write a paper or treatise on the goods available. Rather, you want to make informed choices about what is available to you. Hence a lot of the research on such products is "research-terminating": if you discover that what you're thinking about buying has some (to your mind) fatal flaw, you stop the research and start looking at other items to purchase. The fatal flaw for a car might be initial cost, reliability, availability, availability of service, operating costs—or any of a number of other, more whimsical, factors. For example, I concluded my research on the Aston Martin when I discovered the various negative features already mentioned—the instruments' unreliability, the car's size, and its poor fuel efficiency.

By contrast, in writing an essay about this make and model of car, there is no such thing as a "fatal flaw." I would want to know as much as possible about my subject and topic, and it would take more for me to reverse my position on them. I would have to look at a good deal of the available print material and get a much wider perspective, perhaps concluding that this would be a fine car for someone who was wealthy, who already owned two or more other cars, who had a lot of storage space, and who had or was a good mechanic. Or maybe I'd come up with something different from that, something more complex. One never knows. That's why we do research; that's what makes it fun.

BELIEFS AND PARADIGMS

At the other end of the spectrum from doing research on consumer goods, a situation that can easily reverse previously held positions, lies research about strongly held beliefs. If you are a genuine believer in, for example, the flat-earth theory, or in astrology, or in creation as opposed to evolution, your research is probably not going to reverse these deep-seated beliefs. As Noël Carroll remarks, "belief is not something that is under our control. We cannot will our beliefs. . . . Rather, belief is something that happens to us" (65–66). Hence researching our beliefs is a pointless task: we won't be open to change at all. In some ways, "belief" is a position that I arrived at vis-à-vis the Aston Martin (I believed it to be a poor choice for a used car or an investment): arriving at that belief terminated my research. Perhaps what happened is that the belief encapsulated other beliefs that I don't want to or cannot undo: I think a car should fit in my garage. I think a car should get better than nine miles per gallon. I think a car should have an accurate odometer that records miles it has run. So to overthrow my belief that the car is a poor choice, I'd have to abandon those encapsulated or supporting beliefs.

On the other hand, a large middle ground exists—a ground for research that will not be abandoned when a "fatal flaw" is discovered, yet will also allow one to change or even reverse one's position. This is the ground in which you will do your work. Exploring it will neither undermine nor threaten beliefs you don't want to part with (or cannot part with), nor will it be one where discovery of certain elements will be "research-terminating." In this area, you are not quite sure of what you will discover—you have some idea, but not a complete one—and you are open to various suggestions, various interpretations, various angles of inquiry. You have some hunches and predilections, to be sure, but these are not so strong as to inhibit exploration. Some of your hunches will turn out to be wrong, or ill-informed; some of your predilections, you'll note with chagrin, will reveal themselves as prejudices. But that's OK. That's what doing research should entail.

What's interesting, too—and this is my final point about allowing research to change one's mind—is that once you have a firm idea about a topic, once it has rooted itself in your consciousness, you are actually unable to see disconfirmatory evidence. The philosopher Thomas Kuhn, in *The Structure of Scientific Revolutions*, reports how test subjects who were shown playing cards and asked to identify them would get the identifications wrong if the cards were nonstandard, for example, a red club or a black diamond. It seems that the subjects had established a theory for the kinds of cards—a normal pack, that is—that the experimenter was showing them. Hence the subjects simply did not see the anomalous cards:

> For the normal cards these identifications were usually correct, but the anomalous cards were almost always identified, without apparent hesitation or puzzlement, as normal. The black four of hearts might, for example, be identified as either the four of spades or the four of hearts. Without any awareness of trouble, it was immediately fitted to one of the conceptual categories prepared by prior experience. *One would not even like to say that the subjects had seen something different from what they had identified.* With a further increase of exposure to the anomalous cards, subjects did begin to hesitate and to display awareness of the anomaly. . . . Further increase of exposure resulted in still more hesitation and confusion

until finally, and sometimes quite suddenly, most subjects would produce the correct identification without hesitation. Moreover, after doing this with two or three of the anomalous cards, they would have little further difficulty with the others. (63, my emphasis)

To use Kuhn's terms, the subjects established a "paradigm" of how the experiment worked, and it took considerable disconfirmatory evidence for them to reshape their paradigm. Paradigm reshaping did not happen with the first piece of disconfirmatory evidence, nor typically with the second or third. Yet it did happen with most subjects; that is, the paradigm was not the equivalent of a belief.

Once you have discovered the field or area in which you can be open to the anomalous, and in which there is neither the potential for a "fatal, research-terminating flaw" nor the challenge to a belief you will not or cannot abandon, then you have discovered, I think, the ideal arena for research. Only in this (admittedly large) arena will you always be open to the anomalous. If you have a theory of how something works, or of why something happened, or about the value or importance of an idea, issue, or individual, try to force yourself to seek out evidence that will challenge that theory. Of course, with Kuhn's experiment, the subjects were tricked—they thought that they were dealing with a "normal" pack of cards. Similarly, sometimes the unspoken assumptions about a given issue will be the very ones on which you've established an erroneous theory.

But only truly imaginative research seeks to uncover those false unspoken assumptions or challenge prior paradigms. Your research will involve reading, digesting, and internalizing the material available on your topic—making it your own—and doing so with as open a mind as possible. Ideally, you will have some surprises as you do your research, as you will discover things that you had no idea of. You will show how your paradigms have been reshaped.

DOCUMENTATION AND QUOTATION

Even though you will be dealing with a variety of source material, your writing process should resemble the writing process for any other academic essay: you have to do prewriting, outlining, drafting, and rewriting similar to what I suggested in the early portions of this book. However, you need to deal not only with additional actual points of view—ones that both support your own and that disagree with your position—but also with the issue of how to document the material that you cite.

What do you need to document? And what can you merely assert without having to offer a source to back it up? These questions are often troublesome to students, partly because no easy answers exist. But I want to provide a brief guide here, and to suggest that if you have any questions, ask your professor. In general it's better to overdocument than to underdocument, but overdocumenting can convey that you are uncertain about your work and can thereby weaken your voice and your stance.

1. Things that do not need to be documented:
    a. Common-knowledge facts. George Washington was our first president. The earth is the third planet from the sun. The United States is composed of fifty states. That sort of thing.
    b. Opinions of your own. You are offering an opinion, though I expect it will be an informed opinion, since you are doing research, and that does not itself have to be given documentary support.
    c. Your personal experience. If you are drawing on an experience of your own, this does not have to be documented, unless perhaps it is a lecture that you attended (this can be documented—give date, place, and speaker), or an interview you conducted.
2. Things that are often documented, but need not be:
    a. A meaning of a word. I would avoid quoting a dictionary; this seems to me a somewhat childish ploy, besides which connotations are usually much more interesting than denotations, or dictionary definitions.
    b. General statistics about recent occurrences, unless you are analyzing those statistics as part of your paper.
    c. Material you are fairly sure that your audience would be familiar with, even though it might not be general knowledge per se.

        d. Familiar quotations. (John F. Kennedy once said, "Ask not what your country can do for you, but what you can do for your country.")
    3. Things that must be documented:
        a. Any quoted material from a source.
        b. Ideas that you have gleaned from a source.
        c. Detailed statistics.

In general, I suggest to students that if they are not sure whether to document something, they should probably do so. Published authors tend to be a little less scrupulous about this (an annoying development, I confess), but that does not allow you to be!

Documentation forms vary from field to field. Three common forms of documentation are MLA (established by the Modern Language Association), APA (developed by the American Psychological Association), and *CMS*, or *Chicago* (based on *The Chicago Manual of Style*). Some disciplines require one, some another. You should find out what style manual a given professor wants you to adhere to. Some don't care.In that case, I suggest that you find out, if you can, what style writers in a given discipline prefer, and then adhere to that style. You will need to consult a book (such as the *MLA Style Manual*), and you'll need to *follow exactly* the forms for works cited, notes, internal documentation, and even the look of a keyboarded page.

You will probably be using quotations when you write about literature or use other written source materials. Quotations are useful in that they can provide proof of what you mean and will often capture better than your description a certain aspect of the work that they are from. However, you need to limit your use of quotation. In addition, I recommend that you avoid ending paragraphs on quotations, and also avoid more than two long quotations per paragraph.

I know this sounds a little prescriptive, but my emphasis throughout, as I hope has been evident, has been on maintaining and developing your own argumentative line. If you quote extensively, you tend to fragment your paragraph's ideas. Too, if you end your paragraphs on quoted material, you are not taking advantage of getting the last word in on a given topic; you have, essentially, given over your paragraph to someone else: you've ceded authority. Keep in mind that the author you quote, while likely an authority on the subject, is less important than you and your argument.

Be careful of quoting too much. How much is too much? This is your call, but realize that any quoted material is honored by being quoted and must somehow be something quite special to deserve this honor. You need not quote merely to provide an example of what you mean. And if you can effectively summarize the quoted material, there is no need to quote it. So I recommend that no more than 15 percent of the paper be quoted material. Finally, keep in mind that quoting passages from texts or outside (or secondary) sources does not *prove* your argument. You need to prove your argument with your own words. Sometimes these words of yours will be an elaboration of quoted passages, but still the words need to be your own. And the paragraphs in which the quoted passages appear must remain firmly in your control.

GIVING BACKGROUND ABOUT SOURCE MATERIAL

I often encounter the "dropped quotation" in the student essays I read, namely, the quotation that appears, usually in support of an assertion the paper has made, but without any indication of who is being quoted or why that person has an opinion we might value. I find myself asking in their margins, "Who is it you are quoting?" "Why important?" What you need to do is straightforward, though not really that simple: you need to introduce not just your quotation, as in "Scholes remarks, 'Literature is language used to create an experience that we value for its own sake' (1)," but also something about the person you are quoting: "The well-known literary theorist Robert Scholes, writing in 1969, remarks. . . ." Of course you usually have to do this only for the first quotation from a given source. I used to call this contextualizing material a "source-validation protocol," or a "source protocol," since a "protocol" was initially a series of instructions printed on the flyleaf of a book, and since this particular protocol validates the source you will quote. Now I have moved to a simpler phrase to describe this material: an identifier.

One of the problems with this is that you then have to figure out who it is you are quoting, why he or she is important, and how to economically fit that into your sentence. Students often protest,

"These identifiers make it so wordy!" but I point out that they don't need to. The real problem you will encounter with identifiers is not that they make your prose wordy, but that using them forces you to carefully evaluate your sources, often a lot of work. In addition, when you discover certain things about these sources, you will sometimes discover that you cannot use them—they are biased, out-of-date, or written by nincompoops. This means that you will have to look for other sources.

Another problem that students often mention is that the identifiers I demand are rarely used in published scholarly articles. This is in fact true. While I think an argument can be made that many scholarly articles cannot serve as models of ideal prose, the stronger argument examines the audience these articles address. Most scholarly articles aim themselves at an audience relatively familiar with the academic field. Hence elaborate identifiers are not really needed. When I looked at an article I wrote a few years ago, I discovered that about half the quoted sources are introduced and half are not—I had evidently decided that my audience would probably need orientation of some kind for some quotations but not others. In fact, the sources I quote from outside my field of literary scholarship (that is, the sources I use from psychology, medicine, and other sciences) are exactly the ones that require the identifier.

So once again, you must decide what it is your audience knows, what they will need to be oriented in, how much you need to tell them about your sources. In general, your audience will be the educated nonspecialist, so you won't have to use an identifier such as "The famous philosopher Aristotle writes. . . ." But when you start doing research into areas that are rather specific and probably outside the field of your imagined audience, you will need to use more identifiers, and you will need to make them more complex.

MISCELLANEOUS SUGGESTIONS

Here are some final ideas about dealing with sources:

1. Be fair in how you characterize your sources; don't quote something that, taken by itself, misrepresents the author's opinion or position.

2. Don't just make statements that assert existing research is valid—analyze existing research.
3. Don't automatically assume your sources are either 100 percent correct or 100 percent incorrect. Some can have elements of inaccuracy and accuracy at the same time.
4. Don't assume that later writers or sources are necessarily better than or aware of earlier ones; but don't use out-of-date material when current research has superseded it.
5. Always make it absolutely clear what you have used—words, phrases, ideas, organization—from your sources.
6. Limit quoted material. You may summarize but make it clear that what you are summarizing is someone else's material.
7. If you don't understand a source or passage, don't quote it. First try to figure out what it means. Then decide.

10

Figures and Fallacies, or Being Forceful but Not Cheating at Argument

How you present your ideas is in many ways just as important as those ideas themselves: your argument can be furthered or diminished by the form of your expression and presentation of it. But on the other hand, you don't want your argument to be empty, content-less—all "rhetoric" and no substance. Nor do you want to use language that substitutes for the idea you want to convey. In short, you need to strike some balance between being forceful and being logical; between saying things poetically and saying things plainly.

FIGURES OF SPEECH

Figures of speech are seldom taught in today's schools or universities, except perhaps in specialized courses in rhetoric. But these particular descriptions of ways to arrange sentences—sometimes called "sentence patterns"—are useful to know, if for no other reason than that they allow you to craft more complex and heterogeneous prose. Hence these figures of speech might improve your effectiveness at communicating your ideas.

Some might consider these figures to be rhetorical "tricks" or sleights of hand. Indeed, they can be misused. But at the same time, using them can help you think of new ways to phrase your ideas, and that exercise alone might prove valuable in helping you rethink what you're writing. Too, you need to be conscious of how effective prose contains certain focused areas of intensity, where it is very important that you get your point across. All your prose should not be at the same level, for if it is, it will be flat—lacking in excitement—no matter how carefully honed. Employing figures of speech, where appropriate, will make your prose not only more interesting but more effective as well, allowing you to highlight important areas and shade in significant details in subtle but useful ways.

Finally, it's good to be aware of these figures of speech so that you can identify them in speech or prose you encounter. They are often used to manipulate readers, to persuade them rhetorically—without the use of logic—and thus you need to be wary of them as well. Writing has to be more than just figures of speech. It must have a logical, reasoned basis, specifically, persuasive elements that form the basis of a solid argument. Indeed, the figures can make readers or listeners forget or ignore what is actually being put forth, which should not be your goal, at least not here. Like most things, figures of speech can be overused or misused. But they can also be used effectively and honestly.

Though some rhetoric textbooks will mention figures of speech, the most comprehensive survey is Richard A. Lanham's *A Handlist of Rhetorical Terms*, which you should refer to for more examples or information. Here are a few of the most useful figures, some of which you have certainly encountered and can easily recognize. Others might seem a little alien to you.

1. **Climax.** Arrangement of items in order of ascending importance. For example, "The man was admired, lauded, and finally knighted." "The animals were taught to obey simple commands, to convey their feelings to one another, and, eventually, to speak." Sometimes the order of climax might seem counterintuitive, and this in itself is surprising and effective. For example, a headline in the sports section of the *New York Times* proclaims,

   For Giants,
   Poor Start,
   Poor Finish,
   Poor Season

   Why is this an effective ordering of information?

2. **Antimetabole.** Repeating the idea of a sentence or phrase, but inverting its components in the second half of the expression. For example, "The dragon was fierce,

its breath flame-filled, or was its breath fierce and the dragon flame-filled?" "Rappaccini's daughter was innocent, though her lover was poisoned, but her lover was innocent, and it was she who was poisoned."

3. **Polyptoton.** Repetition of a form of a word that is not the same as the word itself. "The idea of a revolving door revolved in his head." "Be kind, act kindly, reward kindness—and you'll be treated in kind." "Don't be concerned about the goods you can acquire; worry more about the good that you can do."

4. **Asyndeton.** Omission of "and" or "or" when writing out a list: "She was lively, intelligent, noble."

5. **Polysyndeton.** Inclusion of the conjunction between each element: "She was lively and intelligent and noble."

6. **Hypallage.** Lanham defines this as "[a]wkward or humorous changing of agreement or application of words, as with Bottom playing Pyramus: 'I see a voice. Now will I to the chink/ To spy and I can hear my Thisby's face'" (86). "We have long held in this country the Byronic ideal that human nature is essentially good or graceful, that behind the sheath of skin is a little globe of glow to be harnessed for creative uses" (Slater 44). It can also refer to a modified expression of some kind: "Winning isn't everything, it's the lonely thing." "Early to bed, early to rise, makes a man healthy, wealthy, and despised." "Now that the genome project is completed, we're in the DNAge" (Justin Johnson, Princeton University freshman).

7. **Anastrophe.** Nontypical arrangement of word order: "Backward run the sentences till reels the mind" (famous line from *Time* magazine). Yoda, in *Star Wars*, typically uses this figure: "Trust you must."

8. **Metaphor/Simile.** A comparison, implied or stated, between two or more things, but one that isn't so common as to have entered common parlance (in which case it would be trite): "An ogre is like an onion" (*Shrek*). "With minimal overhang front and rear, the [BMW] is as compact and hard as bunched biceps" (Dan Niel, writing for the *New York Times*). "Ships at a distance have every

man's wish on board" (opening sentence of Zora Neale Hurston's *Their Eyes Were Watching God*).

9. **Alliteration.** Repetition of initial consonant sounds in order to call attention to an expression. This can also involve repetition of some vowel sounds (so it can have an element of assonance). The famous baseball player Ted Williams was called, for example, "the Splendid Splinter."

10. **Antanagoge.** Conceding a negative feature of a situation or argument but offering a positive (yet relevant) one to more than compensate. Lanham's example comes from Alexander Pope: "A mighty maze, but not without a plan" (Pope's description of the universe and nature).

11. **Oxymoron.** The pairing of opposites: "burning ice," "calm fury."

12. **Epizeuxis.** Repeating words one right after another. "He cried, cried for all that he had lost and all that he had won." "We are shocked, shocked, at this indiscretion."

13. **Anaphora.** Using the same word at the beginning of multiple clauses: "It was the best of times, it was the worst of times. . . ."

14. **Antistrophe.** Using the same word at the end of multiple, successive clauses. (See example for Anaphora.)

15. **Hyperbole.** Extreme and obvious exaggeration: "If all the Earthy Mass were rambd in Sacks / And saddled on an Emmet small, / Its load were light unto those packs / Which Sins do bring on all" (lines 41–44 of "An Extasy of Joy let in by this Reply returnd in Admiration" [section 17 of "God's Determinations touching his Elect," in *The Poems of Edward Taylor*]).

What practical application might these figures have? How do they transform one's writing—or are they only polysyllabic Greek terms that fill up musty textbooks? One exercise that always proves interesting and fruitful seems at first glance a little mechanical, but bear with me: take a short piece of your own writing—something you are not too pleased with—and, keeping the same "content" or idea base, reword it using figures of speech. Try for ten figures in a paragraph. I know that sounds like a lot, but several might be applied to one sentence alone.

Here's a paragraph that doesn't exactly soar (it's from a college paper I wrote about medical malpractice):

> If the number of malpractice suits goes up, as indeed it ought to, costs would also go up. But with the general trend toward socialization of medicine, this should not be a problem. A more important development of increased malpractice litigation would be the arising of a new form of doctor. These "new" doctors would be less dependent on their own opinion alone and would seek out experts. Numerous and various tests would be conducted on each patient to determine exactly the nature of the disease. Only by elaborate testing techniques can the extent of an illness in a person be determined.

Admittedly pedestrian prose, it's nonetheless generally "correct"; it does make a point, though perhaps rather too circuitously. It uses a "hinge-structure," with the third sentence working as the topic sentence. While this might be better placed earlier on, I won't touch it just now, since I want only to import changes in expression, that is, figures of speech.

Now it's not usually just random what figures you choose. You want to use the best ones. But here I will simply import the above figures to see whether that makes the piece come alive or sing a little, or at least show some signs of once having lived.

> Up climb the costs of medicine, as the number of malpractice suits soars.[1] Yet soar they ought to, and our government, more and more socialized in the places that matter, will both pay that price and impose their authority to create a new, super-breed of medical doctors: less dependent on their own opinions, these doctors will seek out other experts on whose opinions they might depend, will seek out all the current research, will seek out, in a word, the truth.[2] Medical tests—numerous, various, exhaustive, probative—would come to

[1] Anastrophe, alliteration, metaphor
[2] Anaphora, polyptoton

bear, and as an entirety, they would bear what?—the fruit of knowledge: namely, the exact nature of the disease.[3] Using a panoply of tests as their first-line armamentarium, then diagnosing and treating and finally cornering that foe, these new doctors will high-tech disease to distraction, will information-overload it to death, will show that knowledge is indeed power.[4] The power to heal.[5]

Notice how the meaning of the original has shifted somewhat, too, even though I attempted only to change the way that I expressed my ideas. Suddenly, the paragraph seems to be a clarion call for an entirely new kind of medicine, something only hinted at rather listlessly in the original. In the next rewrite, I would strive to tone down the "figures" a little, and strive to make the paragraph a little less apocalyptic in tone. After all, it's just arguing that more malpractice suits might scare doctors into doing more testing and more careful diagnosis; I could easily revert to that particular emphasis, all the while maintaining some of the verbal punch of the rewrite.

Susan Bell provides several interesting examples of how F. Scott Fitzgerald edited *The Great Gatsby*, an enterprise that consisted of doing just what I have done here. Bell suggests that "Fitzgerald was a prose techie who would not merely polish but power up a weak passage" (155). And he does this through skillful manipulation of rhetorical devices.

For example, here is an early version of some musings by the novel's narrator, Nick Carraway, as he listens to his companions' idle prattle:

> I was thirty. Beside that realization, their importunities were dim and far away. Before me stretched the portentous menacing road of a new decade.

Note that Fitzgerald's prose does not completely lack ornament—he uses the road metaphor to describe the next decade of life. But in his revision, he added quite a lot more:

[3] Asyndeton, metaphor, polyptoton
[4] Polysyndeton, hypallage, climax
[5] Epizeuxis

Thirty—the promise of a decade of loneliness, a thinning list of single men to know, a thinning briefcase of enthusiasm, thinning hair. (Qtd. by Bell 156–57).

Bell remarks about Fitzgerald, "He was driven to edit a sentence silly until it punched" (156), and punch this sentence, or sentence fragment, does. In the revision, Fitzgerald has abandoned standard syntax. No longer are there three full sentences but rather just one fragment. Specifically, what figures does Fitzgerald use? I see metaphor, anaphora, climax, metaphor, alliteration, asyndeton, and something very like hypallage—all in a twenty-three-word sentence fragment. What can one do but stand back and clap?

LOGICAL FALLACIES: A SAMPLER

As a counterpoint to the figures, I want to present you with logical fallacies: ways of expression and reasoning that many writers employ in an effort to cloud the issue, distract the audience, shift the focus, or confuse the trivial with the important. As popular as these might be, they do not, finally, meet scrupulous, scholarly standards. Using them constitutes cheating at argument. (Using figures exclusively, that is, relying on them to carry the weight of your argument, is also "cheating at argument.") As I suggested, you must consciously maintain a somewhat precarious (or at least difficult) balance—between being, on the one hand, forceful in expression, saying things in an interesting, engaging way—and on the other, being logical, honest, and fair.

Logical fallacies have inundated our lives, as you might already have discovered; they are especially rife during election years, and in advertising; hence many of my examples will come from either politics or Madison Avenue–based campaigns. I should also point out that there are degrees of fallaciousness; some of these examples are more egregious than others. Note too that fallacies often overlap—or a statement can contain two or more fallacies at the same time.

I provide the following list for a couple of reasons. First, you need to avoid using these fallacies in your own writing. They gravely weaken your argument. Some people might be persuaded by them, but they are not the people you want to persuade, as they either agree with you to begin with or are not looking very carefully at the details of your argument. In addition, by using these you engage in an activity that damages your powers of reason. They suggest a defective logicality, and if you are inadvertently employing such a mechanism, you should probably try not to; if you are using them to manipulate an audience into siding with you, that might be even worse.

Second, as you read and evaluate sources, as you go through your daily life bombarded—verbally, textually—with all sorts of arguments, you need to be able to sort through them. You want to distinguish the strong arguments from the weak ones, the credible claims from the obviously faulty ones. I'm hoping that a knowledge of some of the basic fallacies will help you do this.

Here are the most commonly discussed and easily identifiable fallacies:

1. **Ad hominem.**   Attacking a personality rather than a position. (But sometimes a personality is important: character and personality might be relevant to considerations of how well someone might perform in a position of public office, for example.)
   a. Senator Kerry's ideas about tax reform can't be trusted: he's just too wealthy himself.
   b. How can we take seriously Hemingway's advice about life—he committed suicide!
   c. "Alas, 'Sex, Sex, and More Sex' seems to have been rushed into print to capitalize on [Sue] Johanson's newfound popularity; it's not easy to trust a sex guru who misspells the name of Dr. Ernst Gräfenberg (the first modern physician to describe the alleged G spot) and also Peyronie's disease" (Amy Sohn, "The Elements of Sexual Style," *New York Times Book Review* 26 September 2004: 31).
2. **Ad populum.**   Suggesting that because something is popular, it is therefore good, valuable, or justifiable in any way.
   a. Smoking can't be so bad—millions of people do it!
   b. An argument in the U.S. in 1850: Why, what's wrong with slavery? Thousands of people practice it, and it's

the very basis of our economy—and has been for more than two hundred years!

3. **Circular argument.** Using some key term—or a slightly modified version of it—in both the premise and the conclusion, this is also known as *begging the question*.

   a. "Hawking, the British physicist, claimed to have solved the black hole information paradox. New simulations suggested that the matter and energy jets that spew out of some black holes are caused by their spin" ("Findings," *Harper's* October 2004: 104).

   b. Home ownership is to be valued because owning real estate almost always increases one's net worth.

   c. Almost all cars today are engineered to go at least 100 mph, so speeding must be safe.

4. **Either-or.** Sometimes called the fallacy of suppressed alternatives or the "false dilemma"—usually a tactic meant to alarm the audience. To be a genuine false dilemma, a statement has to offer a pair of "contrary" alternatives— ones different from each other but not absolutely exhaustive of the possibilities. If a statement offers a pair of "contradictory" alternatives, then it is not a false dilemma but in fact an obvious statement that has a tautological ring to it. (Either O.J. committed murder or he did not.)

   a. "Psychoanalysis: Is It Science or Is It Toast?" (title of review of *Secrets of the Soul* by Eli Zaretsky in *New York Times Book Review* 5 September 2004. Review by Daphne Merkin: 9–10).

   b. "We are fast approaching a watershed moment in our social progress. Either we will move forward toward a much more cooperative and coordinated global community, or we will regress into a more and more tribalized, combative, and totalitarian existence. To continue to ignore climate change means putting at risk billions of people around the world. Ultimately, it means consigning our children to a future of chaos and disintegration" (Ross Gelbspan, "Cool the Rage," *Orion*, July/August 2004: 11).

c. Either we buy that house or relegate ourselves to paying landlords for the rest of our lives.

d. Men can be divided into two categories: boxers or briefs.

e. If I don't get the plastic surgery, I'll be doomed to a lifetime of anonymity and blandness.

5. **Red herring or distraction.** A form of statement in which the purpose is to distract the audience or opponent from the issue at hand. One usually resorts to a red herring when one's own arguments are conspicuously weak. This kind of argument attempts to shift the ground rather subtly (or sometimes not so subtly).

a. "Leaving aside the fact that the human race evolved as omnivores and that we most likely would never have acquired our highly proficient brains through vegetarianism, no soy product could ever replicate to any degree a perfectly barbequed steak. I was a vegetarian for many years, and I was never fooled by any of the faux meats. And anyway, if I'm going to eat vegetables, I'm not going to pretend they're meat" (Linda Felaco, letter to editor, *Atlantic Monthly* October 2004: 29).

b. It's true that Mr. Bush didn't capture Osama bin Laden, but he did bring Saddam Hussein to justice.

c. So what if the university exploits part-time adjunct faculty? They're such good teachers! And besides, they don't have to work if they don't want to.

6. **Faulty analogy.** Using a comparison between two sets of circumstances or things that offers no proof of a significant connection between the things compared.

a. "JUDGMENT: The *Indianapolis Star* reports that the Indiana Court of Appeals has dismissed a lawsuit demanding damages from a cellphone manufacturer because of a collision involving a woman talking on one of their cellphones. The judge's reasoning was that people regularly eat while driving and it would be unreasonable to sue the cook if they crash" (David M. Black, "People, Places, and Things," *Road and Track* October 2004: 21).

b. "There really are better times and worse times. The problem is that the better times seem better only when one has a standard of comparison. . . . Did Adam appreciate the paradise handed to him before the fall? How could he? He had nothing to compare it with" (letter to *New York Times* by Gene Asner 24 September 2004: A26).

c. An essay is like a peanut butter and jelly sandwich. The bread's the introduction and conclusion—inside, though, is the good stuff.

d. You say the law discriminates against people of color. One of my coworkers had an accident that turned his skin blue, and yet we still treated him like one of the guys.

7. **Emotive language.** Using terms that prejudge the issue in a certain way, so the argument is made through the terms themselves rather than through logic.

a. "Frankly, I don't care about Formula I [racing] as it abandons Europe to sack the pockets of a collection of dimbulb Far Eastern potentates. But the plight of major-league open-wheel racing in America does concern me as it plunges toward oblivion" (Brock Yates, "Someone Needs to Rewrite Racing Rules," *Car and Driver* September 2004: 26).

b. The monstrous corporation, ever feeding its giant maw with the flesh of average citizens, needs not to be tamed or cut down in size, but exterminated, just as any enemy of society should be.

c. People who brazenly parade their near-naked flesh, while they're making a transparent pretense of sunbathing on our public beaches, should be fined and jailed.

8. **Hasty generalization.** Arriving at a fallacious conclusion about an issue because only a small or nonrepresentative sampling has been examined. Another way of looking at this might be as extrapolation from incomplete data.

a. What are students like here? Well, I've only been to the gym, but in general the students seem more interested in sports than in studying.

b. It's been rainy every day since we moved here. I guess the sun never shines in Seattle.

c. "Rod doesn't have time for people who criticize his taste for roadkill. 'I'm willing to take responsibility for what I eat, while the vegans and vegetarians preaching at me eat vegetables shipped in from other countries and trucked up from down South so they can get the food that's not in season. They are guilty of feeding the monster machines that are creating the roadkill'" (Colleen Wells, "Roadkill Rod," *Orion* July/August 2004: 10).

d. Every philosophy major I've met is a man with a beard—so it's clear that women can't be philosophers.

9. **Post hoc ergo propter hoc.** Suggesting that since one event comes before another, it must necessarily *cause* that event.

a. I had Earl Grey instead of Orange Pekoe tea at breakfast and then got an A on my exam. I think Earl Grey tea must increase intelligence.

b. I lost thirty pounds and suddenly seemed to have no friends. It seems that fat people must be popular.

10. **Straw person/straw man.** Misstating the opposing position, making it seem simplistic, easy to knock down (i.e., like a straw man).

a. "No," the professor said, "we must start the debate about abortion by substituting the word 'murder' for 'abortion,' since that's what it is. Who of you will defend murder?"

b. By trying to increase the writing required for graduation, the college clearly wants to increase levels of student stress, and hence withdrawals from the university.

11. **Non sequitur.** Latin for "it does not follow," this type of fallacy does not really fit into any other category. Lanham defines it as follows: "A statement that bears no relationship to the context preceding."

a. "At the Nashua senior center, a Mr. Kim, who looked well into his seventies, addressed the audience. After apologizing for his English, he said, 'To hell with Lip-itor, a hundred and fifty dollars a month! I decided to hell with it. If I die, I die. I exercised. I lowered cholesterol level. Ran half marathon!'" (P. J. O'Rourke, "The Art of Policy: 'To Hell with Lipitor,'" *Atlantic Monthly* October 2004: 56).

b. That car should prove to be ideal transportation. After all, it's shaped like a box.

c. "Liberal. Conservative. Democrat. Republican. Every opinion in the universe" (ad for iUniverse.com).

12. **Slippery slope.** Saying that taking one action will lead to another, more threatening or grave, situation, but failing to provide a logical connection that could prove such a sequence of events will happen.

a. "In 1972, a night watchman patrolling a hotel-office complex noticed that the basement garage door had been taped open and, attributing this to the carelessness of a maintenance worker earlier that day, peeled the tape off. When, on his next round, he found the door taped open again, he called the police. As a result, citizens of the United States do not enjoy the benefits (or suffer the aggravations) of national health insurance" (Laura Miller, "Imagine," *New York Times Book Review* 5 September 2004: 23).

b. "More and more [politicians] are staking out the rhetorical terrain pioneered by U.S. Representative Tom Cole of Oklahoma last spring: 'If George Bush loses the election,' he said, 'Osama bin Laden wins the election. It's that simple'" (Luke Mitchell, "The Osama Endorsement," *Harper's* October 2004: 89).

c. If we don't increase homeland security, it seems clear that in no time democracy will completely disappear, as each democratic state is toppled by terrorists.

d. The library budget was cut again. At this rate, in fifty years there will be no books.

One of my erstwhile colleagues contended that he would no longer teach fallacies because "fallacies are actually true." I think what he meant is that fallacies often succeed at persuading an audience to your position. My point here, though, is that even though they might persuade your audience, they do so in the wrong way. They don't use logic; they use tricks. They are dishonest. Any practical value that they have—such as persuasiveness—is lost because they do not assess the evidence or analyze a situation in a logical, sober, and disinterested manner. Indeed, they elevate persuasion as the end to be gained at almost any cost, including that of truth. And my contention here is that if people are persuaded by this kind of suspect logic, they might accept it at first, but the truth will, finally, emerge. At the risk of committing a logical fallacy myself (faulty analogy), I feel I must point out that there are many forms of persuasion (torture, coercion, bribery) that we in a civilized society should not employ, and using verbal trickery, while by no means the same thing as putting bamboo splints under someone's fingernails, inhabits the same general galaxy of deceit.

11

The Argument of Style

What makes for a good—or for that matter distinctive—writing style? What do we even mean by a "good" writing style? It seems to me that most often people define a good style through negative characteristics, that is, by suggesting that good writing usually avoids certain linguistic constructions, certain kinds of language, or even certain words. In fact, writing has all too often been taught as if the page were a minefield filled with all manner of hidden explosive devices, any one of which could blow your paper to smithereens.

I'd like to repeat here what kinds of things you ought to avoid, and then I'd also like to make some positive suggestions about what tactics or rhetorical strategies you ought to emulate. My general idea is that style constitutes a significant part of your argument. While many people separate form from content, style from substance, this division seems artificial. Style, especially when distinctive, can make an argument quite separate from the logical points that you make within your writing itself. And, if you work on your style, this argument can be in your favor.

STYLE: SOME THINGS TO AVOID, PROBABLY

On that tentative note, what should you try to avoid? Writing situations vary, but in general, try to avoid indirect, extremely complex, circumlocutious writing. Robin MacPherson captures this notion quite nicely in his textbook *University English*: "First and foremost, lucidity, economy, and precision are overriding considerations: no matter how demanding the subject matter, a good writer of academic English is never verbose or deliberately obscure, and will always try to visualize the reader and go out to him, instead of expecting him somehow or other to construe [the] meaning" (5). In general, academic writing should be direct, forthright, and truthful, though I think you also need to be aware that in some nonacademic contexts (for example, in a letter giving very bad news) such directness might appear to be either too abrasive, harsh, or insensitive. However, learning how to write clearly and directly will also sensitize you to how not to be clear and direct.

But I promised some prohibitions, some things to avoid in writing, some stylistic pratfalls. What follows constitutes a partial list.

1. Avoid frequently using "to be" verbs (is, are, were, was, being, been, be), unless avoiding them makes your writing sound weird or foreign. Often you will find yourself using many "to be" verbs within a paragraph. Such a strategy leads to somewhat leaden, slow-moving, difficult-to-understand prose. Try to avoid using "to be" verbs more than a few times per paragraph. (Note that I probably use too many "to be" verbs here, but what can I say? *Nolo contendere.*)

2. Avoid using many "Th-openers," that is, sentences that begin with words such as *The, This, There, Then, Those, That, Thus.* (Starting with "Though" would be OK, however, as would starting with names that start with "Th-" or with words other than those on the list above). You should probably try to avoid these because using one on top of the other tends to produce sentences with very similar structures, which can lull the reader into a state of mindless passivity—not really your goal, typically.

3. Avoid sentences that use multiple prepositional phrases, especially prepositional phrases linked one after another. Using more than two or three prepositions per sentence effectively slows your prose. Try to keep preposition use to a minimum. Indeed, when you edit an essay, you'll find that the softest, most vulnerable places are prepositional phrases. Instead of writing, "I want to explore how the minds *of* doctors work when they try to listen *to* patients talk *about* problems *with* their health," try something like "This essay explores how doctors hear—or ignore—their patients' stories."

4. As much as possible, avoid using nouns that end in *-tion*,

-cion, *-sion*, which tend to accompany prepositional phrases and tend to muffle a sentence's impact. Often you will find yourself using a lot of these noun forms that have been created out of a verb. "Justify" becomes "justification"; "hierarchize" (which came from "hierarchy") becomes "hierarchization"; "familiarize" becomes "familiarization." I suggest that you not pile up these words (ironic that they're called called "nominalizations"!), for doing so slows down your sentence, clogging the route to understanding.

5. Avoid trite expressions, jargon, catchphrases. What is trite, though? What is jargon? Ideally you need to have some kind of inner monitor that registers when the language you use sounds like a cliché—is old, tired, hackneyed, lacking in originality, ho-hum, boring, flat, colloquial, or just plain blah. However, no one is born with such a monitor; you need to develop one. To do so, be as conscious as possible of what kinds of words you use when you write formal essays. Ask yourself after each sentence, Have I expressed this idea in an original way—or am I borrowing something that's not ultimately worthy of repetition? Can I say this in a fresher, more striking manner? Are there other words I might use? To catch trite (overused) language or clichés, think whether you have heard a given expression—or seen it in print—more than three or four times; if you have, then it is probably trite and should be avoided. Usually these expressions involve a comparison of some kind (*He runs like a deer*), or some metaphorical language use (*He salivated over the prospect of driving the Ferrari*). In general, strive for originality of expression, and try not to rely on phrases that others invented long ago, and that long ago lost their power and imaginativeness. When Henry David Thoreau talked about how people should "march to the beat of a different drummer," the expression had some force, but now it has been used so much, plastered so often on posters and declaimed in so many advertisements, that it has lost any impact it once had. While I in

general disapprove of ending a paragraph with a quotation, I will do so here because I think these words of Martin Amis have especial force: "To idealize: all writing is a campaign against cliché. Not just clichés of the pen but clichés of the mind and clichés of the heart. When I dispraise, I am usually quoting clichés. When I praise, I am usually quoting the opposed qualities of freshness, energy and reverberation of voice" (qtd. by Turner 10).

6. Avoid vulgar slang. Four-letter words and the like are generally not acceptable in formal writing, unless you are quoting from a work of literature that uses such language. Using quotation marks around slang expressions, as in "This novel really 'sucks,'" is also inappropriate; the quotation marks do not justify the use of vulgar slang. In addition, it's fairly clear that formal writing does not exactly replicate speech, with its many pauses, circumlocutions, redundancies, and self-interruptions—not to mention its frequent use of vernacular language. So even though something sounds right out loud, it may not necessarily be correct when put into writing. I suggest you keep a list of all the words that your professors tell you are slang, and try to avoid those words when you write papers. Sometimes, too, words will be understandable within a given context but make little sense outside that context. The following sentence, for example, seems senseless, until the context is made clear: "I'll have an everything with nothing." (Ordering at a bagel shop.)

7. Avoid extremely obscure language. Words like *floccinaucinihilipilification*, *erumpent*, *thigmotaxis*, *sterquilinous*, *anentiomorphous*, or the like, while interesting, tend to obscure meaning. (Of course, if your audience is conversant with such vocabulary, then these words would not be off-limits.)

8. Avoid monotonous repetition, such as following the same sentence structure for almost every sentence, or using the same words over and over in the same paragraph. Typically, English sentences are set up as subject-

verb-object sequences, a pattern that rapidly becomes boring for the reader.

9. Avoid excessive embedding of clauses (hypotaxis) within sentences (see the example from Henry James, below).

10. Avoid highlighting, boldfacing, underlining, italicizing, or capitalizing for emphasis—make your prose clearly set forth what needs emphasis and what does not. If you want to highlight something and you don't feel that your sentence structures do a good enough job, use only one highlighting device (e.g., italics). Mixing the kinds of highlighting serves more to confuse than to illuminate the reader.

11. Avoid emotive language, "emoticons," and typographical eccentricities "It was {{{{{{{{{{Sheila!}}}}}}}}}}." And there you are! ☺

12. In general, avoid passive constructions. You need to know the difference between *active voice* and *passive voice*. In active voice, an agent acts. It performs something. You mention it. "The shopping cart hit John's car." In passive constructions the agent receives the action. "John's car was hit." By what? By whom? Very often no agent inhabits passive constructions, which can make those constructions a little dishonest, as if they were withholding information: "It was decided that you are to be fired"; "The car was evidently hit." Who decided? Who hit the car? Since the passive construction tends to conceal agency, I suggest that you use active voice, unless you intend to conceal agency. Sometimes, though, the passive conceals not only agency but meaning as well. One essay I read contains this sentence: "Clearly, opposition to the cynicism of the qualitative symptoms of the disease is apparent." I don't believe there is any meaning here, or if there is, I welcome you to find it. Once a student asked me, "Is it always wrong to use the passive?" and I thought about this awhile. "Always" statements should probably be avoided in discussions of matters of usage, I decided. In fact some academic fields, particularly in the natural and social sciences, consider the passive voice more scholarly!

Of course, writing evolves and changes as people challenge these "rules." Perhaps in the future, emoticons will be part of the standard formal essay. And in the past, much more hypotaxis was acceptable, even encouraged. Consider, for example, a section of Henry James's "The New Novel," originally published in 1914, in which James discusses some of the novelists of his day:

> The act of squeezing out to the utmost the plump and more or less juicy orange of a particular acquainted state and letting this affirmation of energy, however directed or undirected, constitute for them the "treatment" of a theme—*that* is what we remark them as mainly engaged in, after remarking the example so strikingly, so originally set, even if an undue subjection to it be here and there repudiated. Nothing is further from our thought than to undervalue saturation and possession, the fact of the particular experience, the state and degree of acquaintance incurred, however such a consciousness may have been determined; for these things represent on the part of the novelist, as on the part of any painter of things seen, felt or imagined, just one half of his authority—the other half being represented of course by the application he is inspired to make of them. (189)

Henry James's later writings often employ a style that supplants or supersedes content and argument. Or rather, the style is the argument. Such writing, difficult to read, embodies many of the prohibitions mentioned above. And while it clearly demonstrates James's genius, his uniqueness, it also showcases his flaws—and many of the kinds of things that you should avoid in your own writing. Try to straightforwardly communicate your ideas to an audience. And be aware that while the audience might read your words more than once, they will not likely go back again and again trying to puzzle out your meaning. In fact, I'm still not sure what James was getting at here. You tell me.

CRAFTING A STYLE

Let me offer a few suggestions for what you ought to think about when crafting an individual and lucid writing style. In general, you should strive to make your writing interesting yet communicative. It's really as simple as that. A reader should feel something akin to delight while reading, should want to read on, should in some way forget that he or she is reading and easily engage the progression of ideas on the page. There should be a smoothness, a sense of poetry (maybe), to writing, but at the same time it needs to carry intellectual content. It needs to present the individuality of your insights and your experiences, even though the language it uses is a shared one. You need to make language your own while making that language something others would be interested in sharing.

Retaining the reader's interest, then, conveying ideas, and demonstrating an originality of expression: some people can do this with little difficulty, while others struggle at it for years. For those who don't come to it naturally, let me offer a few suggestions about what to strive for in crafting a writing style. Keep in mind that these are only suggestions, and that this brief list is by no means exhaustive.

1. *Variation.* You need to make sure that your sentences do not follow the same pattern all the time. Employ some figures of speech—but do so judiciously! Make some sentences "right-handed" (i.e., starting with the subject), and others "left-handed" (starting with a modifier or subordinating element). Make some sentences long, some short; others, in between. The linguist John Herum suggested to me once that we should also vary levels of intensity in our prose. If, for example, we cut out of an essay all "to be" verbs, almost all prepositions and nominalizations, the whole piece will be at "the same level" of intensity—hence "flat," not really all that interesting. Perhaps it's best to strive for a "sine-wave" pattern of emphasis or impact (though a sine wave is more regular than you really want), with some areas of the essay more powerfully, tightly, and forcefully phrased than others.

2. *Lucidity.* The windowpane metaphor. In "Why I Write" (1947) George Orwell wrote that "good prose is like a windowpane" (*The Orwell Reader* 395): you should easily see through it to perceive the ideas of the author. You

need to keep in mind that you're trying to convey something to an audience, and that the words should not "get in the way." Often we will talk about writing that is "clear" or "lucid," and this is offered as a virtue: the argument and ideas are easily seen, as if through a windowpane of prose. When you start clouding, frosting, or embellishing the pane, you undermine your ability to convey an idea.

3. *Directness.* Get to your point. Say what you mean. Give clear examples, and try to be specific rather than general. Tangents may sometimes be interesting, but you should probably avoid them when you can—or deal with them in notes.

4. *Musicality.* Can we teach ourselves the music of language? It seems to me we can. Read aloud what you have written. Does it have a musical quality? Does it have a balance, a rhythm, a poetry? Does it sing? Maybe it shouldn't sing. But it almost certainly should have something to it that respects the oral/aural component of language. Look again at the figures of speech and try to listen to the music of various examples. In a way, this overlaps with variation, but the variation needs to be done with the intention of making the reader interested and delighted, not just for the sake of formal variety.

5. *Sense imagery.* You need to realize that, as you write, your appeal should be to many senses, not just to the reader's visual sense, for example. Consider how Vladimir Nabokov appeals to all five senses—including the tactile sense of pain—in his description of a man's situation after having his few remaining teeth extracted:

A warm flow of pain was gradually replacing the ice and wood of the anesthetic in his thawing, still half-dead, abominably martyred mouth. After that, during a few days he was in mourning for an intimate part of himself. It surprised him to realize how fond he had been of his teeth. His tongue, a fat sleek seal, used to flop and slide so happily among the familiar rocks, checking the contours of a battered but still secure kingdom, plunging from cave to cove, climbing this jag, nuzzling that notch, finding a shred of seaweed in the same old cleft. (38)

6. *Cohesiveness.* Good writing flows, one sentence to the next, effortlessly, in a manner of speaking. You need to think about how to connect your sentences, how to make for these smooth transitional moves.

7. *Organization.* Good style has a logicality to it, a progression that the reader can follow.

8. *Verbiness.* Good writing typically uses active verbs, rather than passive ones, which I suggest above that you should avoid. Passive constructions are often used in scientific writing, in social science writing, and in textbooks (I use a lot here, you've no doubt noticed), but I recommend avoiding their use as much as you can. Try to "verb" your reader through your sentences; don't put him or her to sleep by omitting the agent and hiding behind a passive voice.

9. *Grammaticality.* This is neither the last nor the least, but it's quite important just the same. Good writers give the impression that they know the "rules" very well—that they have no trouble with the fundamentals of usage. Your style should display a similar confidence.

10. *Surprise: breaking the rules.* Perhaps I shouldn't mention this here, but impressive stylists not only know the rules; they flout the rules on occasion, when they think it might be effective. Often they are correct—in that this strategy does surprise readers. I don't recommend doing this on a regular basis, but you might think about how to creatively modify the "norm"—making your modification with an eye toward bolstering your argument and achieving an original expression of what you want to say.

ELEVEN EXTRAORDINARY STYLISTS

At this point, what follows will be something of an experiment. Before drafting this chapter, I gathered eleven examples of what I consider "good writing." Many of these writers are among my favorites and have been for years. But I never looked very closely at their writing; I merely enjoyed it, stood in awe of it.

Will these examples of good writing in fact do the very things that I suggest writers avoid? Will they follow the principles I'm recommending? Will they do things other than what I suggest? Finally, perhaps, I wonder whether good prose may inevitably be idiosyncratic, never answering or lockstepping to rules laid out in texts. What I suspect is that these eleven examples are not necessarily ones that everyone should emulate, but that each has a decided individuality. Maybe their violation of the rules shows that the rules may be violated with impunity, but only if the resultant work clearly evinces genius. Or maybe they won't break the "rules" that much after all. We'll see.

Academic writing always has to negotiate among warring imperatives: it should be lucid but at the same time complex; it needs to be engaging but not too informal; it ought to be innovative but not eccentric; informative but not fact-choked, rhetorically rich but not fallacious. Here are my examples. All are nonfiction; some are academic, others less so. And here begins the experiment: do these writers actually perform "prohibited" rhetorical/stylistic moves? And to what extent does their writing exemplify the virtues I have outlined?

William James, *The Varieties of Religious Experience*, 1899

The normal process of life contains moments as bad as any of those which insane melancholy is filled with, moments in which radical evil gets its innings

[1] Note interesting use of colloquial and formal (here using a baseball metaphor to describe "radical evil").

and takes its solid turn.[1] The lunatic's visions of horror are all drawn from the material of daily fact.

[2] Passive throughout does not seem to diminish James's impact one whit.

Our civilization is founded[2] on the shambles, and every individual existence goes out in a lonely spasm of hopeless agony.[3] If you protest, my friend, wait till you arrive there yourself![4] To believe in the carnivorous reptiles of geologic times is hard for our imagination—they seem too much like mere museum specimens. Yet there is no tooth in any one of those museum-skulls that did not daily through long years of the foretime hold fast to the body struggling in despair of some fated living victim.[5] Forms of horror just as dreadful to their victims, if on a smaller spatial scale, fill the world about us to-day. Here on our very hearths and in our gardens the infernal cat plays with the panting mouse, or holds the hot bird fluttering in her jaws.[6] Crocodiles and rattlesnakes and pythons are at this moment vessels of life as real as we are[7]; their loathsome existence fills every minute of every day that drags its length along;[8] and whenever they or other wild beasts clutch their living prey, the deadly horror which an agitated melancholiac[9] feels is the literally right reaction on the situation.[10] (152–53)

[3] "Lonely spasm of hopeless agony": extraordinary turn of phrase, one that's frighteningly musical and unforgettable.
[4] Switches form of address to comment directly to audience. When read aloud, this comment beautifully anticipates how audience had reacted to previous line. (And this work was initially delivered as a lecture, I might add. Often reading a work aloud will stimulate in the writer a particularly nice turn of phrase.)
[5] James treads on the edge of the sentimental here, but doesn't slide in.

[6] Note use of multiple sense imagery.
[7] Use of specific examples—museum skulls, cat, mouse, crocodiles, etc.—brings his insights to a concrete level.
[8] The day dragging its length recalls the length of crocodiles and pythons, tying the concepts together visuo-spatially.
[9] Suddenly bringing back the "melancholiac" in the last line surprises the reader but recalls the topic sentence, which now seems invested with even greater weight.
[10] Note the use of *-tion* word: OK here. So much for that prohibition!

This book, compiling the Gifford Lectures, which James delivered in Scotland in 1899, stands out for the vigor of its style and the freshness of its language. William's writings stand in sharp contrast to those of his brother, Henry (see above). (William was called the "philosopher who wrote like a novelist," and Henry, "the novelist who wrote like a philosopher.") The passage I have quoted comes at the end of the chapter called "The Sick Soul."

W.E.B. Du Bois, "Abraham Lincoln" (1922)

Abraham Lincoln was a Southern poor white, of illegitimate birth, poorly educated and unusually ugly, awkward, ill-dressed.[11] He liked smutty stories and was a politician down to his toes.[12] Aristocrats—Jeff Davis, Seward and their ilk—despised him, and indeed he had little outwardly that compelled respect. But in that curious human way he was big inside.[13] He had reserves and depths and when habit and convention were torn away[14] there was something left to Lincoln—nothing to most of his contemners. There was something left, so that at the crisis he was big enough to be inconsistent—cruel, merciful; peace-loving, a fighter; despising Negroes and letting them fight and vote; protecting slavery and freeing slaves.[15] He was a man—a big, inconsistent, brave man. (1196)

[11] Note asyndeton. Also, a rather striking list.
[12] Du Bois now moves into a somewhat less formal register.

[13] Very simple language, "big inside," but at the same time very evocative. What does this mean? A stark contrast to the ugliness of Lincoln that had been painted by the first few lines. Such a reversal is often effective.
[14] Vivid metaphor—as if habit and convention were merely clothing.

[15] Again, a creatively shaped and interesting list. Du Bois surprises the reader by pairing attributes we don't expect.

Writing in the NAACP journal (*The Crisis*) that he himself founded and edited, Du Bois felt it was important to tell the truth about Lincoln, even though that truth was perhaps not what his readers genuinely wanted to hear. Several months later, he wrote an explanation of his piece on Lincoln, and he elaborated some on his position. He ends that editorial, "The scars and foibles and contradictions of the Great do not diminish but enhance the worth and meaning of their upward struggle: it was the bloody sweat that proved the human Christ divine; it was his true history and antecedents that proved Abraham Lincoln a Prince of Men" (1199).

Ruth Benedict, *Patterns of Culture*, 1934

In our generation extreme forms of ego-gratification are culturally supported in a similar fashion.[16] Arrogant and unbridled egoists as family men, as officers of the law and in business, have been again and again portrayed by novelists and dramatists, and they are familiar in every community. Like the behavior of the Puritan divines, their courses of action are often more asocial than those of the inmates of penitentiaries.[17] In terms of the suffering and frustration that they spread about them there is probably no comparison. There is very possibly at least as great a degree of mental warping.[18] Yet they are entrusted with positions of great influence and importance and are as a rule fathers of families.[19] Their impress both upon their own children and upon the structure of our society is indelible.[20] They are not described in our manuals of psychiatry because they are supported by every tenet of our civilization. They are[21] sure of themselves in real life in a way that is possible only to those who are oriented to the points of the compass laid down in their own culture. Nevertheless a future psychiatry may well ransack our novels and letters and public records[22] for illumination upon a type of abnormality to which it would not otherwise give credence. In every society it is among this very group of the culturally encouraged and fortified that some of

[16] Benedict uses passive voice, but still her prose retains clarity and elegance.

[17] A striking contrast—Puritan divines and convicts, along with the "egoists" who form the subject of the paragraph.

[18] "Mental warping" is a good phrase.

[19] Climax effectively used here.

[20] "Impress . . . indelible"—another strong metaphor.

[21] Anaphora is effective.

[22] Interesting idea and metaphor—a "future psychiatry" "ransacking" our culture for understanding.

the most extreme types of human behavior[23] are fostered. (256)

Edward Kasner and James Newman, *Mathematics and the Imagination*, 1940

To grasp the meaning and importance of mathematics, to appreciate its beauty and its value, arithmetic must first be understood, for mostly, since its beginning, mathematics has been arithmetic in simple or elaborate attire.[24] Arithmetic has been the queen and the handmaiden of the sciences from the days of the astrologers of Chaldea and the high priests of Egypt to the present days of relativity, quanta, and the adding machine.[25] Historians may dispute the meaning of the ancient papyri, theologians may wrangle over the exegesis of Scripture, philosophers may debate over Pythagorean doctrine, but all will concede that the numbers in the papyri, in the Scriptures, and in the writings of Pythagoras are the same as the numbers of today.[26] As arithmetic, mathematics has helped man to cast horoscopes, to make calendars, to predict the risings of the Nile, to measure fields and the height of the Pyramids, to measure the speed of a stone as it fell from a tower in Pisa, the speed of an apple as it fell from a tree in Woolsthorpe,[27] to

[23] At first the vagueness of this might seem too indirect, but upon closer inspection "extreme types of human behavior" works well—has evocative power. What does she have in mind? One can only speculate, but leaving it unsaid makes the horror even greater.

[24] Nice use of metaphor: at first it seems trite, but applied to numbers it has an originality.

[25] "Queen" and "handmaiden" are somewhat ordinary, but the specificity of Chaldea, relativity, and the like, more than make up for it. "Adding machine" dates the piece, I might add.

[26] Again, excellent use of examples set in elegant parallel form.

[27] I like the specificity of "Woolsthorpe," Isaac Newton's hometown.

weigh the stars and the atoms, to mark the passage of time, to find the curvature of space.[28] And although mathematics is also the calculus, the theory of probability, the matrix algebra, the science of the infinite, it is still the art of counting.[29](28)

[28] Effective use of asyndeton.

[29] Striking conclusion to the paragraph: it brings the whole idea back to the opening, but now that idea has become enriched and complicated.

George Orwell, "Politics and the English Language," 1946

The inflated style is itself a kind of euphemism. A mass of Latin words falls upon the facts like soft snow, blurring the outlines and covering up all the details.[30] The great enemy of clear language is insincerity.[31] When there is a gap between one's real and one's declared aims, one turns as it were instinctively to long words and exhausted idioms, like a cuttlefish squirting out ink.[32] In our age there is no such thing as "keeping out of politics." All issues are political issues, and politics itself is a mass of lies, evasions, folly, hatred and schizophrenia.[33] When the general atmosphere is bad, language must suffer. I should expect to find—this is a guess which I have not sufficient knowledge to verify—that the German, Russian, and Italian languages have all deteriorated in the last ten or fifteen years, as a result of dictatorship.[34]

(*Shooting an Elephant* 173–74)

[30] Nice use of metaphor. One can almost see the snow fall.
[31] "Insincerity" is a surprising word here to use as the complement. It's impressive that Orwell brings issues of language use down to such personal, intimate terms.
[32] Again, a strong metaphor. The cuttlefish is repulsive and primitive, at least in this context. (Today's reader might have a greater affinity for it, though, as more and more ocean creatures become threatened or extinct.)
[33] Obviously I am partial to stylists who use lists effectively, and Orwell is one such writer.

[34] A surprise ending, especially given the opening sentence. The paragraph has evolved in a quite unexpected way.

Erving Goffman, *Stigma*, 1963

[I]n an important sense there is only one complete unblushing male[35] in America: a young, married, white, urban, northern, heterosexual Protestant father of college education, fully employed, of good complexion, weight, and height, and a recent record in sports.[36] Every American male tends to look out upon the world from this perspective, this constituting one sense in which one can speak of a common value system in America. Any male who fails to qualify in any of these ways is likely to view himself . . . as unworthy, incomplete, and inferior;[37] at times he is likely to pass and at times he is likely to find himself being apologetic or aggressive[38] concerning known-about aspects of himself he knows are probably seen as undesirable.[39] The general identity-values of a society may be fully entrenched nowhere, and yet they can cast some kind of shadow on the encounters encountered everywhere in daily living.[40] (128–29)

[35] "Complete unblushing male" is an odd, yet captivating phrase, at once metaphorical and precise.

[36] The last attribute lends a comic effect, because usually the most important feature appears last in a list (i.e., if we abide by the formula of climax). The list overall is extraordinary because almost no one reading it will have all these attributes, which might cause a blush!

[37] List includes three adjectives all very close in meaning but subtly different and strategically ordered.

[38] Interesting pairing of opposite attributes.

[39] Goffman packs an enormous amount of information into this sentence. It rewards rereading.

[40] Interesting use of shadow metaphor. Something that does not really exist can cast a shadow—almost illogical, but perhaps effective for that very reason.

John Updike, "Hub Fans Bid Kid Adieu," 1965

Fisher, after his unsettling wait, was low with the first pitch. He put the second one over, and Williams swung mightily[41] and missed. The crowd grunted, seeing that classic swing, so long and smooth and

[41] Updike risks the trite here. This "swung mightily" recalls "Casey at the Bat." But like Ted Williams, Updike knows what he's doing. The clumsy appearing language replicates the clumsiness of Williams's first swing.

quick,[42] exposed. Fisher threw the third time, Williams swung again, and there it was. The ball climbed on a diagonal line into the vast volume of air[43] over center field. From my angle, behind third base, the ball seemed less an object in flight than the tip of a towering, motionless construct, like the Eiffel Tower or the Tappan Zee Bridge.[44] It was in the books while it was still in the sky. Brandt ran back to the deepest corner of the outfield grass, the ball descended beyond his reach and struck in the crotch where the bullpen met the wall, bounced chunkily,[45] and vanished. (316)

Bela Hap, "Structuralist Meta-Analysis," 1972

As a starting point of our present analysis, we only ascertain that the first sentence of the analysis in question comprises twenty-three words. Further quantitative research will point out that the number of words in the following (that is, the present) sentence is only twenty-two.[46] Our working hypothesis, or what Mukařovsky called "semantic gesture," is that the number of words diminishes by one in consecutive sentences.

$$S_x = S\ (x - 1) - 1 \qquad [47]$$

The correctness of our hypothesis should be first checked in this sentence: the number of words, as ex-

[42] Polysyndeton effective. Mirrors swing of bat.

[43] "Vast volume of air" is a lovely expression, alliterative and vivid. It calls to mind the largeness of Fenway, the potential expansiveness of all outdoor baseball parks.

[44] This vivid metaphoric imagining conveys the author's awe at the same time that it describes the high, majestic arc of the ball. I like the choice of the Tappan Zee, too, since that slows the reader down, allowing you to grasp the bridginess of the Tappan Zee, rather than letting you glide over it, as you might were it the Brooklyn Bridge, say. Also the Tappan Zee doesn't have the same historic associations as the Brooklyn Bridge, at least not for me, and can be just an architectural construction, not so much a cultural one.
[45] "In the books . . . in the sky": syntactically parallel but stylistically contrasting and striking. "Chunkily" is interesting, a strange usage I would label hypallage, though it might be used onomatopoetically here.

[46] Clearly, this is a humorous piece, though its not announcing that fact immediately is a good stylistic maneuver.

[47] The equation is hilarious, still seriocomic, but just the sort of thing that you'd find in literary theory of the last generation.

pected, is twenty. The present sentence, by necessity, consists of nineteen words, as it will be borne out by a careful examination. The task that remains is then to check through the methodical analysis of each further surmise, the hypothesis. In other words, the following sentences should be the verbal equivalents of the mathematical formula given above. Examples for examination need to be brought in from a sufficiently wide ranging field of utterances. The validity of the formula will of course greatly depend on the liberality of selection. This view was kept in mind when choosing the present sentence of fourteen words. As the investigation advanced, the validity of the formula tended to become evident. This sentence, consisting of twelve words, was found at an advanced stage.[48] Even more promising results came when we explored a new medium. Like the present statement, unquestionably made up of ten words. Then, not surprisingly, followed an evidence of nine words. The eight words here came almost as natural. Expectedly, there are seven in this one. One, two, three, four, five, six. One, two, three, four, five.[49] There are four here. This seems reasoning. Proved indeed. Undeniable.[50] (310)

[48] By now, you've figured out the organizing "trick" to the passage, so Hap must conceive of a way to further surprise and amuse.

[49] Now you are wondering: how silly will this get? Why do I read on? But read on you do.
[50] Ending on one word is effective—it gives an added punch to the paragraph. Since the whole paragraph is absurd, though, the ending is ironic: it has rhetorical punch but lacks semantic justification.

It struck me that when a piece is "pure style" or is composed simply to exemplify some kind of stylistic theory—a situation that rarely arises—the results are quite remarkable, even humorous. According to Bela Hap, what he wrote forms "part of a single work, called

Meta-Anthology; the common idea in the single parts of it is the endeavor to draw (perhaps somewhat ironical) conclusions from the philosophical condition of today, in which *thought is reduced to language*" (qtd. by Kostelanetz 464).

Wisława Szymborska, "A Tale Retold," 1989

Job, afflicted in body and possessions, curses his fate as a man. That is great poetry.[51] His friends come to him and, rending their mantles, probe Job's guiltiness before the Lord. Job cries out that he has been a righteous man. Job does not know wherefore the Lord has smitten him, Job does not want to speak with them. Job wants to speak with the Lord.[52] The Lord appears riding the chariot of a whirlwind. Unto that man, open to the very bone[53], He praises His creation: the heavens, the seas, the earth and the beasts. And especially Behemoth, and in particular Leviathan, pride-inspiring monsters. That is great poetry.[54] Job listens—the Lord does not speak to the point, for the Lord does not wish to speak to the point. Hence Job makes haste to abase himself before the Lord. Now events follow swiftly. Job regains his asses and his camels, his oxen and his sheep, all increased twofold. The grinning skull begins to take on flesh. And Job assents. Job resigns himself. Job does not want to spoil a masterwork.[55] (49)

[51] The short sentence as the second one in the paragraph has a strong impact. Usually the second sentence of a paragraph is lengthier.

[52] Note use of anaphora—effective.

167

[53] An odd turn of phrase and striking metaphor.

[54] Note how this repetition of the second sentence ties the paragraph together.

[55] Ironic ending, I would say. It is a logical ending that ends up being a bit surprising just the same. The repeated use of anaphora again ties the paragraph together cohesively.

Charles Frazier, Introduction to the
Book of Job, 1999

But his [God's] long speech offers hope for an alternative reading, one that proposes quite a different channel of communication than the one Job recommends. What God holds out for consideration is Creation, all that is the world, its bigness and smallness, its infinite detail, its differing statements of motif and theme, their complex variation and repetitions,[56] beauty and terror intermixed.[57] It is a construct so finely made that even its wild and violent and enormous elements—Leviathan is an example God offers with particular pleasure—contain in their details the smallest and most delicate elements, for the eyes of the monster are "like the eyelids of morning" (41:18). God is rightfully pleased with the concept and execution of water in its various forms, rain and dew and ice and frost. His pride is the understandable pride of the artist who has succeeded in creating a whole world. The details of horse anatomy, he feels, worked out particularly well:[58] "The glory of his nostrils is terrible" (39:20). . . . Look at it all, God seems to be saying. Don't trouble me with reason; what you need to know is there in the arts and the mystery and the ultimate unknowableness of my elegant design.[59] Love it and fear it. Submit to it.[60] (xv–xvi)

[56] Good list here using asyndeton. Note also use of climax.
[57] Use of appositive is also effective. At first it does not appear to be an appositive (i.e., a repetition of noun phrases), which makes it stand out even more.

[58] Frazier is being a little humorous here, I think, but it's effective to see the Book of Job in this light, since it's so often taken with such dread seriousness.
[59] Note use of polysyndeton.
[60] Last two sentences are short, strong, punchy: they contain and convey the authority that God has over Job, indeed, over all creation, Frazier seems to suggest.

David Foster Wallace, "Consider the Lobster," 2004

As I see it, it probably really is good for the soul to be a tourist, even if it's only once in a while.[61] Not good for the soul in a refreshing or enlivening way, though, but rather in a grim, steely-eyed, let's-look-honestly-at-the-facts-and-find-some-way-to-deal-with-them way.[62] My personal experience has not been that traveling around the country is broadening or relaxing, or that radical changes in place and context have a salutary effect, but rather that intranational tourism is radically constricting, and humbling in the hardest way—hostile to my fantasy of being a real individual, of living somehow outside and above it all.[63] (Coming up, is the part that my companions find especially unhappy and repellent, a sure way to spoil the fun of vacation travel:)[64] To be a mass tourist, for me, is to become a pure late-date American: alien, ignorant, greedy for something you cannot ever have, disappointed in a way you can never admit.[65] It is to spoil, by way of sheer ontology, the very unspoiledness you are there to experience.[66] It is to impose yourself on places that in all noneconomic ways would be better, realer without you. It is, in lines and gridlock and transaction after transaction,[67] to confront a dimension of yourself that is as inescapable as it is painful: As a tourist, you become economically significant but existentially loathsome, an insect on a dead thing.[68] (56n)

[61] Note the conversational opening.

[62] A sentence fragment, effective here in that its fragmentary nature not only calls attention to itself but also emphasizes the unusual modification: stringing together fourteen words connected with hyphens in order to make an adjective works suprisingly well.

[63] This sentence with its "ideal/real" halves—the first half mentioning the supposed benefits of tourism, and the second half noting the actuality of how it makes Wallace feel—mirrors Wallace's mixed feelings and discomfort.

[64] A total prohibition in most writing, announcing in a parenthesis a comment on what it is you are going to do. But it works: it makes me eager to see what "repellent" comment he intends to make. He ends with a nonstandard punctuation, a colon inside a closed parenthesis, furthering the oppositional nature of his position.

[65] Asyndeton and climax. The shift to the second person also has the effect of redirecting the emphasis: it's not just about Wallace and his experience, but about yours, too.

[66] "By way of sheer ontology" and "unspoiledness" push this sentence into hypallage, I think— and it's effective in its deformation of language.

[67] Polysyndeton.

[68] Climax.

Wallace is writing hard here. "[E]conomically significant but existentially loathsome: an insect on a dead thing" powerfully juxtaposes abstract idea and vivid image. And the insect image brings us back to the essay itself, recalling one of its best sentences: "The point is that lobsters are basically giant sea-insects" (55), and the funny footnote to *it*, relating how in Maine, people invite others over for lobster by saying, "Come around on Sunday and we'll cook up some bugs" (55n). I should mention here that this is a footnote in an essay about the Maine Lobster Festival. It appeared in *Gourmet*, perhaps an unusual venue for such a piece. (In the October issue it emerges that the magazine received more letters to the editor about Wallace's piece than they had ever received about a single article.) Wallace examines how we as a nation deal with food, and with all the largely hidden from us information as to where it comes from. He traveled to Maine on assignment from the magazine; he was, essentially a paid tourist. Hence the footnote about tourism serves as a comment on the country and a reflection on self.

Keep in mind that style cannot totally displace or usurp the argument because then—well, then there'd be no argument. (You've heard the phrase "empty rhetoric.") But style can scaffold, buttress, drive home argument in a forceful and memorable way, and that's the effect of Wallace's prose here. It's an imaginative style that complements an imaginative argument. Read the passage again, and you'll see: its homespun, aw-shucks opening and the cagey conversational parenthetical only serve to make more surprising and palpable the shock of the last image: tourist as maggot. Scary. But that's the point: tourism is scary, for what it does to the places being visited, for what it does to the tourists themselves.

*   *   *

What can I add after having looked at these examples? First, I'm surprised by how many of the figures of speech they employ. I hadn't thought these examples would be quite so formally ornate. In addition, I notice that metaphor stands out as being one very powerful tool, and virtually all of these writers use it exceptionally well. These writers also show impressive variation in the way that they use lists, often bringing together rather disparate items. Too, there's an attention to making the language of the writing, even the sound of the writing, replicate something of that writing's content. And finally, what I am not surprised about, really, is the very element of surprise: these writers all catch the reader off guard, using some surprising turn of phrase, metaphor, or linkage—or sometimes returning to the thought that started their paragraph, now that it has been modified in a surprising way.

But more surprising still is the way these authors do all sorts of things that I listed among "prohibitions." They use passive voice, "to be" verbs, prepositional phrases, even some slang and trite language. So much for the "rules." I don't think this means, however, that you should violate the rules with abandon, but rather, certain moves you make can more than compensate for your breaking those rules. Or maybe I mean something larger, more amorphous: a good style doesn't consist of following rules or taking care not to violate prohibitions; it consists of finding an original, striking, and genuine voice—your own—and giving that voice the opportunity to make an impression on your reader.

12

Concluding a Manifesto: The Future of Writing

In his above-quoted and rightly famous essay "Politics and the English Language" (1946), George Orwell contends that "the present political chaos is connected with the decay of language" (*The Orwell Reader* 366). I wonder how right he is, how prophetic his words have really been. My suspicion is that if everyone spoke and wrote completely lucid prose, or prose even better—say, on the superb level of Orwell's own—we would still be troubled with war, inhumanities, disease, poverty, and famine.

Of course Orwell does not contend that political chaos caused decay of language, only that the two events are connected. Yet I think the two elements cause each other, are linked in an ever-downward-spiraling vortex. I believe, for example, that to use logical fallacies is to damage the public discourse, as it creates an atmosphere that diminishes freedom of thought. It adds to the overall mechanism in our culture that grants the fake more value than the actual, and that demonstrates what matters is putting things over on an audience, engineering cons, or flat-out lying to get what you want. As Lauri M. Mattenson writes in a trenchant piece, "Teaching Student Writers to Be Warriors," "Unfortunately, [students] are learning that success means mastering the system rather than their own impulses; that they should seek money, not meaning; and that as long as they shut up and figure out what the teacher wants, they'll get their stamp of approval" (B10). And later, Mattenson distills the situation even further. She says that students have "become calculated, not motivated" (B10). It's as if we as a society—even in college classrooms—are endorsing the credo of the late Vince Lombardi, "Winning isn't everything, it's the only thing."

I strenuously disagree. Winning is not everything. What about

Pyrrhic victory—the victory at incalculable cost and enormous loss: hardly worthwhile, is it? What about cheating? If you win a debate but argue unfairly, is this a good thing? If you win a game by cheating, is that good? What would Lombardi himself say? In a society in which winning is the only thing, one might think that cheating to win is acceptable. When did obsession with winning eclipse our interest in the truth? Even the arena that uses argument as a staple—namely, the law—is not interested in discovering the truth. Rather, it's interested in what a jury can be convinced of. Federal Appeals Court judge Jerome Frank captures this idea when he writes,

> [T]he lawyer aims at victory, at winning in the fight, not at aiding the court to discover the facts. He does not want the trial court to reach a sound educated guess, if it is likely to be contrary to his client's interests. Our present trial method is thus the equivalent of throwing pepper in the eyes of a surgeon when he is performing an operation. (736)

This description of our legal system suggests that Mr. Lombardi's doctrine is revered not only in high schools or on football fields, but also in that supposedly sacrosanct arena of justice—the courtroom. Frank's attack on our arbiters of the truth and justice does not stop there: he contends that, even worse than manipulating facts in the interest of winning, our system unfairly denies access to the facts to those who lack the funds for legal discovery. And remember, a trial, one would think, is intended to uncover "what really happened." Indeed, when I taught in the prison system in Indiana, the standard inmate joke was that convicts could pay their way to a shorter sentence, and those behind bars were only the ones who lacked sufficient funds. Admittedly, none of this seems too surprising in the post–O. J. Simpson trial United States, but I bring it up to remind you that if a society values winning above all else, then logic, reason, and careful argument are only tiny fingers in a dike whose entire structure is as susceptible to pancaking as were the Twin Towers.

Our own age, saddled as much as Orwell's with political chaos—what age has not been?—differs, perhaps, from that of sixty years ago in the following manner: too many people don't want to challenge the system and show where it is unfair, crazy. They have become complacent, self-satisfied—indolent with their own relative success. They don't want to confront existing assumptions. They don't want to challenge the president or the Supreme Court. As entertainer Britney Spears remarks in *Fahrenheit 9/11*, Michael Moore's great but tendentious 2004 film, "I think we should trust the president." Yes, that's the mantra: trust those in authority, especially in times of duress; let them make the decisions that will affect our lives. People don't want to do their own thinking, much less their own writing, about the issues of the day. People don't want to read material that will shake up their preconceived ideas—it's not too surprising that they don't habitually do a lot of research or thinking on their own.

Well, that's natural, isn't it? We have jobs to do; we have lives to live. What am I recommending here—that people spend huge amounts of time in libraries or hammering out manifestos?

No. What I want to convey, though, that writing about things—books, art, ideas, relationships, houses, poems, politics, movies—represents an important first step. It seems a small step, but it really can be that "giant leap for mankind," in the words of Neil Armstrong. Writing can allow you to discover what you really feel about the world around you, and once you discover this, maybe you can work for change. Try it: go to a movie and then write up a review of it; send it to your local paper. Odds are it won't get published, but that isn't the important thing. Watch a speech on TV and then write a review of it for an Op-Ed page, as if you were a pundit. What's important is that by writing the review, you will have discovered something about yourself, something that you didn't know before. At the same time, you will have discovered (or do I mean "uncovered," "excavated"?) details about the movie, the speech, that you had forgotten. In short, you will have made your experience more valuable because more complete, more understood, more articulated. And your review might get published at that.

Many people just don't have to write anymore, except in schools and colleges, experiences that are for most too brief. What happens when people don't write? They have others do their thinking for them. They have computers fix their sentences and correct their spelling. They accept written communications from companies or organizations and submit to the authority of that institutional rhetoric. They hire attorneys to write for them, attorneys who themselves often have to rely on associates or paralegals to do the actual composition. Writing is passed down and passed down, and the result is that no one thinks for himself or herself, and society lurches along more and more mindlessly. Once I had a student (whose name I've slightly changed to protect his identity) submit his paper with his own name grievously misspelled. His name was, let's say, Don Wavely, yet his paper had on it "Don Waffle" "What's this?" I demanded in front of the class, perhaps a little peremptorily. "Didn't you write this? Don't you know how to spell your own name?" "Yes," he stammered. "It's just that the computer highlighted my name as a misspelling and suggested 'Waffle' instead. I automatically took its suggestion." Everyone laughed; they had been there.

"Automatically took its suggestion": is this the latter-day version of the Nuremberg Defense? Computers, which when they first appeared seemed like a technology without much application to our daily routines (people stored recipes on them), have now begun to dominate our lives, especially our writerly lives. We're doing a lot of writing now that we used not to do—consider the omnipresence of email, for example—but the things that computers focus on differ from what we as humans focus on. I can't log in to my email unless, for example, I spell my password exactly right. It has to be in the right case too—all lowercase, for mine. If I put in my name into Google but misspell it Coiffi, I get nothing, except perhaps "do you mean *coffee*?" The computer demands accuracy, repeatability ("What is your password? Retype your password"), simplicity. And if you as a computer user meet its demands, you are amply rewarded; you can get information from a Web site; you can compose an email; you can do on-line shopping. But these are relatively simple, not to say simplistic, goals. What has happened to the complex crafting of language?

I have subtitled this work a "manifesto" for various reasons. Primarily, it seems to me you are no longer so willing as you used to be to voice an opinion. At the same time that you shy away from argument, you are surrounded by disputatiousness and incivility, especially in the media and in the political arena. Perhaps that's why you have shied away from argument—you're sick of it! You want answers, to be sure, to various problems, just so long as they are not circuitous, windy "long answers." You want straightforward answers. This is reasonable enough. But when it comes to composing your own work, you also shy from "long answers"; you don't want to fight and struggle to defend a position. You don't want to be afflicted with what the critic David Bleich calls "chronic on-the-other-handism." It's much easier for you—and it's also often rewarded—to come up with short versions, with the already established, the somewhat derivative, the unassuming: with what you have been told to do or write.

I'm encouraging you to break out of this attitude. We as a culture bolster it, I know, forcing you—and everyone else—into a position of being cowed by information, knowledge, words. Think of how the media intervenes, tells us what to think: after every speech, after every play in every game, an "expert" is on hand to explain significance. This hardly encourages your freedom of thought. What happened to the days of yore—did these ever exist?—when people could just listen to a baseball game or political speech and make of it what they would? Of course, we might turn to the most articulate or the most informed among us to hear what she or he had to say, but at some point, each of us would play that very role.

And it is just that role—the amateur but revered thinker—that seems to be disappearing in our culture. Why think "outside the box" if the box thinks so very well for us and does so in color, to boot? Why imagine a solution if in fact eighteen thousand different solutions emerge at the right cue of a search engine? Why not change the inquiry so that one of those answers will work? Indeed, perhaps the writing class of the future will work on honing student "search phrase" skills, so that students can suck information from the Internet (or whatever it will be called) with greater efficiency and speed. Actually, this isn't a bad thing, just so long as it doesn't usurp independent thought.

Perhaps, though, we can take a page or maybe a silicon chip out of the computer's book. Consider, for example, what's known as fuzzy logic. Can this help with writing, with creativity?

In a lecture at Bard College in August of 2004, computer science professor Sven Anderson laid out two important principles of fuzzy logic:

1. An agent must sometimes act nonoptimally to explore his or her world.
2. Agents in fact develop representations and actions via experience.

To put these ideas into alignment with some ideas about writing, it seems to me that the second suggests that while writing (i.e., going thought the experience of setting out your thesis, laying out the evidence for it and against it, etc.), you need to leave yourself open for modifying your ideas, developing them via the experience of writing. (Think of the blueprint or road map thesis in relation to this!)

Anderson's first idea, about agents acting "nonoptimally," has even more relevance, since indeed, as you do your writing, you'll be best off if you explore stuff that might not first off seem directly relevant, if you go down some apparent blind alleys, if you write in tangential relation to or around an issue rather than necessarily directly to it. This might involve taking the other side, inventing a new persona to deal with the issues at hand, possibly even embracing areas of your subject that seem most hostile to your sensibilities, full of sharp spikes and thorns, in a manner of speaking. Using some equivalent to fuzzy logic allows you to handle material that you can't immediately classify; it forces you to engage a broader range of possible examples. Mathematician Deborah J. Bennett gets at the same idea: "Fuzzification," she writes, "takes into account the imprecision of data, the vagueness of language, and the uncertainty inherent in systems. Where two-valued Boolean logic is sufficient for worlds with two states such as true and false, fuzzy logic allows us to deal with shades of gray" (173). Indeed, the argumentative paper's structure itself replicates how fuzzy logic works: as writers of argument, we live, we thrive, in that gray zone.

But fuzzy logic really applies not only to writing but to the creative process as well. I mean, how is it that people come up with new ideas? How is it that that "aha!" experience works for some so often, so regularly, while for others that experience is a rarity? When Thomas McMahon writes (in *Ira Foxglove*), "ideas always show up like that, absolutely free . . . , very often, in a nearly final form," is he describing only the experience of the creative genius, or does what he suggests apply (at least potentially) to everyone? It seems to me that all too often that experience is indeed a rarity—people basically just repeat what they have heard. Our culture has deposited in us all a certain residue, but that residue, it seems, has begun to crowd out ourselves. Or to use a different metaphor, culture speaks through us, as if we were loudspeakers, and now we've all been reduced to bookshelf-sized units.

Can we provide an output that really exceeds, goes beyond what was "programmed in" by culture and education? John Stuart Mill suggests that we are getting more and more trapped by culture (and this was in 1859—what would he think today?):

> The circumstances which surround different classes and individuals, and shape their characters, are daily becoming more assimilated. Formerly, different ranks, different neighborhoods, different trades and professions lived in what might be called different worlds; at present, to a great degree, in the same. Comparatively speaking, they now read the same things, listen to the same things, see the same things, go to the same places, have their hopes and fear directed to the same objects, have the same rights and liberties, and the same means of asserting them. . . . Every extension of education promotes it, because education brings people under common influences and gives them access to the general stock of facts and sentiments. Improvements in the means of communication promote it, by bringing inhabitants of distant places into personal contact. The increase of commerce and manufactures promotes it, by diffusing more widely the advantages of easy circumstances . . . [T]here ceases to be any social support for nonconformity—any substantive power in society which, itself opposed to the ascendancy of numbers, is interested in taking under its protection opinions and tendencies at variance with those of the public. (70–71)

Mill's got his finger not only on the touch pad but on the pulse of what's going on today. No one wants to be different, nonconformist. And the way this plays out in writing is that no one wants to take the unusual path, the not-obviously-optimal solution.

Maybe we need to go beyond the idea of fuzzy logic, of making inferences based on incomplete data or of doing stuff that is not immediately or obviously relevant to the task. That's the fuzzy logic of computer programs, of refrigerators. We need what I'm going to call a "fuzzy subjectivity." We need not just to write around an issue, not just to dig a hole in a new place rather than dig the same hole deeper (*pace* Edward deBono); no, we need to reimagine the shovel, the hole, the act of digging, even the self. We have to see creativity as involved with reimagining who we are, leaving our subjective self behind, inhabiting not just other personalities but other races, other species. Hence the act of imagining isn't just one of digging a hole yourself but of say, gyring and gimbling in a wabe, of finding the most apt slithy tove, of total self-Jabberwockification. I don't yet know what any of that means: you tell me.

If there were a formula for exceeding our cultural programming, then that would not be exceeding our cultural programming. Just bending down, grasping your legs and looking through them behind you at an upside down world—as Henry David Thoreau supposedly suggested we do—is not quite enough: we need also to use different eyes, and something other than the usual parts of our brain need to record what it is that's perceived.

But I don't think the battle must be lost. There is a lot of "headroom" still left for most of us, and I hope to have suggested some positive ways to tap into it.

First, you need to allow yourself the opportunity to be creative, on your own. Think of that nine-dot grid, and then think, just for fun, of five ways other than those I mentioned earlier to solve the problem. The key to thinking outside the box is just this: there is no "outside" and no "inside"—it's all just thinking; the box itself is a mere construct. And what is "the" box? In what sense is the deictic "the" meant? Are inside and outside in real opposition? Think about this: could you think both inside and outside simultaneously? Isn't the whole model just a little too three-dimensional in a multidimensional universe? Don't be afraid to pursue paths that seem to lead nowhere. Go down them, explore them; look for interesting flora and fauna along the way. Maybe you'll meet something odd too— an iguana, a dodo, a tapir, a tapir that talks, an android dodo from the future. Lots of things emerge, not only serendipitously, but because taking the odd path is in itself a creative act.

Yet you can't allow yourself to be seduced by your own ideas, your own cleverness or creativity: question what you're doing, what you've written, what turns of argument you have taken. Don Quixote makes a flimsy helmet for himself early in Cervantes' novel, and then he goes after it with his sword to see whether it can stand the rigors of combat. He destroys it utterly. He rebuilds it, but the second version he decides not to test, assuming that it will work just fine. To offer ideas to an audience without subjecting them at least to your own toughest testing strikes me as equally deluded. My second suggestion, then, is that you very seriously consider what kinds of objections will be raised against your ideas, what sorts of counterexamples might be brought to bear, what ways you will have to accommodate these wrinkles, modify your own position, backtrack, or defend yourself—remember Mill's 75 percent rule. I know these are all challenging, potentially exhausting things to put yourself through, but what creative endeavor is not?

And that creativity applies to research, too. My third suggestion is that you don't want to just accumulate small mountains of data, piles of books, printouts, photocopies. No. You want to make some sense of it all. You do this by having some angle on the issue before you do research, or by discovering an angle early in your investigation. Don't worry about material that you discover and don't use: waste is as necessary to the research/writing process as it is to life. And what you think might be wasted could in fact turn out to be useful at some other point. In your research, you need to direct your inquiry, looking not just for material or evidence, but for issues that have some controversy for you, some points of fracture, some fault lines. You say, "How can I challenge existing research, research by experts in the field?" and my response is that as you do research, you will discover that there are many angles and points of view; scholars ("experts") challenge and undermine and argue with one another all the time. There really is something wonderfully democratic (or maybe I mean meritocratic) about scholarship, for as you do research, you become a scholar too. As you discover what it is that others are arguing about, you at once clarify your own point of view and open up a new area for research.

At the same time, you need to be honest in your research, honest with how you present the opposition, honest in the language that you use. As the economics writer and editor Peter J. Dougherty remarks in a recent article about globalization studies, "flimsy arguments can have disastrous worldly consequences, but . . . sound and innovative ideas can yield untold benefits" (chronicle.com). You might think that your ideas don't matter, that no one is listening, or that the impact you create will be negligible, a tree falling in a forest on an uninhabited planet. Think again. To vary Henry Adams's dictum about teachers, a *writer* never knows when his or her influence will stop—or even start. Professor Mark Edmundson remarks sagely: "Words are potent. Ten years after the fact, people often can't remember a grievous pain. . . . But a decade on, they'll remember every word and tonal twist of a painful insult" (12). No, words have tremendous power, and the Jim B.'s of the world, who think that "wordsmithing" should be left to minor functionaries (see chapter 2), might consider not just the impact of powerful written documents but the anguished anfractuosities of everyday discourse.

A fourth suggestion: you need to keep your audience in mind, but you also need to balance your sensitivity to them against the freedom to tell them something they do not know beforehand. If you intend to disagree with the audience's opinion, or with "received opinion," that's fine—you can respect that view and show in what ways it is not adequate or true. But too often it seems to me people say or write only what they think others will want to hear, that is, only a confirmation of the audience's perceived values and ideas. How does that kind of activity advance knowledge, complicate thought about an issue, solve ongoing problems? If your audience does not want to be challenged, not even a little, here's my suggestion: find a new audience. If the nonchallengeable audience is your college professor, drop the course. If it's your parents, don't engage them in debate. If it's your friends, run with a new crowd. If it's your boss, get another job. I know this might be hard. Think of my suggestion as tough writing instructor love.

And finally, I make an appeal here for some attentiveness to language, to its style, its music, its beauty. Probably half of my impulse in writing this book was to find a vehicle by which I could quote from authors such as James, Nabokov, Goffman, Updike, Orwell. As I wrote, I found that what links most of these writers' work can be distilled into a single word: surprise. They surprise me. Their writing, even when I reread it for the seventeenth time, catches me up short, makes me catch my breath. Their works do not follow predictable verbal circuits; they spark up insights that I could not have foretold. You can find your own touchstones, your own authors who speak to you and for you.

And that, perhaps, is what heartens me, what makes me think that writing, that argument, that "style" are not obsolete notions, dying icons worshiped only by fuddy-duddies who still read books. Rather, many years after having been composed, the words and the works they're from still breathe, still give off the pungent odor of well-wrought things that require labor to make, and still send their idea-infused tendrils into our modern brains. And they link us, if briefly, to the genius of inventiveness, the weird unknowability of language well used, the vision of which will always be the human condition—to live in an instantly dissolving present informed by a not-well-enough-understood past and face a projected but ultimately unpredictable future. In a metaphysical sense, it's as if the near infinity of all past space-time has suddenly pinched in to a single point—a vanishing point, a present at which you now sit—and on the other side of this point looms an equally vast, or maybe even vaster, expanse of space-time, a projected future. Your writing can capture that present and solidify it, freeze-frame it, imbue it with meaning for the imagined future. And if your writing says something new, you can change that future, can make it worth living in and into. You can make it—yours.

I

Sample Essays

I include here two sample papers, one a comparison-contrast essay by Ryan Marrinan, and the other a research paper by Lisa Korn. The students wrote these in my freshman writing seminar at Princeton University, Medical Narratives. In glosses, I append some commentary of my own. Both of these are good papers, and the students did well in the class. Their papers manipulate complex concepts and grapple with genuinely difficult issues. However, the papers are not "perfect" ones: Ryan's could use a stronger argumentative edge, and Lisa's could offer a somewhat clearer line of development. Both need to have stronger conclusions. And both would benefit from the inclusion of more counterarguments, which would provide a better means of arriving at some conclusion that matters.

The format of the papers—the use of notes, the works cited, the reference form, spacing of quotations, and the like—will be somewhat different for you, since these pages are typeset. Make sure that you follow the form your professor or discipline requires.

Ryan Garrett Marrinan
April 1, 2004
Professor Cioffi
WRI 132

Thin Ice above the Atomic Flux Genius and Madness in "Gehenna" and "Carcinoma Angels"

Humans organize.° Inherent to our very nature is the endless struggle against hateful disorder. As a result, we have divided our world into continents, countries, provinces, counties, and cities. Each of these divisions has a name

This seems to me a strong start—a two-word sentence that really grabs the reader.

and can be neatly classified in such comfortable terms as population, gross domestic product, per capita income, culture, government, and language. The many faces that form our societies are striated into classes, hierarchies, and authorities. Even our very bodies amount to nothing more than manifestations of this propensity to order, as the metabolic functions floating us above the atomic flux are organized into the conveniently packaged baggies of haphazardly moving molecules that we call organs. In essence we are nothing more than compartmentalized chaos, units of staggering genius and rational order dangling precariously over a sea of cellular madness.°

Though our hearts and minds are constantly bent on combating this chaos, few of us even realize that a war is underway. Those aware of our fragile situation we laud as geniuses. With their singular understanding they simultaneously comprehend the disparate patterns and hierarchies that define our universe. Conrad Aiken's "Gehenna" and Norman Spinrad's "Carcinoma Angels" describe with striking similarity two such individuals of unparalleled understanding, of genius, though superficially the two short stories seem as though they should have little in common. Despite their exceptionally keen conception of the world, the nameless protagonist of "Gehenna" and Harrison Wintergreen of "Carcinoma Angels" demonstrate that no matter how assiduously human beings endeavor to greatness, striving to synthesize the macrocosm into a cohesive and ordered whole, they will ultimately and inexorably be reduced to their chaotic internal biology. Moreover, the further we proceed in this quest for perfection, the more we think we transcend our random chemical processes, the closer we come to transgressing the thin barrier that separates genius from utter madness.°

A comparison between the works of Conrad Aiken and Norman Spinrad is an unlikely one. Aiken, an American Pulitzer Prize–winning poet, served during his lifetime as the poetry consultant of the Library of Congress, a position that has now become the United States Poet Laureate,

A bit overwritten here. While this paper demonstrates a great power with words, Ryan has a tendency toward slightly ornate language. It's fun to read, but it's a little excessive for the kind of paper he's writing. I guess what it comes down to is a very simple issue: does the language distract from what he's trying to say? Here, and elsewhere, it does, a bit. But this is a good kind of problem.

These last ten lines are the paper's thesis. It seems argumentative and challenging. I would prefer it be a little more focused on the works themselves, but it's clearly imaginative, well placed, and *challenging*.

and his editing of the *Selected Poems of Emily Dickinson* was largely responsible for Dickinson's rise to fame. Spinrad, a relatively obscure science fiction writer, has gained some meager notoriety, if he is known at all, for his raunchy° short stories, the likes of which have been considered too lascivious for *Playboy* (Ellison° 543). Furthermore, the divergent lives of the two authors stand in stark contrast and emerge strongly in their respective writings. When Aiken was only a boy, his father murdered his mother and immediately took his own life afterward. The young Aiken was the first to find the corpses.° Understandably, such a trauma tints Aiken's stories with a certain tenebrous morbidity that unsettles the reader and tends to push him or her away from the work. It is a struggle to empathize with the solitary, nameless, and disquieting character of Aiken's "Gehenna" as he wrestles with the paradox of his own consciousness.

Conversely, Spinrad embodies much of what has become known in popular culture as "The American Dream," leading his editor to call him "a street kid, with the classic hunger for achievement, status, and worldly goods that drives the have-nots to the top" (542). This familiar and classic hunger, rooted deeply in popular culture, manifests itself clearly in Spinrad's heroic character, Harrison Wintergreen, who in only forty-one years succeeds in accomplishing what most individuals could not in forty-one lifetimes.° Employing such a common American success-story archetype, in addition to opening his story with the traditional expression "the world was his oyster" (546), immediately makes Spinrad's "Carcinoma Angels" more welcoming than "Gehenna" and sweeps the reader away on a pop-culture joyride. Thus, "Gehenna" and "Carcinoma Angels" oppose each other not only in terms of genre and authorial biography, but also in terms of their central characters.°

Yet, both characters are fraternal members of an extraordinarily select group, the order of genius. Much more than extreme intelligence defines genius, however, as the

Slang: avoid.

Ryan alludes to the introduction to Spinrad's story, and he should probably provide an "identifier" to explain who Ellison is. Moreover, as the Works Cited is currently set up, a reader seeking an Ellison work will be frustrated.

Source for this information should be given.

Note effective repetition of "forty-one."

I don't think any other student picked these two stories to compare—they are really quite different, and just the fact that Ryan chose them to discuss side by side evidences a creativity on his part: this is an original conception.

"Word" or "label" might be better here.

sacred name° also implies phenomenal creativity and singularity stemming from a thoroughly unique conception of the world. Whether such creativity and unique perspective arise out of great intelligence, diligent labor, or a stroke of luck is irrelevant, for the only way to become a genius is to perceive the world in ways others would never imagine, and a necessary concomitant of this perception is isolation. Without such an unparalleled vision Albert Einstein never could have conceived that space and time formed a continuum in his theory of relativity, nor could Picasso have been called a genius had he not seen the material world through the novel lens of harsh geometric shapes. But because of this same extraordinary conception, such figures are destined to be alone.

Good use of climax.

The simultaneously multi-named and nameless character of "Gehenna" embodies the solitude that defines genius, as he is separated physically, temporally, and perspectivally from the world.° His singularity is apparent from the very first sentence of the narrative: "How easily—reflected Smith, or Jones, or Robinson, or whatever his name happened to be—our little world can go to pieces!" (236). At first glance, having three names seems to imply anything but singularity. Furthermore, the idea that his name is irrelevant seems to immediately convey unto° the story a universality that entices the reader to identify with the character as an extension and personification of the reader's own self. The whole of humanity becomes examples of Smith, or Jones, or Robinson. In actuality, however, the three names' simultaneous namelessness establishes the unparalleled uniqueness of the character, for despite the prevalence of poverty and want in the world, every boy or girl is at least endowed with a name at birth. Thus, the absence of a name establishes the uniqueness associated with genius.° But in fulfillment of the eternal human need to define and categorize, I will refer to the character as Smith for the rest of this paper. More than just namelessness isolates Smith, however, as he is physically separated from the outside world, alone in his small

A bit archaic?

I think Ryan goes on a bit too long about this point. But it's imaginative.

apartment. Moreover, time forms a barrier around the character as well: "It is now—thought Smith, or Jones, or Robinson—past midnight, and this apartment house, with all its curious occupants, is asleep" (238). Thus, Smith's isolation in terms of his name, lonely apartment, and nocturnal nature hints that he may be suffering from the same sort of disconnection with the world that afflicts all men and women of genius.

Isolation does not lead to genius, however, but instead springs from the extraordinary gift of seeing the world in a unique way, and such a gift manifests itself clearly in the character of Smith. From the same quotation at the outset of the story,° one captures a glimpse of Smith's novel perspective characterizing genius, as he puts forth a universal truth about the world—that it can so easily go to pieces. Much of the rest of the narrative serves to emphasize this unique insight, as the character describes his apartment with an extraordinary skepticism that highlights an alternate perception of reality:

> What in heaven's name are all these walls, this floor, the books on my mantelpiece, the three worn wooden chairs, the pencils in a row on my red table? Arrangements of atoms? If so, then they are all perpetually in motion; the whole appearance is in reality a chaotic flux, a whirlwind of opposing forces; they and I are in one preposterous stream together, borne helplessly to an unknown destiny. (238)

Few people see the universe of inanimate material objects as one of chaotic flux, and even fewer perceive humans as beings swept up in the same swiftly moving stream that guides the atoms constituting this piece of paper. Furthermore, one of these precious few is none other than the famed Albert Einstein, whose theories explain the chaotic material flux of light and the parallel stream of time and space. Thus, Smith embodies the fundamental quality of genius with his unique apperception of the world's prepos-

Ryan might remind us what this quotation is. I don't want to flip back to look it up.

terous current and also shares the principal affliction of genius, isolation.

So too is Harrison Wintergreen of "Carcinoma Angels" blessed, or cursed, with a preternatural insight into the nature of the world, and this unique perspective allows him to accomplish the fantastic feats that characterize individuals of genius. His gift is present from a very young age, a frequent indicator of genius perhaps most clearly seen in Mozart. Just as Aiken chooses to do in "Gehenna," Spinrad establishes this novelty of perspective at the very outset of the story, stating in the first sentence: "At the age of nine Harrison Wintergreen first discovered that the world was his oyster when he looked at it sidewise" (544). When Wintergreen perceives the world from a peculiar sidewise point of view he can discern the patterns and truths that allow him to master the universe and capture it in into his very own oyster. The choice of the specific word "sidewise" to qualify the character's perspective is significant as well, as it alludes to the way one tilts one's head when regarding something perplexing—or even ridiculous. Thus, Wintergreen's conception of the ludicrousness of the world, as exemplified by his looking at it sidewise, ties him back to Smith in the realm of genius with the latter's understanding of the "preposterous stream."° Wintergreen not only possesses this extraordinary faculty, however, but harnesses it to his advantage as well, as he succeeds in every endeavor he pursues including becoming filthy rich, doing good, and leaving his footprints in the sands of time.° He emerges as "the J.P. Morgan of baseball cards" at the humble age of nine, "[wins] seven scholarships with foolish ease," launches a successful career in erotic stories after a mere month of study (autobiographical of Spinrad), commands the substantial sum of $200,000 for his first painting, wipes out syphilis in eighteen months with a mutated virus that was "spread by sexual contact" and was a "mild aphrodisiac" (546) and ultimately cures cancer. Impressive even for a man of genius.° Because of a singular sidewise perspective, an ability to laugh at the preponderance of

I don't follow this. Maybe rephrase?

These phrases ("filthy rich," etc.) need to be in quotation marks, since they are directly out of the story.

Note use of sentence fragment for effect.

the ridiculous in the world, Wintergreen discerns the esoteric paths leading to worldly success and as a result should be exalted among the ranks of the geniuses.

Further similar to Smith and other men of superb insight, Wintergreen is utterly alone and estranged from the world. Ultimately, because of the ease with which he surmounts any obstacle placed before him, the macroscopic material world essentially has nothing to offer him, and Wintergreen succumbs to boredom: "At the age of thirty-eight Harrison Wintergreen had Left sufficient Footprints in the Sands of Time. He was bored. He looked around greedily for new worlds to conquer" (547). The claws of isolation envelop Wintergreen on an inter-personal level, as there are no other characters present in the narrative; though if there were other personalities, they would be hopelessly overwhelmed by Wintergreen's own power and charisma, leaving him alone in any case. Spinrad puts a final accent on this separation with his description of the character's state-of-the-art laboratory erected for his battle with cancer, "an air-conditioned walled villa" situated "in the middle of the Arizona desert" (547). Thus, Wintergreen is not only isolated spatially in an indeterminate location, lost amidst an expanse of sand and shrubbery, but he, like Smith, is isolated physically as well, by the walls that surround his residence.° One might be tempted to assert that Wintergreen engenders his own isolation, as he elects to brave the desert and construct his massive, walled complex there.° While it is certainly true that Wintergreen ultimately makes the decision himself, he is compelled to isolation because of his cancer. This compulsion to isolation resulting from an internal physical state is an all too familiar characteristic of disease, and it is exemplified perhaps most clearly in the case of quarantine and in instances of the diseased separating themselves from loved ones because of their immense pain, as in the story of "The Death of Ivan Ilych."° So, through its emphasis of Wintergreen's isolation, "Carcinoma Angels" intimates that genius is somehow linked to disease.°

These two types of isolation don't seem to me sufficiently discrete.

Start of a counter-argument.

Maybe mention that this is a story by Leo Tolstoy.

I'm not sure about the placement of this sentence. It seems to me that it would work better as the topic sentence of a separate paragraph. In fact the whole paragraph might be tightened up some.

Such a relation between genius and disease arises not from causation but from the direct opposition of order and chaos in the microscopic world of our internal bodies. Smith and Wintergreen's perspicacity in discerning the patterns of the macroscopic world leads the two geniuses to the infinitely thin barrier that separates the familiar material world from an internal hell of molecular madness, in which both are reduced strictly to their physical biology.°

Smith is initially much more aware than Wintergreen of this fine barrier. In fact, Smith's entire narrative consists of flirting with this fragile balance between the rational outside world and his own hellish internal Gehenna. Revisiting the first sentence of the story, Smith remarks about the ease in which "our little world can go to pieces" (236), thus establishing the fragility of the microscopic world of the body from the outset. Furthermore he states:

> In an instant it will be as if I had stepped through this bright cobweb of appearance on which I walk with such apparent security, and plunged into a chaos of my own; for that chaos will be as intimately and recognizably my own, with its Smith-like disorder, as the present world is my own, with its Smith-like order. (237)

Here, Smith puts forward the notion of the minutely thin barrier, the cobweb, that separates the illusory security we gain in rationally organizing our world from the utter chaos that lies just under the surface. Furthermore, the fact that this chaos is Smith's very own implies that it is an internal chaos, which further implicates the molecular madness inside his own body as the source. Another example, the troubling image of a marine organism struggling in an aquarium,° illustrates the inevitable reduction of the rational consciousness to the infernal chaos of physical biology:

> In this dream, I am standing before a small glass aquarium, square, of the sort in which goldfish are

kept. I observe without surprise that there is water in one half of it but not in the other. And in spite of the fact that there is no partition, this water holds itself upright in its own half of the tank, leaving the other half empty. More curious than this, however, is the marine organism which lies at the bottom of the water. [. . .] Moreover, I see that this advancing surface is as if sliced off and raw: it is horribly sensitive: and suddenly, appalled, I realize that the whole thing is simply—consciousness. (244)

Thus, consciousness—the human understanding of ourselves and the world that allows us to accomplish the great feats that distinguish us from the bestial world of mere biology—is reduced to a nondescript marine organism lying at the bottom of an aquarium. Moreover, the choice of a marine organism is symbolic because, according to modern biological science, life originated in the seas. Therefore, the fact that consciousness becomes an organism of the ocean makes the link between consciousness and biology painfully obvious. Further, consciousness's resting immobile at the bottom of the tank, an abode for the lowliest of creatures, establishes this relation as one of reduction. Finally, the suspension of the dependable physical force of gravity suggests that a sort of irrationality, or chaos, dominates the situation. Thus, through its reduction of consciousness, the most prized human faculty, to pure and irrational biology, Aiken's "Gehenna" illustrates the truth that no matter how far human beings rise above the chaotic molecular world from which they spring, they will never be capable of overcoming their physicality.°

Though Wintergreen does not initially seem to be as acutely aware of the fragile relationship between success in the macroscopic world and internal biological chaos, he ultimately gains experience of this truth firsthand as he descends into his own body to undertake a hellish battle with cancer. Spinrad's choice of cancer as the disease that ultimately triumphs over the great Harrison Wintergreen

Interesting idea— well phrased. But again, we need to have a counterargument here somewhere.

is crucial to elucidating the truth that molecular chaos will ultimately undermine even the most creative employments of the fruits of human consciousness. Harlan Ellison, Spinrad's editor, refers to cancer as "psychosis on a cellular level" (552), which is a perfect description of perfectly° normal cells in the body making the senseless transformation into cancer, as they essentially go mad and disobey the body's usual requirements for cell replication and achieve immortality. Thus, cancer is the apotheosis of the atomic madness present in our bodies, and it is only fitting that this biological insanity defeats the seemingly invincible Harrison Wintergreen. Exactly like Smith, Wintergreen recognizes the fragile "cobweb of appearance" that separates humankind from this internal cellular madness, as he transgresses the "atom-thin interface ... the analogical translucent membrane between his mind and his internal universe" (551) and enters into his own body. There he finds "white blood cells [careening] by him like mad taxicabs" (551) and cancer cells embodied in bikers clad in all black, the "Carcinoma Angels" that are the internal universe's analog of the Hell's Angels. Thus, Wintergreen comes to realize that the substance of his body is nothing more than molecular chaos, complete with red-eyed cancerous monsters and insane taxicab drivers. Though we are meant to believe that Wintergreen somehow defeats his cancer, as he succeeds in enduring past his allotted cancerous life-span, the battle leaves the character as a "catatonic vegetable" (553); he becomes the marine organism lying on the bottom of the tank, reduced utterly to its own biology.

Human beings are obsessed with order, classification, and rationality because we have an inherent sub-conscious conception that we are somehow defying the laws of nature. The universe moves inexorably to entropy, to disorder, and our physical bodies, bags of molecular chaos° harnessed into the ephemeral clarity we call life, stand in stolid disagreement with this universal truth. Though the average person cannot perceive this reality, geniuses, with

APPENDIX I

Polyptoton.

What a wonderful phrase!

their phenomenally keen perception of nature, can discern the absolute fact that we, as human beings, teeter on an unstable promontory above a vortex of microscopic chaos. The truism asserting that genius is intimately intertwined with madness has arisen for precisely this reason. Geniuses alone perceive the precarious nature of the human situation, and they are therefore left in solitude before the reality of an atom-thin translucent barrier that separates humankind's consciousness from molecular chaos. Thus, "Gehenna" and "Carcinoma Angels," with their characters of genius, serve as cautionary tales warning human beings to be ever mindful of the frightful turbulence that lurks below.°

Works Cited

Aiken, Conrad. *Among the Lost People.* "Gehenna." NY: Scribner's, 1934. 236–245.

Spinrad, Norman. "Carcinoma Angels." *Dangerous Visions.* Ed. Harlan Ellison. NY: Berkley Publishing Corporation, 1967. 541–553.

The conclusion is well phrased, full of interesting language, but ultimately not enough of a ΔT is present.

Lisa Korn
5/3/04
Medical Narratives
Dr. Frank Cioffi

Perceptions and Realities: Patient Attempts to Regain Control after a Cancer Diagnosis

We believe that we have control over the course of our lives.° We live with the expectation that our actions today will have some influence over what happens to us tomorrow. A diagnosis of cancer drastically changes such a perception; as one magazine writer comments, "And frankly, if you're diagnosed with cancer, you have every right to be

A good opening sentence here. It immediately catches the reader's attention.

pissed off. The future you'd been counting on [. . .] could be stolen from you" (Pittaway 36). With "the future" no longer guaranteed, for the patient a sensation of losing control follows. In a study on reactions of couples to a diagnosis of prostate cancer for the husband, Sally L. Maliski, a researcher at UCLA, broadly describes the initial reactions to cancer diagnosis "as loss of control" (393). When cancer disrupts their lives, people attempt in many different ways to regain control. Maliski further distinguishes between types of control: "Actual control exists when a person has the ability to regulate or influence outcomes, whereas perceived control exists when there is the *expectation* of being able to participate in making decisions in order to obtain desirable outcomes" (396). Maliski mainly refers to the fact that patients ultimately must relinquish control to a doctor during surgery. They cannot achieve the self-determination necessary for actual control, and thus can only strive to perceive control over cancer. Yet, in a fictional story by Norman Spinrad, a character with apparent actual control loses, and in real life, when patients use different methods to attain perceived control, different outcomes in quality of life or treatment result.° When examined, the boundary between perceived and actual control easily blurs.°

I don't quite follow this sentence.

Thesis statement. It seems to me that this should be phrased in such a manner that it's more clearly the thesis. The first few times I read the paper, I missed it. It also might be extended: why is the "blurring" so important?

Harrison Wintergreen of Norman Spinrad's "Carcinoma Angels" serves as a model of a patient with actual control over his illness, yet in the end he is no better off for all his autonomy. In fact, Wintergreen seems to control the course of his life: "At the age of thirty Harrison Wintergreen had had it with Do-Gooding. He decided to Leave His Footprints in the Sands of Time. He Left His Footprints in the Sands of Time" (546). Wintergreen effortlessly transforms his decisions into his reality. When he discovers that he has cancer and has one year to live, he refuses to accept death, and executes a series of actions culminating in his mentally entering his own body to cure himself. In this way Wintergreen appears to exert actual control over his cancer; through his actions and attitude he affects the course of the disease. Wintergreen first asserts control by gathering information: "Wintergreen spent the first month of his last year searching for an existing cure to terminal cancer" (547). Accumulating information on his disease empowers him: "He had eliminated the entire external universe as a factor in spontaneous remission in one fell swoop. Therefore, in some mysterious way, the human body and/or psyche was capable of curing itself" (549). Even when he cannot find an existing cure his reading helps inspire him to find his own.

With all the information at his disposal, Wintergreen also transforms the cancer from mysterious and incomprehensible to familiar.° When Wintergreen enters his own body to fight the cancer, he sees "speeding towards him a leering motorcyclist" (551). He has transformed a single cancer cell from a simple cell into a mayhem-wreaking motorcyclist, an intimidating but more familiar sight to human eyes. Wintergreen literally fights his personified cancer: "Wintergreen fought his analogical battles in an equal number of incarnations, as driver, knight, pilot, diver, soldier, mahout, with a grim and savage glee, littering the battlefields of his body with the black dust of the fallen Carcinoma Angels" (552). Though Spinrad writes of "analogical battles," Wintergreen can actually change the course of the cancer through the battles; his analogies give him actual control. Wintergreen's attitude, his fighting spirit and refusal to give up, and also his literal fight with the cancer cells within himself, help him defeat the cancer. Yet Wintergreen's triumph is tinged with tragedy: "Go to the finest sanitarium in the world, and there you will find Harrison Wintergreen, [. . .] catatonic vegetable. Harrison Wintergreen, who stepped inside his own body to do battle with the Carcinoma Angels, and won. And can't get out" (553). Despite his control over the course of his life and his actual control over his cancer, Wintergreen remains trapped in his own body. Perhaps Spinrad attempts to show that true actual control remains unachievable despite evidence suggesting otherwise.° Wintergreen

Clear use of topic sentence. But I'm wanting to see more argument, less summary.

Yes, a good point, perhaps worthy of its own paragraph.

achieves actual control only by retreating into a universe of his own creation.

Like Wintergreen, patients, doctors, and society in general attempt to increase the perception of control over cancer by making cancer seem more familiar in their thoughts and language.° In his book *How We Die: Reflections on Life's Final Chapter*, Sherwin Nuland writes, "Cancer, far from being a clandestine foe, is in fact berserk with the malicious exuberance of killing. [. . .] Its cells behave like the members of a barbarian horde run amok—leaderless and undirected, but with a single-minded purpose: to plunder everything within reach" (207). Nuland personifies cancer, transforming the disease into a formidable enemy, but a beatable one; civilization usually conquers so-called "barbarian hordes." In speaking of cancer's "exuberance" in killing, calling cancer "malicious," and later "wicked" and "malevolent," Nuland appeals to our instinct that good wins over evil (211). If patients see themselves as heroes battling against cancer as a traditional foe, they are more likely to think they are in control. Unlike Wintergreen, however, in real life patients cannot take their redefinitions literally. In recounting her experiences with breast cancer, Barbara Ehrenreich familiarizes cancer even as she mocks the war imagery often used: "The 'enemy,' I am supposed to think—an image to save up for future exercises in 'visualization' of their violent deaths" (68). From her strategic use of quotation marks and emphasis on what she is "supposed" to believe, Ehrenreich makes her sarcasm clear. Yet she soon writes, "I try beaming them [the cancer cells] a solemn warning: [. . .] Keep up this selfish rampage and you go down, every last one of you, along with the entire Barbara enterprise" (69). Ironically, Ehrenreich also personifies cancer, only she gives the disease a different personality than Nuland does. Thinking of cancer as a comprehending, though not necessarily compliant, entity, even in jest, may make Ehrenreich feel more in control.°

In another effort to gain control, patients often re-

Maybe this would be a better thesis statement, if placed a little earlier on. It does have a strong argumentative edge to it.

Nuland's and Ehrenreich's ideas are nicely integrated into paper.

spond to their diagnoses of cancer by gathering information. In the Maliski study, couples first responded to the diagnosis of prostate cancer by researching the cancer (394). Maliski notes that such "data gathering [. . .] increased their perception of control" (395). The couples' research allowed them to conclude that prostate cancer is easier to treat than other cancers, making them feel even more in control, "even though they had no actual control over the cancer or the surgeon" (394, 395). After initially stating that she did not want to gather information on breast cancer as other women did, Ehrenreich writes: "I can't seem to get enough of these tales, reading on with panicky fascination about everything that can go wrong [. . .] I compare myself with everyone, constantly assessing my chances" (69, 73–74). Ironically, Ehrenreich does engage in information gathering despite her initial assertion. Like the prostate cancer patients and their wives, Ehrenreich wants to know "her chances," perhaps in an attempt to perceive control. However, the line between perceived and actual control blurs when patients make decisions based on the information they have gathered.° Ehrenreich, for example, seeks information not only to help determine her chances, but also to find practical advice "on hair loss, lumpectomy versus mastectomy, how to select a chemotherapy regime, what to wear after surgery and eat when the scent of food sucks" (73). The treatment she chooses may affect the course of the cancer, and the clothes she chooses to wear and the food she chooses to eat will affect how she feels, her quality of life. For the prostate cancer patients and their wives in the Maliski study, the couples also searched for the best treatments and surgeons. In making decisions that change their conditions, patients have some form of control.°

The very act of understanding cancer may also affect the results of treatment. In a study conducted by Hitoshi Okamura, from the Psycho-Oncology Division of the National Cancer Center Research Institute East in Japan, breast cancer patients who reported that they did not un-

The "blurring" mentioned in thesis. Perhaps it should've been alluded to earlier.

Last sentence effectively ties together Maliski and Ehrenreich.

derstand the nature of their disease had a lower survival rate than those that did, with all patients having similar medical factors (149). The correlation between understanding and mortality does not imply direct causation. However, there may be an indirect link; patients with inferior understanding may not have been able to speak as well or honestly to their doctors or may not have developed proper "health habits" to combat the cancer (149). Though Okamura does not directly refer to the information gathering emphasized by Maliski, from his results it follows that when patients gather information in attempts to perceive that they are in control, they actually can indirectly help control the cancer through their informed actions and responses to treatments. Okamura also suggests that for patients who did not understand, "It is possible that the patients may not have wanted to understand the bad news" (150). The search for information is a choice on the part of patients; even when patients choose an option less conducive to treatment and survival, they still exercise control.

The separation between perceived and actual control becomes even less distinct as patients choose the attitudes that they use to approach cancer.° Spinrad's Wintergreen adopts a positive attitude: "He knew that some terminal cancer patients had been cured. Therefore terminal cancer could be cured" (548). Wintergreen appears to exert actual control in that he intends to find and implement the cure for cancer by himself. In real life, patients adopt a range of attitudes towards cancer, all attempts to perceive control. In a study conducted in Australia by Jenny O'Baugh, a clinical nurse consultant specializing in cancer care, on the attitudes of cancer patients and their nurses, patients even partly defined "being positive" as "taking control" (262, 265). The nurses in the study said that giving patients choices "would provide them with a feeling of power and control" (268). Thus the nurses appreciated the patients' needs to perceive control, even as the patients relied on the nurses for care. Yet patients also exercise con-

APPENDIX I

This is a crucial distinction that Lisa makes, and it marks a new direction that the paper is going.

trol over outcomes through their different attitudes; in the O'Baugh study nurses spoke of "destructive attitudes and states of mind" (263). For example, refusing to comply with treatment can make it less effective. Ironically, though, when patients questioned their treatments nurses deemed them "negative," yet the questioning seemed to be just another attempt to understand and to exercise some control over treatment.

Patients' "destructive attitudes" in general are alternate methods of seeking to perceive control.° In *On Death and Dying*, Elizabeth Kübler-Ross recounts the interview of a difficult patient who "fluctuates in her willingness to accept help and her denial of any need for help" (229). Kübler-Ross concludes that much of the patient's inconsistency stems from her belief that complaining equals death, but she also mentions the patient's wish to remain as active and functional as possible (243). Perhaps the patient attempted to feel in control by denying her disease when she felt well enough. In a commentary in a London magazine, the author writes, "Some patients prefer to cope by denying the reality of their life-threatening diagnosis. Who is to deny that living in the present is the most satisfactory way of coping with any disaster?" (Anonymous). In truth, a patient can continue "living in the present" while acknowledging the existence of cancer. Denial, a separate issue, is another attempt to perceive control by feigning normalcy. If the denial persists, however, the patient may not cooperate with or even receive treatment. The attitude influences the outcome. Most would consider even terminally ill patients' wishes to die sooner another negative attitude. A study by Brian Kelly of the Department of Psychiatry at the University of Queensland discusses such patients, and reported that such patients had more "feelings of hopelessness and loss" than other dying patients (344). Kelly also considers "inadequate symptomatic treatment," poor relationships with doctors, missing social support, and other possible causes for the wish of patients to end life (340). But perhaps the patients

This might be seen as a "con" argument.

who want to die have lost their perception of control, a distinct possibility if they feel a great amount of pain and lack social support. Ending life, then, is the final way to exert control.

It must be conceded that even if patients' choices change their conditions, patients have little or no control over exactly how their lives will change.° Eating certain foods during treatment does not guarantee a calm stomach, responding in a cooperative manner to doctors does not guarantee successful treatments. Choosing one treatment over another or one doctor over another can turn out well or poorly. Surgeons and medicines can fail. Cancer patients with positive attitudes can die, and angry patients can survive; adopting the kind of positive attitude encouraged by nurses and society does not mean a patient will win. Ehrenreich, for one, writes that "what sustained me [. . .] was a purifying rage" against insurers, polluters that dump carcinogens into the environment, and even the "sappy pink" breast cancer awareness ribbons (87, 80). It could be further argued in this way that not only is the distinction between perceived and actual control blurry, but that actual control does not even exist. Yet Ehrenreich's ire must affect her quality of life; as a fellow patient responded to her angry posting on the Internet: "I hope you can find some peace. You deserve it" (81). Her decision to adopt an angry attitude affects her reality, and in this way at least she exercises control.

When we have the ability to make choices, perceived and actual control begin to become the same. Not all cancer patients are lucky enough to be able to make decisions, and of course outside factors influence the choices we make. But it seems that even if we cannot control outcomes, we often can control the decisions we make. Our decisions do, if only indirectly, affect the courses of our lives. Even if in truth we have actual control over nothing in our lives, if we think we have control, our perceptions determine our realities. Thus when we consider Maliski's distinction at a broader level than perhaps she even in-

This is a con argument that will move the paper's argument forward.

tended, the difference between perceived and actual control becomes meaningless. It is our perceptions of the world that matter, because our perceptions are all we have.°

Works Cited

Anonymous. "The Refractory." *The Lancet.* 24 Nov 2001. 1822.

Ehrenreich, Barbara. "Welcome to Cancerland." *Best American Essays.* 2002.

Kelly, B. "Terminally Ill Cancer Patients' Wish to Hasten Death." *Palliative Medicine.* 2002. 339–345.

Kübler-Ross, Elisabeth. *On Death and Dying.* New York: Macmillan, 1969.

Maliski, Sally L. "From 'Death Sentence' to 'Good Cancer': Couples' Transformation of a Prostate Cancer Diagnosis." *Nursing Research.* Nov/Dec 2002. 391–397.

Nuland, Sherwin. *How We Die: Reflections on Life's Final Chapter.* New York: Knopf, 1994.

O'Baugh, J. "'Being Positive': Perceptions of Patients with Cancer and Their Nurses." *Nursing.* 2003. 262–270.

Okamura, Hitoshi. "Patients' Understanding of Their Own Disease and Survival Potential in Patients with Metastatic Breast Cancer." *Breast Cancer Research and Treatment.* May 2000. 145–150.

Pittaway, Kim. "It's No Cure for Cancer." *Chatelaine* (English edition). Feb 2003. 36.

Spinrad, Norman. "Carcinoma Angels." *Dangerous Visions.* Harlan Ellison, ed. New York: Berkley Publishing, 1967.°

Interesting conclusion—one that does offer something of a ΔT. But it lacks full development, hints more than really drives the point home, and, when placed side by side with the thesis, fails to show enough by way of development. However, it's on the right track and needs only a little bit of modification to fully succeed.

Lisa's paper is impressive in that it draws on quite a bit of research. It's interesting, too, in that it uses works that are both "popular" and "professional" in an attempt to argue the thesis.

II

Writing Prompts

1. Take one of the assigned texts and look for a book review of it, one written at about the same time the book appeared. Next, look for a scholarly article about the book. Compare and contrast the two pieces, showing in what way the review and article differ, and how that difference can be connected to the idea of a different conception of audience.

2. Look for a contemporary review of a book similar (same theme, genre, author) to one of those from the reading list so far. Using it as your starting point, try to develop a similar evaluation of the book on the reading list, using criteria similar to those advanced by the reviewer, but in your paper strive for a more balanced approach than that offered by the review.

3. Many works of fiction are "thesis" stories. They present an idea or thesis themselves, are arguing for a particular position. Write a paper in which you argue that *a subsidiary or correlative thesis* underlies the book's main thesis. (The main thesis of the books is typically more or less evident, even obvious, but looking for underlying assumptions or theses is ultimately a much more difficult and rewarding task.)

4. Many "thesis" novels are ones that could be accused of propagandizing rather than functioning as "art." Using one or more of the works on the reading list, explore the differences between art and propaganda.

5. Earlier on, I used the concept of the "writing production device"—the mechanism you use to generate prose (see chapter 3). Describe your WPD: How does it work? What kinds of unusual features might it have—or how do you think the way you go about writing differs from how most people do, or from how I describe it here?

6. One of the sections of this book went through thirty drafts. Lit-

erally. Is this a good idea, do you think? What do you think is the ideal relationship of drafting to a finished version of a piece of writing? Can a piece of writing be rewritten too many times? At what point does it not behoove you to rewrite any more, presuming of course that you still have time before a deadline?

7. Do a "newrite," then "freewrite" about it (see chapter 3), and turn that work into an argumentative paper about one of the works on the reading list. Include all the prewriting with the final version.

8. Use one of the suggested methods of coming up with ideas (aporia, disjunction, etc.) in order to generate a paper about one of the course texts.

9. As I mentioned in chapter 4, the humorist Dave Barry once suggested that the best way to write papers in college writing courses was to make the most outlandish comparisons possible. Try inventing such an outrageous thesis and then attempt to modify it, through the course of revision and rewriting, into a reasonable but argumentative thesis. Start, that is, with the zany, self-consciously out-there idea, and mold it into something of analytic value.

10. Take one of the texts that seriously challenges some deeply held personal belief—for example, one involving religion, the family, morality, or the like. Generate a paper around a thesis showing how this text's challenge to your personal belief has some validity, how it should not be dismissed, and how it might have advanced your belief structure in a significant way, even though it did not force you to entirely abandon that belief. Make sure, though, that you still focus on *analyzing* the text—revealing something important about it.

11. Play around with a sphere/disc metaphor with regard to thesis: how is a ΔT really like a sphere? What attributes are "sphere-like" and make for a good conclusion?

12. Taking a work of nonfiction that is relevant to the course (or is one of the course texts), analyze and evaluate its structure. Develop an argument as to why the author chose the structure she or he did, and show in what way that structure either is successful or could be improved.

13. Again, using nonfiction works that are on the reading list, look

at two argumentative essays and isolate their thesis statements and conclusions. In what way or ways do the conclusions of the two pieces represent an evolution over their respective thesis statements? Which thesis-conclusion relationship seems to you superior? Why?

14. Take one of the stylists' passages in chapter 11 and do a detailed stylistic analysis of it. Why is it effective? Could it be better? What "virtues" of style does it possess (as enumerated earlier in the chapter)? What faults does it have? What new ways does it allow for us to talk about style, or what new virtues can you infer from it?

15. Sentence combining: When students study writing, they often develop a fear of using any kind of elaborate sentence structure. They end up writing essays in sentences as simple as the following: "My puppy is cute. He has a long tail. He wags this a lot. He also has a sweet and warm pink tongue. He licks me all over my face. I love my puppy a lot." While all these sentences are correct, and while the paragraph that contains them also has details and some sense of development, this writing can hardly be considered college-level work. What's needed is complexity as well as correctness. It is important that you write correct prose, but it seems to me every bit as important that you develop an individual and distinctive prose style, one that reflects the patterns and complications of your thought process. And to make matters even more challenging, at the same time that your prose is complex and correct, it must also be lucid.

Write a brief story based on the simple sentences that are provided below. Try to put paragraph breaks in where appropriate. And strive for lucidity as well as accuracy. Use more complex sentences than the ones provided, though you may (if you like) retain some of the simple sentences. This is basically a story for children, so the narrative structure should be simple. However, the challenge is to make the story interesting and much more complex on the sentence level, putting the sentences in paragraphs, including revisions, and the like. Try to use a variety of ways to connect the sentences too (subordination, coordination, etc.). Make sure that you capture all the ideas the sentences present. For example, you might combine the first six sentences in this way: "It was comfortable and dark in the Queenston house, even though the sound of cars and trucks passing on the street that was so close to the house occasionally broke the stillness." There are lots of ways to combine them, preserving the details; feel free to use your own imagination and inventiveness as you combine the sentences. I have made this example kind of wacky, since I'm hoping that will unleash some creative juices!

The Glymphiad, or The Frfrlungenlied

1. The Queenston house was dark.
2. It was very comfortable there.
3. There was an occasional sound.
4. The sound was of trucks or cars.
5. These cars passed on the street.
6. A street ran very close to the house.
7. No noise came from the wormhole.
8. The wormhole was in the house.
9. The wormhole led to Bim sub-two.
10. Bim sub-two is a planet.
11. Bim sub-two is very far away.
12. G'Narth is Supreme.
13. G'Narth is a Philosopher.
14. G'Narth is the Leader of Bim sub-two.
15. G'Narth is very jolly.
16. G'Narth is basically dinosauric in origin.
17. G'Narth is interested in the Queenston house.
18. Asleep in the house are Frfrnrfr and Glymphyr.
19. Also asleep is Biinken.
20. Biinken is a deer.
21. Actually he is not a deer.
22. He is an android replica.
23. Jathy and Frak snore softly.
24. Their snores hardly disturb the air.
25. In the household there are others.
26. There are the dinos.
27. The dinos are pets.
28. They frolic.
29. Now they too are asleep.

30. Suddenly a sound rips the air.
31. The sound is loud.
32. It is piercing.
33. It is confined to the house.
34. It is a flying saucer.
35. Flying saucers often visit the Queenston house.
36. Aliens come out of the saucer.
37. They are not very chatty.
38. They shoot all the entities and people.
39. Their ray guns are set on stun.
40. Biinken does not get stunned.
41. Androids cannot be stunned.
42. Biinken pretends to be a stuffed animal, though.
43. The aliens drag all the stunned entities aboard their saucer.
44. It is cold in the saucer.
45. The aliens do not feel the cold.
46. Biinken is left behind.
47. The saucer takes off.
48. Biinken thinks quickly.
49. Biinken goes into the wormhole.
50. He goes through it to Bim sub-two.
51. Biinken finds G'Narth.
52. G'Narth is tall.
53. G'Narth is benevolent.
54. G'Narth is especially interested in the story.
55. G'Narth wants to help.
56. G'Narth goes to earth via the wormhole.
57. G'Narth brings the Bim sub-two scientists with him.
58. The scientists are middle-aged.
59. The scientists are very advanced over earth scientists.
60. The scientists bring instruments with them.
61. The instruments are very sensitive.
62. The instruments can record energy residues.
63. Energy residues are all over the Queenston house.
64. These residues tell the scientists information.
65. The information pertains to the abduction.
66. Evidently a very powerful technology was behind the abduction.

67. The Bim sub-two scientists are scared.
68. G'Narth is not scared.
69. Biinken is not scared.
70. Androids do not feel fear.
71. Biinken experiences a simulacrum of fear.
72. The Bim sub-two scientists can say where the saucer is.
73. They cannot say exactly where it is.
74. They can give a rough radius of where it might be.
75. This radius is large.
76. This radius is not insurmountable.
77. They need a plan.
78. Once they locate the saucer, they need to decide.
79. They need to decide how to capture it.
80. They cannot destroy it because of its earth occupants.
81. It would be best to make contact with the alien abductors.
82. Suffice it to say that they locate the saucer.
83. They make contact with the abductors.
84. The abductors are not evil.
85. They are not good.
86. The abductors are only seeking information.
87. The abductors want the contents of the brains of the abductees.
88. The Bim sub-two scientists offer an exchange of information.
89. They offer this instead of the contents of the brains.
90. The alternative is that the abductors can be reduced to Z-particles.
91. Z-particles are types of weakons.
92. Z-particles are very small indeed.
93. The aliens return their abductees.
94. The group is returned to the Queenston house.
95. Everyone is OK.
96. Glymphyr has taken something.
97. What he has taken is a key piece of technology.
98. This piece of technology is very significant.
99. This piece of technology allows Glymphyr to monitor the whereabouts of the aliens.
100. It indicates that they are on a return path.

WORKS CITED

Adams, James. *Conceptual Blockbusting*. New York: Perseus, 1990.

Baker, Sheridan. *The Practical Stylist*. 7th ed. New York: Harper, 1990.

Barry, Dave. "College Admissions." *Dave Barry's Bad Habits: A 100% Fact-Free Book*. New York: Owl Books, Henry Holt, 1987. 200–203.

Becker, Alida. "The Inventor, His Wife, Her Lover, and a Tomato." Review of *Ira Foxglove*, by Thomas McMahon. *New York Times Book Review* 21 March 2004: 10.

Becker, Carl. *Heavenly City of the Eighteenth Century Philosophers*. New Haven: Yale UP, 1992.

Beers, Mark H., and Robert Berkow, eds. *The Merck Manual of Diagnosis and Therapy*. Whitehouse Station, NJ: Merck, 1999.

Bell, Susan. "Revisioning *The Great Gatsby*." *Tin House* Summer 2004: 48–57.

Benedict, Ruth. *Patterns of Culture*. New York: NAL, 1934.

Bennett, Deborah J. *Logic Made Easy: How to Know When Language Deceives You*. New York: Norton, 2004.

Biblioctopus. 17 June 2004. <http.www.biblioctopus.com/pages/html/cat18a.html>.

Bleich, David. *Subjective Criticism*. Baltimore: Johns Hopkins UP, 1998.

Booth, Wayne, et al. *The Craft of Research*. Chicago: U of Chicago P, 1995.

Bowling for Columbine. Dir. Michael Moore. Starring Michael Moore, Charlton Heston, Dick Clark, and George W. Bush. United Artists, 2002.

Brown, Goold. *The Institutes of English Grammar*. New York: William Wood, 1863.

Carroll, Lewis. *Alice's Adventures in Wonderland and Through the Looking Glass*. Baltimore: Penguin, 1962.

Carroll, Noël. *The Philosophy of Horror, or Paradoxes of the Heart*. New York, Routledge, 1990.

Chismar, Douglas E. "Heidegger's Critique of Empathy." 13 March 2003. <http://www.chowan.edu/acadp/Religion/pubs/heidegger.htm>.

Columbia Encyclopedia. Ed. Paul Legassé. 6th ed. New York: Columbia UP, 2000.

de Bono, Edward. *Lateral Thinking: Creativity Step by Step*. New York: Harper, 1973.

Denham, Sir John. *The Poetical Works of Sir John Denham*. Ed. Theodore Howard Banks, Jr. New Haven: Yale UP, 1928.

Dickens, Charles. *Hard Times*. 1854. Rpt. Ed. George Ford and Sylvère Monod. New York: Norton, 1966.

Doolittle, Hilda. *H.D.: Collected Poems, 1912–1944*. Ed. Louis Martz. New York: New Directions, 1983.

Dougherty, Peter J. "The Wealth of Notions: A Publisher Considers the Literature of Globalization." *Chronicle Review* 16 July 2004. <http://chronicle.com/temp/email.php?od-6hpevpOnstwplgwo7yvxjl34qxhm13ue>.

Du Bois, W.E.B. *Writings*. Ed. Nathan Huggins. New York: Library of America, 1986.

Dubrow, Heather. "Thesis and Antithesis: Rewriting the Rules on Writing." *Chronicle of Higher Education* 6 December 2002: B13.

Edmundson, Mark. "The Risk of Reading: Why Books Are Meant to Be Dangerous." *New York Times Magazine* 1 August 2004: 11–12.

Elbow, Peter. *Writing without Teachers*. New York: Oxford UP, 1998.

Eliot, T. S. *Selected Prose of T. S. Eliot*. Ed. Frank Kermode. New York: Harcourt, 1975.

Emerson, Ralph Waldo. *Essays and Lectures*. Ed. Joel Porte. New York: Library of America, 1983. 469–92.

Fahrenheit 9/11. Dir. Michael Moore. Starring Michael Moore and George W. Bush. Lionsgate Films, 2004.

Frank, Jerome. "On Lawsuits as Inquiries into the Truth, from *Courts on Trial*." *The World of Law: The Law as Literature*. Ed. Ephraim London. New York: Simon and Schuster, 1960. 731–53.

Franzen, Jonathan. "My Father's Brain: What Alzheimer's Takes Away." 10 September 2001. <http://newyorker.com/fact/content/?010910fa_fact1>.

Frazier, Charles. Introduction. *The Book of Job*. King James Version. New York: Grove, 1999. vii–xvii.

Goffman, Erving. *Stigma: Notes on the Management of Spoiled Identity*. New York: Simon and Schuster, 1963.

Gorrell, Donna. *A Writer's Handbook from A to Z*. New York: Allyn and Bacon, 1994.

Gould, James. "Science Writing." Unpublished paper.

Gould, James, and Peter J. Arduino, Jr. "Is Tonic Immobility Adaptive?" *Animal Behaviour* 32.3 (August 1984): 921–23.

Graves, Robert, and Alan Hodge. *The Reader over Your Shoulder: A Hand-book for Writers of Prose*. New York: Macmillan, 1943.

Hall, Donald. *Writing Well*. 9th ed. Boston: Addison, 1997.

Hap, Bela. "Structuralist Meta-Analysis." Trans. Gyula Kodolanyi. *Essaying Essays: Alternative Forms of Exposition*. Ed. Richard Kostelanetz. New York: Out of London Press, 1975. 310.

Harvey, Gordon. *Writing with Sources*. Indianapolis: Hackett, 2000.

Histomobile. 14 June 2003. <www.histomobile.com>.

Huyssen, Andreas. *Present Pasts: Urban Palimpsests and the Politics of Memory*. Stanford: Stanford UP, 2003.

James, Henry. *The Art of Fiction and Other Essays*. New York: Oxford UP, 1948.

James, William. *The Letters of William James*. 2 vols. Ed. Henry James. Boston: Atlantic Monthly Press, 1920.

———. *The Varieties of Religious Experience. William James: Writings, 1902–1910*. Ed. Bruce Kuklick. New York: Library of America, 1987.

Kafalenos, Emma. "The Power of Double Coding to Represent New Forms of Representation: *The Truman Show, Dorian Gray*, "Blow-Up," and Whistler's *Caprice in Purple and Gold*." *Poetics Today* 24.1 (Spring 2003): 1–33.

Kasner, Edward, and James Newman. *Mathematics and the Imagination*. New York: Simon and Schuster, 1940.

Keats, John. *A Critical Edition of the Major Works*. Ed. Elizabeth Cook. Oxford: Oxford UP, 1990.

Kostelanetz, Richard, ed. *Essaying Essays: Alternative Forms of Exposition*. New York: Out of London Press, 1975.

Kuhn, Thomas. *The Structure of Scientific Revolutions*. 2nd ed. Chicago: U of Chicago P, 1970.

Lagondanet. 14 June 2003. <http://freespace.virgin.net/roger.ivett/>.

Lanham, Richard A. *A Handlist of Rhetorical Terms*. 2nd ed. Berkeley: U of California P, 1991.

Lipsyte, Robert. "Athletes Offer Straight Talk about Cancer." *New York Times* 25 November 2001, late ed., sec. 5: 11.

MacPherson, Robin. *University English*. Warsaw: Wydawnictwa Szkolne i Pedagogiczne, 1994.

Marius, Richard. *A Writer's Companion*. New York: McGraw, 1995.

Mattenson, Lauri M. "Teaching Student Writers to Be Warriors." *Chronicle Review* 6 August 2004: B10–B11.

Menand, Louis. "Comp Time." *New Yorker* 11 September 2000.

Mill, John Stuart. *On Liberty*. 1859; rpt. Indianapolis: Hackett, 1978.

Miner, Horace. "Body Ritual among the Nacirema." *Apeman, Spaceman: Anthropological Science Fiction*. Ed. Leon Stover and Harry Harrison. New York: Doubleday, 1968. 238–42.

Muir, John. *Nature Writings*. Ed. William Cronon. New York: Library of America, 1997.

Nabokov, Vladimir. *Novels (1955–1962)*. Ed. Brian Boyd. New York: Library of America, 1996.

Orwell, George. *The Orwell Reader: Fiction, Essays, and Reportage by George Orwell*. New York: Harcourt, Brace, 1949.

———. *Shooting an Elephant and Other Essays*. London: Secker and Warburg, 1950.

Ramsey, Frank P. *Philosophical Papers*. Ed. D. H. Mellor. Cambridge: Cambridge UP, 1990.

Richards, I. A. *Principles of Literary Criticism*. New York: Harcourt, 1925.

Robertson, William O. "Poisoning." *Merck Manual of Diagnostics and Therapeutics*. Ed. Mark H. Beers and Robert Berkow. Whitehouse Station, NJ: Merck, 1999. 2619–55.

Sanders, Scott. "Invisible Men and Women: The Disappearance of Character in Science Fiction." *Science Fiction Studies: Selected Articles on Science Fiction*. Ed. R. D. Mullen and Darko Suvin. Boston: Gregg, 1978.

Scholes, Robert, and Karl Klaus. *Elements of the Essay*. New York: Oxford UP, 1969.

Slater, Lauren. "The Trouble with Self-Esteem." *New York Times Magazine* 3 February 2002: 44–47.

Stoppard, Tom. *Jumpers*. New York: Grove, 1972.

Szymborska, Wisława. "A Tale Retold." *Poezje/Poems*. Trans. Magnus J. Krynski and Robert A. Maguire. Cracow: Wydawnictwo Literackie, 1989.

Taylor, Edward. *The Poems of Edward Taylor*. Ed. Donald E. Stanford. New Haven: Yale: UP, 1960.

Turner, Jenny. "The Amis Papers." Review of *The War against Cliché: Essays and Reviews, 1971–2000*, by Martin Amis. *New York Times Book Review* 23 December 2001: 10.

Updike, John. "Hub Fans Bid Kid Adieu." *Baseball: A Literary Anthology*. Ed. Nicholas Davidoff. New York: Library of America, 2002. 301–17.

U.S. Department of Energy. 14 June 2003. <www.fueleconomy.gov>.

Van Leer, David. "Hester's Labyrinth: Transcendental Rhetoric in Puritan Boston." *New Essays on* The Scarlet Letter. Ed. Michael J. Colacurcio. Cambridge: Cambridge UP, 1985. 57–100.

Wallace, David Foster. "Consider the Lobster." *Gourmet*. August 2004: 50–64.

Weinstein, Arnold. *A Scream Goes through the House: What Literature Teaches Us about Life*. New York: Random House, 2003.

Winchester, C. T. *Some Principles of Literary Criticism*. New York: Macmillan, 1914.

Woolf, Virginia. *A Room of One's Own, Three Guineas*. Oxford: Oxford UP, 1992.

INDEX

Becker, Carl, and "climate of opinion," 4, 25

begging the question. *See* circular argument

belief, as influence on writing and research, 127

Bell, Susan: on prose of F. Scott Fitzgerald, 140–41; on rewriting, 114

Benedict, Ruth, example of writing by, 161–62

Bennett, Deborah J., on "fuzzification" and fuzzy logic, 177

Bleich, David: "chronic on-the-other-handism" and, 176; identifying emotional response of reader and, 32

Booth, Wayne, 97

Brown, Goold, John Denham and, xiv

Bunch, David, writing style of, 15

Bush, George W., and "Bushisms," 17

Carlyle, Thomas, belletristic writing and, 2

Carroll, Lewis, meaning as expressed in novel by, xv

Carroll, Noël: on belief, 127; on horror stories, 92–93; on macro-questions and micro-questions, 97–103

cause-effect, as genre of argument, 6

censorship, of self in writing, 71

Cervantes Saavedra, Miguel de, character of Don Quixote and, 180

Cioffi, Frank [Salvatore], and "we-discourse" vs. "they-discourse," 25

circular argument (logical fallacy), 143

claim, 89. *See also* thesis

classification, as genre of argument, 6

climax (figure of speech), 136, 140n.2; Benedict's use of, 161n.19; Fitzgerald's use of, 141; Goffman's use of, 164 nn. 36 and 37; Wallace's use of, 169 nn. 65 and 68

colloquial language, use of by William James, 158n.1. *See also* slang

comparison-contrast, as genre of argument, 6

con argument, 5. *See also* counterargument

Conceptual Blockbusting (Adams), 35, 62–63

"Consider the Lobster" (Wallace), writing style of passage from, 169–70

consumer desire, and contradictory feelings about, 66–67

"correctness," of language, 13–17

counterargument, 100–103, in creative nonfiction, 113; infeeling and, 100, 102–3; Mill on, 100–102, 115

creative nonfiction, 2, 111–13; defined, 112

creativity, xvi, 177

Cummings, Donald W., and paragraph cohesiveness, 79–80

database, use of in research, 121–22

deBono, Edward, 179; creativity as expressed by, 35

"delta-thesis," as conclusion to essay, 5, 59–60, 107–10, 115

Denham, John, and "The Tree of Knowledge," xiv

description, as genre of argument, 6

Development Demon, 96–103

Dickens, Charles: and *Hard Times,* xiii, xiv, xviii; use of anaphora by, 138

Dillard, Annie, belletristic writing and, 2

discourse environment, 25–26; fractures within, 26–27; working within, 30

disjunction, as invention strategy, 33

distraction. *See* red herring (logical fallacy)

documentation, of research paper, 130–33; styles of, 131

Dougherty, Peter J., 181

drafts, of writing, 40–42

Du Bois, W.E.B., example of writing by, 160

"Earnest Liberal's Lament, The" (Hemingway), 64–65

Edmundson, Mark, 181

effect, arguing for, 10

either-or (logical fallacy), 143

Elbow, Peter, "freewriting" and, 36

Eliot, T. S., on "genuine" poetry of Dante, 46

Emerson, Ralph Waldo: belletristic writing and, 2; on facts, 77

emotional response: and contradictory feelings within, 65–67; and writing, 32–33

emotive language (logical fallacy), 145

epizeuxis (figure of speech), 138, 140n.2

erotesis, as way to develop argument, 92–93, 95–96

ethos, 19. *See also* self image

evidence: confirmatory vs. disconfirmatory, 1; in body of essay, 90

example-supportable assertion, 93–94

explanation, as goal of argument, 6–10

extrapolation: as type of explanation, 10; as invention strategy, 33

Faulkner, William, style of, 15

faulty analogy (logical fallacy), 144

figures of speech, 135–41; as rhetorical tricks, 135–36. *See also individual figures of speech*

Fitzgerald, F. Scott: process of revising of *The Great Gatsby* by, 140–41; use of figures of speech by, 141

"forethought," as necessary for argument, 47–50, 110

Frank, Jerome, legal system described by, 173

Franklin, Benjamin, 8

Franzen, Jonathan, and paragraph incoherence, 82–83

Frazier, Charles, example of writing by, 168

"freewriting": and "automatic writing," 36; as way to overcome Writer's Block, 36

Fuller, Margaret, belletristic writing and, 2

fuzzy logic, 176–79

"fuzzy subjectivity," 179

Garrison, Philip, on creative nonfiction, 113

generalization, as explanation, 9

"Glymphiad, or Frfrlungenlied, The," 205–7

Goffman, Erving, 181; example of writing by, 164

Google, 175; as used for research, 117, 126

Gould, James: language use of, 28; and Peter Arduino, 24; on science writing, 25, 27

Graves, Robert, and Alan Hodge, *The Reader over Your Shoulder*, 96

Gurr, Ted Robert, 116

Hall, Donald, on thesis, 44

Handlist of Rhetorical Terms, A (Lanham), 136–37

Hap, Bela, example of writing by, 165–67

Harvey, Gordon, 97

hasty generalization (logical fallacy), 145–46

Hawthorne, Nathaniel, 39, 88

H.D. (Hilda Doolittle, pseud.), considerations if writing about, 48. *See also* "Pool, The"

Hemingway, Ernest, 64–65, as anticipating minimalism, 65; literary forebears of, 65

Herum, John, 155

Heston, Charlton, in *Bowling for Columbine*, 26

Hoban, Russell, style of, 15

Hodge, Alan, and Robert Graves, *The Reader over Your Shoulder*, 96